CW01637930

# No One To Change But Self

## Series Revised & Expanded

Edward Art

FIRST EDITION

Artwork by Edward Art

ISBN - Book: 979-8-9918575-4-3

**Author's Contacts**

Website: www.edward.art

Email for 1 on 1: Edwardartsupplyhands@gmail.com

Youtube: www.youtube.com/@EdwardArt

Reddit: www.reddit.com/r/EdwardArtSupplyHands/

X: www.x.com/@EdwardArtt

Instagram: www.instagram.com/edwardartsupplyhands/

*This book is addressed to the Inner Man of Imagination, and that is the* ***real you****.*

*“Why doubt the power that brought you here?”*

# Preface

This entire book revolves around one central theme: *there is no one to change but self.* This truth will be stressed repeatedly throughout these pages, because this book is addressed to the Inner Man of Imagination, not merely the outer-man in physical form. It speaks to the inward being, who is made entirely of imagination. That is who this book seeks to set free.

Everyone tries to change everything but themselves. This is not a disparaging remark but rather an acknowledgment of an observable reality amongst Man. Most do not feel any need to change anything inside, but for Neville's ideas to truly work for you, you must want to be different. What happens when you desire to be different, during your journey of transformation, you discover you already were that which you were just momentarily seeking. This is how it will always be. You will be desiring to be someone, only to discover you already are. That is why this book is solely about changing Self and seeing that the Self is within.

If you can hold this idea firmly in your mind, that this book is for the Inner Man, and when I speak of freedom and having things, you apply it to that Inner Man, this book will begin to liberate you. You will start to see that you are freer than you ever imagined. You are not just a fleshly being; you are an imaginative one, a creator dwelling within your own imagination.

When you bring something to your awareness, making it present to you in your imagination, you are practicing the principle that God's name is *I Am*, not *I Was* or *I Will Be,* or *He is* and *She is.* If you can get the name, the tense correct and hold steadily to the assumption that you *are* who you wish to be, then you will inevitably become that. For *I Am* hardens into fact.

What most people do, however, is postpone their desired state to some future moment. They think of themselves as someone who *will be* successful, who *will be* loved, who *will be* free, one day. But this is not how imagination works. In the outer-world, it may appear that events unfold across time, happening on particular days and in specific sequences. But in imagination, everything is *now.* What you assume yourself to be in this present moment is what you are, and it is *this* present assumption that casts its shadow forward into your experience.

This is why Neville insisted so strongly on the importance of thinking *from* the wish fulfilled rather than *of* the wish-fulfilled. When you think *of* your desire, you are acknowledging separation from it. You are viewing it as something distant, something outside yourself that you hope to obtain. But when you think *from* it, you are assuming the feeling of already being the person who possesses it, who lives in that reality. You are no longer reaching for it; you are resting in it.

Your imagination does not deal in future promises. It only knows the eternal *now*. Whatever state you occupy in your imagination *now* is the seed from which your future experience grows. If you persist in dwelling in the feeling of your wish fulfilled, if you make it so real to yourself that it becomes your natural inner way of being, then things will start to rearrange in your life according to that new natural state. Not because you are forcing it, but because the inner and outer are one.

This is not to say you must pick up certain behaviors. It is not about behavior modification. It about being in the wish-fulfilled meaning you have a conviction that you are or have what you desire, and you walk that way everywhere. So if you choose to be free, you are not free some of the time, you choose it everywhere in your life. If in some areas, you are not free, then that is the area you must start with. Do not wait for any outer change to take place before you have a change in imagination. You start to be free in every aspect if freedom is what you want. Let the behaviors be the same in the sense that you do not focus on them but only on your freedom. Let the circumstance remain the same, you leave it all alone and feel internal freedom. Then this new, free Self must start to take form and emerge.

Consider what it means to truly choose a state. If you choose to be free, you cannot be free only some of the time, in certain comfortable areas of your life while remaining bound in others. Freedom, or any state you wish to embody, must be claimed in totality. It must permeate every aspect of your being. If there are areas where you still feel trapped, limited, or dependent, those are precisely the areas where you must begin your inner work. These are not obstacles to overcome later; they are invitations to deepen your assumption now.

Do not wait for any outer change to occur before you experience a change in imagination. This is where most people stumble. They believe they will feel free once the circumstances shift, once the external world gives them permission. But this is backwards. Your imagination is not meant to only react to your world, it is also meant to create it.

You must start to be free in every aspect of your inner life right now, even while the external world appears unchanged. Let your behaviors remain as they are for the moment. Let the circumstances stay exactly as they are. You do not need to manipulate or control anything on the outside. Instead, leave it all alone and turn your attention inward. Feel internally the freedom you seek. Inhabit that feeling as your natural state. Make it so familiar to yourself that it becomes *who you are*, not something you are trying to become.

Trees bear fruit of their own kind. An apple tree cannot produce oranges. A fig tree cannot yield grapes. The fruit is determined entirely by the nature of the tree itself, by what lives within its roots and trunk, by the essence of what it is. In the same way, your imagination is the great mental tree, and you, your lived experience, your circumstances, your relationships, everything you encounter in the outer-world, are its fruit.

The fruit you bear in your life is a direct reflection of the image you hold of yourself within your imagination. This means that if you persistently imagine yourself as limited, unworthy, or trapped, your outer-world must reflect those inner assumptions back to you either through situations or your own behaviors. Some reflection will happen. For *it is not what you are looking at that matters but what you see*. If you see bondage, then you are in bondage, and you must free yourself all on the inside.

This is why there is *no one to change but self*. When you change the tree, when you transform the self-concept held in your imagination, the fruit changes automatically. You do not have to figure out *how* the fruit will change or force it to be different. You simply tend to the tree by changing what you assume yourself to be, and the fruit takes care of itself. The tree produces according to its nature, and so do you. If you want different fruit in your life, you must become a different tree in imagination. For tree's bear fruit of their own kind. You imagination is the great tree and you are its fruit. The fruit you bear is the image you hold of yourself.

Just as a chef reduces wine in a meal, simmering it down to concentrate its essence, distilling its flavor into something potent and pure, this book is a reduction of Neville's work. It takes the vast body of his teachings and condenses them into these pages. Since we must live this out and practice it in life, this book is a reduction of that life. It is not meant to replace the fullness of Neville's original lectures and writings, but to serve as a concentrated guide, a distillation you can return to again and again. You are going to have to do things, speak to people, make inner decisions while you walk this world. This book is a tool that you can use and should be seen as that. A method of reading should not be to read it as a novel, but as a small jolt of contemplation. So open the book randomly, find something valuable and contemplate on it and ask questions about yourself. Why did you find that valuable you? How does that free you?

So take what you find valuable discard what you do not, but know that the practice of it and the reading of it are two different things. Reading about these principles can inspire you, clarify your understanding, and point you in the right direction. But the real work, the transformation, happens only when you *live* it. When you apply these ideas persistently in your own imagination, when you dwell in the state of the wish-fulfilled despite appearances, when you change yourself within, that is when the teachings become real. That is when they bear fruit.

Use this book as a way to guide and uplift you. Let it remind you of what you already know deep within: That your imagination is the only creative power, that assumption hardens into fact, and that there is no one to change but self. Return to these pages when you forget, when doubt creeps in, when the outer-world tempts you to bow to it. But never mistake the reading for the doing. The map is not the territory. The recipe is not the meal. This book is the reduction, but you must be the one to taste it, to embody it, to let it nourish and transform you from within.

***Edward Art***

# No One Or Nothing To Change But Self

A FEW YEARS AGO, I received a thoughtful question about revision. I was asked, "If revision changes the past, does that then change the future?"

> ***My answer:*** *"Well, you change your attitude towards the past, which inevitably changes your future relationship to that event. It is not about changing the past or future specifically.* ***There is no one or nothing to change but Self, and Self and Imagination are one.****"*

This explanation makes sense conceptually, but it does not fully capture what Neville is teaching.

When you recall an unpleasant experience from years ago, where is that experience *actually* taking place? When you worry about the future, where does that worry exist? All of it happens within your imagination, which we are making synonymous with Self. Both the past and the future exist in imagination, and you have complete freedom to change whatever you wish within your imagination.

This is why Neville emphasizes that there is no one or nothing to change but Self. The "past you" is not "out there" somewhere, it exists as a present activity of imagination. The "future you" is not waiting somewhere ahead, it too is a present activity of imagination. When you revise the past or imagine the future differently, you are not reaching backward or forward in time. You are changing Self *now*, in the only place where change can occur: within your own imagination.

Understanding this dissolves the confusion about whether revision changes the past or future. You are not manipulating external events in a timeline. You are transforming your present state of imagination, which is the only reality you ever experience. The past and future are simply concepts you hold *now*. Change the concept, and you change Self.

This is why Abdullah told Neville to "start with self" and to "find self." The Self you discover is not bound by time. It is the eternal *now* of imagination, where all experiences, whether labeled "past," "present," or "future" exist simultaneously as states of imagination you can occupy or abandon at will.

So avoid getting caught up in terms like "past" or "future." These labels only complicate understanding what to do. The reason is simple: thinking in terms of past and future implies that these are separate realities existing outside of you, which must be manipulated through some external mechanism. This misleads you into believing you need to "go back" to change the past or "reach forward" to change the future.

But there is nowhere to go. There is nothing outside of Self to manipulate. Everything exists within imagination now. When you think you are revising the past, you are actually changing your present feeling about a memory. When you think you are creating the future, you are actually changing your present state of being. The goal is always the same: to change Self, *here and now*, within imagination.

This is why Neville repeatedly brings us back to the present moment of imagining. Not because the past and future do not matter, but because they only exist as present states of imagination. Change what you are conscious of being now, and the entire framework of your perception of the past, present, and future, transforms accordingly. You will see the past in a new way, a compassionate way, and you will see your future in a new way, something to be embodied *now*.

Remember:

*"No one or nothing to change but Self."* - **Neville**

To change Self, you must imagine with feeling anything you genuinely want. Not what you think you *should* want or *have* to want, but what you truly desire. Removing the feelings of 'should' and 'have to' liberates you internally. Free yourself from consequences, punishments, and guilt for imagining what you genuinely desire. Release the pressure of needing to achieve things, for within yourself there is no pressure to achieve anything, everything already exists. Eliminate that stress in imagination by simply imagining what you want while feeling completely free to do so.

Your imagination is your private kingdom where you reign supreme. No law of the outer-world applies here. No one can enter this space uninvited. No consequence follows from what you imagine. This is where you are truly free, where you can be, do, and have anything without limitation. Yet most people bring the restrictions of the outer-world into this sacred space. They imagine with one eye on "reality," constantly checking whether what they imagine is "realistic" or "possible." This defeats the entire purpose.

When a troubling memory surfaces, I have learned a valuable approach. When those cringe-inducing thoughts appear, I ask myself: "Where is this taking place? Within me. Who is cringing? Me. Who is imagining this? Me." Once I recognize it is all within me, then I can change it. Until then I will forever remain a victim of my imagination. I then ask: "Can I change my feeling? Yes. Can I transform this into what I want? Yes. Can I release it entirely if I choose? Yes. Can I imagine what I wish? Yes." Then I act immediately, without delay, even if the thought persists.

I do not fight against unwanted thoughts. Fighting them only gives them more attention and energy. Instead, I simply shift to what I *want*. This is not suppression, it is redirection. When I focus on precisely what I want, a natural surge of feeling follows. This happens automatically, without forcing it. Why would I need to force it? When I imagine *exactly* what I want, the feeling emerges naturally because I am giving myself what I truly desire.

It must be exactly what I want, or I will struggle to feel the reality of this new state of imagination. If I compromise even slightly, if I imagine something close to what I want but not quite, the feeling will be weak or absent. This is because I am not truly satisfied. My goal is to create my own heaven in imagination, not a tolerable compromise.

Neville teaches us not to remain in desire. The Bible tells us to stop sinning (*missing your mark).* William Blake warns against suppressing desire, calling it the path to misery. Take these words to heart. If you have even the tiniest desire, Neville advises fulfilling it mentally. Do not leave it unfulfilled. Do not tell yourself you cannot have it. Do not postpone it to some future moment. Fulfill it now, in imagination, where all things are possible.

Start to prune your imagination daily. Remove the rules, the consequences, and the outer-world when you imagine. Discard all notions of what you "should do" or "have to do" here. Do instead precisely what you want, because it can always be done in imagination. There is no risk, no cost, no punishment for imagining freely. Yet we impose these restrictions on ourselves out of habit, out of conditioning, out of fear.

Through practice, I have discovered the answer is always the same. Whenever I am not feeling well or imagining well, the reason is: *"I am not imagining what I want."* This is consistently my answer. The moment I move toward exactly what I want, I become fulfilled. Fears dissolve and bliss emerges.

I do not concern myself with others' opinions, my circumstances, whether it will express, or what fears arise. None of that matters because those concerns all belong to the outer-world, the world of effects. *All that matters is fulfilling it within me.* This is what transforms me. This is how I find happiness inside. So I make imagination my only reality that concerns me.

> For example, Neville said: *"You want to be free of all embarrassment?* ***How would you feel this night if you were not embarrassed, that not a thing in this world could embarrass you?*** *How would you feel where it so?"*

This quote deserves serious consideration. For years, I felt the world was fundamentally unsafe. I acted upon this feeling, constantly experiencing uneasiness and creating thoughts of being harmed by the world. This was my dominant state of imagination, the lens through which I interpreted every experience.

When I attempted to imagine that my world is safe, conflicting thoughts immediately arose: *"Sure, you can imagine that but come on... there are crazy people out there." "It would be nice to believe that but you know people can be harmful,"* and so on. These objections felt reasonable, even necessary. They seemed like wisdom, like being realistic about the dangers of life.

But here is what I failed to recognize: These objections were not coming from "the world." They were coming from within me. The unsafe world I was protecting myself against existed entirely in my imagination. The "crazy people" and "harmful situations" I was defending against were thoughts, images, feelings within my own imagination. I was fighting against my own imagination while believing I was fighting against external reality.

Yet safety is what I truly desired. I wanted to feel it, experience it, imagine it, and believe in it. That is what I genuinely wanted. Why would I deny myself this experience in the one place where I have complete freedom? Neville is asking, *"What if nothing could embarrass you?"* What if your world was safe? What if your world always worked toward fulfilling your desires instead of opposing them?

These questions initially seem naive or foolish. But they are actually profound. They reveal where we have given up our power. Every time we say, "but I have to consider the facts," we are choosing to remain bound by our current state of imagination. We are refusing to change Self.

The irony is striking for we understand that our past unpleasant memories exist in imagination, yet we treat our fears about the future as if they are facts rather than imagination as well. We know we can change how we feel about something that happened years ago through revision, but we resist imagining a different future because "we have to bow to the facts." This inconsistency reveals our confusion about where reality actually exists.

When I assume this new state, when I dare to feel that my world is safe, I do not worry about how or when it will happen, or even if it is possible. I focus solely on shifting my entire feeling and awareness to exactly what I want. Then, in its own mysterious way, it starts to take form in the world. Not because I forced it, not because I figured out the right steps, but because I changed Self.

This is what I mean by giving yourself what you truly want. Find something deep that you desire, and dare to assume it. This is what truly changes the "Self," and that transformed "Self" will be expressed in your reality. The reason this works is simple yet profound: Self is always being expressed. We always experience ourselves inside, not what we want separate from ourselves. However, we can change ourselves into what we desire if we want to receive our desire. Since there is no one to change but Self, this is how we approach it.

When you give yourself complete freedom, complete safety, complete fulfillment in imagination, when you become that in imagination, then that is what expresses. Not because the outer-world changed first, but because *you* changed, and our world conforms to what we are. Understand that imagination is the true reality, and everything else is its expression.

> *"I have seen scientists, doctors, lawyers, bankers, from every walk of life seek an audience with old Abdullah, and everyone Who came thought themselves honored to be admitted to his home and to receive an interview. If he was ever invited out, and he was, he was always the honored guest. He said,* ***"Neville, you must first start with self. Find self. Don't be ashamed ever of the being you are. Discover it and start the changing of that self." - Neville***

There is no shame in the being that you are. You are fundamental, the being *behind* all conceptions. You can always outgrow the conception but you can never outgrow the Conceiver. Or another way of saying this is that you can always outgrow the dream you but cannot outgrow the dreamer. The Conceiver does not need to shame themselves for what they have conceived themselves to be. What tends to happen is the Conceiver loses themselves in their conception and forgets who they are. When they find themselves in an unwanted state, they think they *are* that state. Then they shame themselves for being inadequate, broken, or unworthy.

But this shame is based on a misunderstanding. You are *not* the state you occupy. You are the one occupying it. Just as an actor is not the character they play, you are not the conception you have assumed. The actor can put on any costume, speak any lines, embody any role, yet they remain themselves underneath. Similarly, you can occupy any state, assume any feeling, conceive yourself to be anything, yet you remain the Conceiver, the one doing the conceiving.

The way out is to acknowledge that you are never the state itself, you are the Being occupying it. Just as you are not your thoughts and feelings, you are not the state you occupy. Thoughts come and go. Feelings rise and fall. States are entered and exited. But you, the one aware of all these movements, remain constant. You are the awareness in which all these experiences appear.

When you realize you are not the unwanted state but merely the one occupying it, shame dissolves. How can you shame yourself for temporarily wearing something you can remove? You would not shame an actor for playing a villain in a performance. Why shame yourself for occupying an unwanted state when you have the power to occupy a different one?

So rather than shame, understand and change. Understand your thinking and feeling. Understand the states you occupy. When you find something you want to change, change it. Not through force or struggle, but through understanding that you are the operant power, the one who chooses which state to occupy.

When you understand this deeply, you stop seeking outside yourself for change. You stop waiting for circumstances to shift, for other people to change, for the world to give you permission to be different.

You never encounter the world directly. You encounter your conception of the world, filtered through your state of imagination. The person who feels unworthy finds evidence of their inadequacy in every situation. They are not seeing the world as it is, they are seeing their own state expressed in the world.

So you will no longer seek outside yourself to change Self, for Self is not on the outside. Self has never been outside. You are within yourself, always have been, and that is where all change occurs. That is where freedom lies. Not in controlling the outer-world, but in growing the inner world from which the outer springs.

*"So what would it be like this night if we, as we are seated here, were now the embodiment of the man, the woman that we would like to be? I tell you it is possible to do everything that you want to do. For the believer—and you're a believer—and God of the universe are one... they aren't two. All things are possible to God and all things are possible to him who believes...so they are equated. So don't now divorce yourself from God. Well, who is God? Say "I am," that's he. "Unless you believe that I am (is) God, then you'll remain in your sin," (Jn. 8:24). Sin is called "missing the mark." You'll miss the mark—the mark is simply a goal in life, that's what the mark is.* ***You'll miss it because you do not believe that you are already the one you would like to be. It's just as simple as that. I'm not saying that it's the easiest thing in the world, no, I would not tell you that; but I tell you, you and I must practice...***

*Here we are in a world I call educative darkness learning to play the instrument which is God; and God is your own wonderful human Imagination. Now reason's going to deny it, I know, so what? You'll simply assume that you have it. And you may say, I don't know anyone in this world who can give me, say, $10,000. I have no relative who is alive that could ever mention me in his will; I have no one to whom I could turn, so what? Are all things possible to God? Yes! Oh, you'll say yes to that right away. Well, do you believe that God is your own wonderful human Imagination? "Oh, hold it a minute, no, I can't believe that, because God is all love and I can* *imagine the most unlovely things in this world. I have and still do, so that couldn't be God.*

*Then, therefore, God is not all powerful. If you can imagine something that he cannot, because of your own stupid concept of what God is, then he can't produce a discord. He is not as good as that violin...he can't produce a discord, and if you can produce a discord you transcend him. You can hit, even by accident, a chord that is beautiful, well, you did it, it's a harmony; and then you strike a discord, but he can't strike a discord, you are greater than God because he can't hit one. Well, you can't be... I can take any discord if I know how to play, which I do not, but if I knew I could resolve it into a beautiful dissonance to the ear that is trained to appreciate a dissonance. So everything can be resolved, even though in our learning we make the most horrible mistakes in the world.* ***So don't condemn yourself for anything that you have ever done or that you're doing or that you may do. Learn to play this instrument. The instrument is God himself and that instrument is your own wonderful human Imagination, and there is no other God.*** *There is no other creative power in this world."* - ***Neville***

**Artwork Commentary:**

This artwork depicts a man who has encountered many pearls and different beliefs throughout his life. At the center of the composition, a pearl rests between two doors. These are the doors of imagination. Outside these doors, he encounters countless beliefs in his outer life, each claiming to explain the cause of things. But when he goes within and opens the doors, he discovers the pearl of all pearls: The source of himself, the source of the pearls, the source of the doors, the cause of all. There, he finds peace.

The doors represent a threshold, the boundary between the external noise and the inner sanctuary. Most people never open these doors. They spend their entire lives sorting through the beliefs outside, debating which ones are true, which ones are valuable. But the real work is crossing that threshold, daring to look within, and confronting what lies at the center.

If you observe carefully, there is chaos outside the doors. Some beliefs cling to the dark-painted walls, representing ideas that are harmful to Self, they keep you trapped in illusion. Others rest on the ground keeping you lower than what you are, not necessarily evil, but not the truth either. They are distractions, partial truths, or comfortable lies we tell ourselves. The outer-world bombards us with explanations, philosophies, and systems of belief. Some are seductive in their darkness, pulling us toward cynicism or despair. Others are simply incomplete, they offer comfort or structure but do not reach the fundamental truth. We collect these beliefs like pearls, thinking each one brings us closer to understanding, but they only accumulate on the floor of our imagination. It is only when you go within that you find the real pearl, the pearl of great price, and when you look at it, you will see yourself.

The reason the final realization, that the pearl is you, can be difficult to grasp is because we have spent so long looking outward for answers. We have been conditioned to believe that truth exists somewhere external to ourselves: in books, teachers, religions, sciences. But the pearl of great price is not something you acquire or learn, it is something you recognize. It is the awareness that has been present all along, the imagination that observes all the beliefs, all the chaos, all the seeking. When you finally see it, you realize it was never hidden, not really. You were simply looking in the wrong direction. The pearl is not an object to be found in space but the in subject doing the finding. It is the "I" in Man. And in that recognition, all the other pearls lose their luster, because you have found the the pearl of great price from which they all derive their meaning.

# Let Go Of Control And Control Self

*"If you go to jail, and say you get five to ten years, all right you know five years, and maybe you get off in six for good behavior, but when you are drafted into the army, there is no date that you are promised where they let you out. You're in for the duration.*

*Well, I was drafted into the army with seventeen million men, where* ***I did not ask the permission of anyone, I only consulted myself. I looked around, I knew what the world knew, it was something that had to be done. But I must be honest with myself, I didn't want any part of it, but no part of it.***

*Others would tell me, "Is that the act of a coward?" I didn't care what they said, is that being a good citizen? .. I didn't care what they said." -* ***Neville***

When Neville was drafted into the army, he did not want to go. Critics asked him, "Isn't that the act of a coward?" He simply felt, "I didn't care what they said."

Why? Well for one, the concept of cowardice varies from person to person. Everyone perceives things differently. You might appear heroic to some but villainous to others. Also, Neville knew that his desire was to not be in the army, and so he will use the law to fulfill his desire in imagination. So in this case we see Neville disregard the critical labels thrown on him and to imagine what he truly desires. Your imagination must become a place to protect with gates that reject the doubtful words of others.

A side note before the army story: when Neville wanted to be with his second wife, he caught himself worrying about *how* it would happen. He describes thinking about *how* he would get a divorce from his current wife. They had not spoken in a while, so *how* would he approach her? What would she say? And so on.

He admits he forgot to apply this law, yes, Neville himself, forgot to apply it. It happens to everyone, even teachers. Instead of blaming himself, or feeling down for not applying it, he returned directly to using the law. He released all concerns about *how* and simply slept in the assumption that he was already married to that woman. That he was no longer Neville unmarried, but Neville the husband. He fell asleep embodying the person he wanted to be. This was his heart's true desire. He applies the same principle in the army story.

*"Never blame, only resolve."* - ***Neville***

*"I was convinced I wanted out. I didn't ask anyone's permission, I did not discuss it with anyone as to why I should want out when seventeen million men are being drafted, such numberless girls to make a tremendous effort against this monstrous thing that was in Europe. I still wanted out. I did not take anyone into my confidence, as to why I wanted out."* - ***Neville***

*"I was drafted. I did not oppose it. They drafted me. Took me down to Camp Polk, Louisiana, for my basic training. And while I was there, I didn't want any part of it.* ***And I dare to assume that I am out of it and*** *made my normal natural application, as you have to do in the world of Caesar.* ***Within twenty-four hours, it came back and it was simply rejected****. It was signed disapproved and signed by my colonel."* - ***Neville***

Returning to the army story, Neville had clearly learned to let go of the "how." Despite others implying he was a coward, he remained unconcerned. He understood that fulfilling his heart's desire was paramount to him. Who else can fulfill the desires of your heart, other than you?

So Neville's desire was to get out of the army and go back to New York and be with his family. So Neville imagined where he wanted to be (*New York*) as though he was *already* there. While physically sleeping in a crowded room on a tiny bed, in his imagination he slept in his own room in New York. In imagination, he lived in the end result he wanted. Yet after doing this, he faced rejection. So he imagined he was out, but then was quickly rejected.

This is where many of us miss a crucial lesson. How did he

respond to this rejection? Did he think, "This doesn't work. I imagined and nothing happened. In fact, I was rejected. The world is more powerful than my imagination. I never get what I want?" Did he react in a powerless manner? Perhaps slightly, but who wouldn't? But did he complain or believe he could not get what he wanted? No. It would be natural to feel disappointed, but Neville understood we are not called to be natural but to not sin *(miss your mark).* To rise above natural reactions and instead take action by imagining.

Take note that Neville did not read books to get out. Any book can say to "imagine what you desire," but if we do not do it, then what is said does not matter. Sometimes we may feel we are making progress by solely reading, yet we remain the same on the inside. True rearrangements on the outside are a results of a true change on the inside.

> *"It was too early to disturb the twenty-five other fellas sleeping there, but I waited until the very first moment that I could leave that room, went down to the latrine and* ***shaved bade early and came up filled with the glow that the whole thing was done****.*
>
> ***All that I walked in that assumption for the next five days****. Nine days later, the same Colonel that disapproved my request, called me in. He said close the door Goddard – I closed the door – he said take a seat. And he never asked me to take a seat in his presence before. I was a private, you always stood in his presence.*
>
> *He gave me all the reasons in the world why I should still be in the army. He said you still want to get out – I said Yes Sir. Give me another reason – still want to get out – I said Yes Sir. Another one. When he exhausted all the reasons why I should be in the army and I am still saying yes sir, the said all right, bring me another application, have your captain sign it. Which I did. That day I was honorably discharged and out of the army. I didn't run away, I was honorably discharged." -* ***Neville***

Neville was able to not react even after rejection because Neville was not imagining to "get out," in a sense. He was imagining who and where he wanted to be. This is a huge difference. Had he merely imagined escaping and controlling external circumstances, his rejection would have devastated him. If his sole purpose was just to "make something happen on the outside," then the rejection would have meant failure.

Instead, he imagined to change himself in his imagination. To change his feeling of "I", or to rearrange the inner structure. He imagined to change the only thing being expressed, *himself*. Neville understood that he could change reality by changing himself. Because he focused exclusively on changing his *feeling*, he could persist regardless of circumstances. He remained indifferent to others' opinions, his physical location, or his rejection. He only cared about imagining what he wanted. This acceptance of the whole thing being done, allowed him to glow and feel radiant for 9 days. Even while doing physical training for the army, he experienced ecstasy and glow. He was not feeling what he "must feel" or "have to feel" to get out. Neville simply embodied what he wanted in his imagination, completely trusting the whole thing was done.

He released control of the outer-world and controlled himself instead. The world merely reflects the Self when you use it, and "Self" encompasses everything you think you have and are. Rather than feeling after, "I am stuck. I have to stay here," after rejection, he changed himself from the inside out and believed he possessed his desire. He now believed he was back in New York, had his bed back, his wife back, and so on. While his physical body was at the camp, his imaginal body was back at home and that is who he associated himself with.

> *"We are witnesses against ourself for the Lord's only name is I AM. Well, who was actually assuming that he was, in his own apartment 2,000 miles away? I AM. I am assuming I am where physically I am not.*
>
> *But the reality of me is not this, the reality of this speaker is his imagination. And I must be where I am in imagination.* ***So the***

***body was in Camp Polk, the reality of me was in that apartment of mine in New York City****. You will take this story and multiply it thousands of times. But here, while you are here I would like to make it so clear that you and you alone are responsible for your own selection."-* ***Neville***

*"Who is pharaoh in this world?*

*But then I believed in scripture. I believed that with God all things are possible, and I firmly believed that God is I AM. There is no other God. I will not in eternity know another God. But the God that I know is a present-tense, first-person experience: "I am the Lord thy God"—first person, present—and so I firmly believed him and I trusted him. So he clothed himself in me and made me alive, that's how I became alive. And now I will trust him implicitly. His name is I AM, he has no other name. There are other names but the real name is I AM. And so I will now trust him and test him.*

*And so, while in Egypt—Egypt means Camp Polk, Louisiana. So that's Egypt—I am in a compound, can't get out of it—a pass to get me out of the gate and then to get back, show the pass again, and there you are, completely restricted. My pharaoh whose heart was hardened... when I applied for an exit from this land called Egypt, it was denied. Same story as told us in the Old Testament. So pharaoh said "no" to the children of Israel, "You cannot go. I will not let you depart from Egypt." And so, all the pleas in the world would not soften his heart. He said no to my application.* ***So while this night, believing in the scripture, that the only name of God is I AM, I assumed that I am the man that I wanted to be. I assumed that I am where I would be were my assumption realized, and there I slept****." -* ***Neville***

There is also a symbolic quality to this story. Neville saw the colonel, the president of the time, the denial of his freedom as pharaoh. While there is no literal pharaoh in our world today, the pharaoh of scripture lives on as part of the drama in our lives. The moment we find ourselves trapped in a situation we cannot escape, that becomes our Egypt. When we try to leave only to be told "No," that refusal becomes our pharaoh with a hardened heart.

So what do we do when Egypt comes upon us? We turn to the only God there is: I AM. For the name of God is I AM, and that is the name forever and forever. Is that not your name? When you say you are anything, even your own name, you say "I am..." Where does I AM exist if not within you? So when you are trapped and cannot leave, you do not go to another pharaoh and ask for permission. You leave pharaoh alone, you leave Egypt alone, and you assume a new arrangement of I AM.

This is the mysterious revelation: pharaoh, caesar and the president of the time, has no power over I AM. The hardened heart of pharaoh, the locked gates of Egypt, the denial that seems so final, none of these can touch the creative power of I AM. When Neville assumed *"I am honorably discharged,"* he did not ask permission from the colonel. He did not plead with pharaoh. He simply rearranged his conception of himself and trusted in the only power that exists.

Do you see the power of this story? Are you witnessing the power of symbology? On this inner level, truth is symbolic, not literal. Millions will look outside and think that since there is no literal pharaoh ruling in the world today, then pharaoh does not exist. The literal mind will eventually become trapped, creating its own walls. It will not be able to see past them, let alone through them. But the one who sees the symbology, the one who recognizes pharaoh in their own life, can overcome it!

The symbolic mind sees that pharaoh is alive today *(this is what Blake calls "double vision").* Pharaoh is the authority you believe has power over you. Any authority! Pharaoh is the circumstance that tells you "No." Any circumstance! Pharaoh is the person, the institution, the condition that appears to have the final word on your freedom. When you go to your boss asking for a raise and he denies you, that is pharaoh. When you apply for your discharge from a situation and receive "disapproved," that is pharaoh. When the world tells you that you cannot be what you want to be, that is pharaoh.

The literal mind will always find reasons why this cannot be true. It will point to the colonel who denied the application, to the laws of the land, to the locked gates of Egypt. It will say, *"But pharaoh said no. But the world will not allow it. But circumstances are against me."* And in saying this, the literal mind hardens pharaoh's heart even more. It gives power to the very thing it fears.

But you who read these words, you who have followed and now know the story, you are being invited to see symbolically. You are being invited to recognize that when Neville was drafted into the army, he was not just telling a personal anecdote. He was revealing a universal principle. He was showing you what to do when your own Egypt appears. When your own pharaoh says "No." When your own circumstances seem impossible to escape.

You do what Neville did. You leave pharaoh alone. You do not fight against the outer-world. You do not plead or beg or try to convince anyone of anything. You simply turn to the only God there is, the I AM within you, and you assume that you are already the person you want to be. You assume that you are already free. And then you do nothing but remain convinced of your freedom. You let the creative power of I AM rearrange the outer-world to match your inner conviction.

This is not weakness. This is not passivity. This is the most powerful thing you can do. To imagine beyond the walls of Egypt! Because I AM does not conform to the nightmare. I AM is above the nightmare. I AM is the Dreamer, and the world is the dream. When you remember this, when you truly remember the I AM, no pharaoh can hold you. No Egypt can contain you. No circumstance can limit you. You are free the moment you assume you are free. You are not asking pharaoh for permission. You are not waiting for Egypt to release you. You are claiming your freedom by assuming it within yourself.

This is why Neville heard the voice say, *"That which I have done I have done. Do nothing."* Once you assume the state, once you rearrange I AM, the motion has been set.

> *"This is how I do it:* ***When I close my eyes this world is shut out and I, like Isaac, am blind to the outer-world****. Then I* ***feel*** *myself into the state of my desire. With my inner eye I see it all around me. I sense its solidity, and when my five senses are awakened I have the feeling of relief, knowing it is accomplished."* - ***Neville***

Notice carefully how when Neville imagines, he eliminates the concept of an "outer-world." He simply *feels* and *sees* what he desires.

This great secret is profoundly liberating. It is to do anything you wish in your imagination. Within your imagination, you are truly the highest power. You are so powerful in imagination that nobody can imprison you, you can only imprison yourself. No one can free you as well, only you can free yourself. In your imagination, you are the absolute ruler. You can choose to either rule over your assumptions or be ruled by them. It depends entirely on what you desire to be in your imagination.

So when you imagine, do not think in terms of things coming to you. Imagine in terms of things coming *from* you. This means it was within you all along.

**Artwork Commentary:**

In this artwork, I love its shadowy quality. The orb represents Neville's imagination and inner eye as he sleeps in the army camp, surrounded by men. In that moment, he blocks out the entire world and transports himself to the room he longs for in New York.

I see each sphere as a different dream. Outside the room, it is snowy and everything appears dead. His Egypt, his prison, appears frozen, solidified. Within that solidified reality, Neville imagines himself elsewhere, adding layer upon layer of sensory vividness until the imagine room no longer feels imaginary.

The image appears shadowy and dark, as though he is illuminating a realm within himself that remains dim, unseen by the mortal eye. Yet he persists until he sees it clearly. That is why the room appears warped, he is still striving to see this vision as vividly as possible. He is quite literally trying to be where he is in his imagination.

And this is how life can feel, can it not? Life often feels solid, immovable, dead to our desires. The camp is real, the snow is real, the duty is real. But within that seemingly fixed reality, there exists another dimension, imagination. And imagination, when persistently occupied, becomes fact.

So this image gives me both an eeriness and redemption. The eeriness comes from recognizing how much of what we call "reality" is actually a prison, a solidified dream the appears to have no escape. The redemption comes from understanding that we can dream a new dream. While the outside may appear solid, cold and dead, you can imagine yourself where you want to be. You bring light and life to your imagination, and in doing so, you bring light and life to your world.

# He Who Will Not Live By Love

*"Imagining with love is imagining without fear. With no fear, there is no doubt, no expectations, no confusion. For love is clear, honest and free, always."*

When I wrote this series a few years ago, there was a particular night that and I felt the safest and most loved I have ever felt in my life. I was literally laughing with joy in same bed I have gone to sleep depressed. It was a joy that came simply from removing fears and loving what I imagined. I was not even thinking of anything specific; I just could not contain myself. I was laughing freely, feeling completely at ease. While experiencing this deep freeing love, several thoughts emerged that I want to share.

Let me emphasize this point: You can release your fears if you do what you want in your imagination.

Loving what you do inside yourself will unlock a level of mental freedom you never knew existed. Your body will feel open, and you will develop an entirely different perspective on your desires. You will recognize how much greater you are than those desires and that you are actually creating everything in your imagination.

Let's touch upon fear. William Blake said this:

*"He who will not live by love must be subdued by fear."* - ***Blake***

This is absolutely true. If you are not focusing on what you love, you must be subdued by fear. Fear will eventually creep up on you, even if gradually, when you are not filling your imagination with what you love. If you do not choose love, fear must take its place. Surely you recognize this by now. How often do we think fearfully, believing it will protect us? When has fear ever truly protected us? Since when has feeling fearful become our definition of safety?

The first manifestation of fear is within the body. The body becomes afraid, the gut tightens and the muscles tense. Breathing becomes shallow and frustrations start to form. These irritations then come back to the imagination and the imagination naturally starts to think of things it dislikes. Fear bears fruit of guilt, paranoia, uneasiness, sabotage, rage etc. But at the root of all these emotions is fear.

So the goal is to *not* change each and every fearful thought. It is not to argue and contemplate on the fear. However, doing that is not in itself harmful, but it is more of a detour. To get to the true heart of the issue, we must let go the fear.

You think fearful thoughts because in the depths of yourself you are claiming to be afraid. Without feeling afraid, you would never think fearful thoughts and these thoughts would lose their potency.

So how does one overcome their fears?

By recognizing that you are the creator inside yourself, no longer just a reactor. This means you are creating that fearful thought. When the fearful thought comes up, take full responsibility for it! See it as your creation! This means you are always greater than what you are creating in your imagination. The fearful thought is only there because you created it to be there. It has no power of its own. It is truly all your dream. Feel these words to be true, *"I am in control. I am the Creator in here."* You do not have to justify why you are in control or why are you choosing to feel love (*that which has no fear*). You can just feel it and intensify it. No need to rationalize, or judge, just feel.

Second, once you take responsibility for that fearful thought as your creation, ask yourself this simple question: *"What would I love to imagine/feel after instead?"* From this Creator perspective, you can move toward love. Love is the most powerful force within you. Why? Because it never fails to change the Self. For fear creates stagnation, but love always transforms.

Why is this important?

Remember the reason why we are doing this. We are not trying to manipulate reality or force some change upon this physical world. That will happen *naturally*. Why? Because you have to express yourself in the world.

Since imagination is being expressed, how can we transform imagination *(Self)* most effectively? Through love. By going within our imaginations and experiencing what we love, having what we love, being what we love, we change at our core. *And it will never fail, for love never fails.*

From this new feeling of freedom and love, you will find it incredibly easy to imagine what you want. You will even find it harder to feel fear. This ease and love starts to become your natural state. There will be something will be lighter about you. You will not even have to imagine every little thing going your way, it just will start to go that way. Things you wanted months ago, start appearing in your world. Things that bothered you deeply, has little to no effect on you anymore. Why? Because you are no longer fearing. You are living in fulfillment and love. You are actually living what you love within, and this love expresses itself without.

To reiterate, when you are doing these meditations, and you get "resistance" which is just fear, remember the words of Neville:

> *"To repent is simply man's ability to entertain the nature of the opposite." -* ***Neville***

Can you entertain the opposite of fear? Can you embrace love instead? Is that not what you truly desire?

I used to have this terrible mindset. My imagination was cluttered with these rules: "I must do SATs (state akin to sleep) correctly or else. I must read this book and do these self-help actions or else. I must understand every concept flawlessly. I must discover that elusive key."

> *But here is the truth: your Self is the key. Change your Self by experiencing what you want in your imagination first. Do everything you desire in your imagination and do not allow any doubts to stop you in here.*

I do not mean this as a one time action. Do not just imagine what you want once. I mean that you start to now imagine what you want as a new way of living inside. You move from a place of imagining of what you fear to a place of what you love. This is not something you do once but it is actual change in how you imagine. From imagining this way, you will start to become what you are imagining which will be a lovely fulfilled Self. So it is not about imagining a lovely thing once, but imagining many lovely things throughout your life.

Once you understand this, you will see how unnecessary many rigid practices are. You might hear advice like: *"Wake up at 5:30 am, run 10 miles weekly, do this technique and that one..."* While there is nothing wrong with discipline (*in fact, I respect such dedication*), but ask yourself: do you really believe that running is the God that creates in your life? That performing SATs five times daily guarantees results? The fundamental truth is that you only receive what you first give yourself. *If you do not have it, then you have not given it to yourself.*

This is why so many people struggle with Neville's teachings despite following every technique perfectly. They are imagining to *get* something rather than to *have and be* something. They perform their imaginal acts mechanically, thinking that on some future day when they will finally receive what they have been imagining themselves as. Instead, they must see themselves actually *being* what they desire in their imagination right now. They must experience themselves *already* possessing what they desire. Not imagining so that they can one day have it, but imagine they already have it. If you are going to be it one day, then why not be it now?

Let me give you an example for clarity: Say one person imagines their desire 100 times, thinking "If I do this enough times, eventually it will express and then I will become what I am imagining." Another person imagines themselves *being* that thing in imagination, as in seeing themselves *already being it*. Do you see the crucial difference? The first person is perpetually postponing their fulfillment in imagination to some future outer moment. They are imagining *from* a state of postponement, hoping to eventually reach fulfillment somewhere and sometime outside. It is all vaguely stitched together. The second person is imagining *from* fulfillment itself. They are not waiting to become, they imagining themselves *already* being what they want. No postponement, but experiencing themselves as they wish in imagination.

*"God gives man what man first gives himself."* - ***Neville***

When you do not imagine with love, you naturally become subdued by fear. This is not a punishment, it is simply the nature of imagination. The forgetfulness of love creates a vacuum that fear rushes to fill. How does one imagine with love? Imagining in love does not necessarily have to do with morals, although it can. It more has to do with freedom, freedom from judgment, from expectation, from control.

Imagining with love can be as simple as imagining something you genuinely love. For me, it is the freedom to imagine without any expectations or pressures. If I see a memory that I love, I love it. If I imagine a scene that brings me joy, I love it. If I imagine the possession of what I desire, I love it. It can be elaborate as a constructed scene, or as simple a color that I love. Regardless of the complexity or simplicity the action is the same, you love it.

*I love what I am imagining.*

This distinction must be understood. I am *not* imagining what I *think* love is. I am *not* imagining things that I was told is love. No, I *love* what I am imagining. I love it as if it is a person or an artwork that I love. It naturally feels joyful, free.

When you try to imagine what you think love is, or what you were told it is, then you will start to doubt. You will wonder if it is really love, or if you are doing things well enough, or if your scene it perfect enough etc. This is all coming from anxiety.

This is a key many miss. They imagine their desire while simultaneously imagining all the reasons they cannot have it, all the obstacles, all the doubts. They imagine with fear rather than love. They imagine while judging themselves: "Am I doing this right? Is this good enough? What if it doesn't work?" This is *not* imagining with love, this is imagining with anxiety. And when you imagine with anxiety (*doubts*), you receive more for things grow after their own kind.

When you imagine with love, you are not trying to manipulate. You are not performing a technique to force changes. You are simply enjoying the experience of possessing what you desire in your imagination. You are loving it and feeling it. No ulterior motives, just simply love.

This state of loving your imagination is your natural state. It is who you were before fear taught you to doubt, before the world convinced you that imagination was powerless. When you return to this state, when you simply love what you imagine without needing it to prove itself, you discover that imagination was never powerless at all. It was always creating. You were just creating from fear instead of love.

Now, we may not be perfect at this. There will be times when we do not love what we imagine, when we fear it instead. It creeps back in and we find ourselves imagining limitations, obstacles, and worst-case scenarios. When this happens, we naturally begin to move toward fear. But here is the beautiful truth: the only answer to fear is to return to love. Not to fight the fear, not to resist it, not to shame yourself for feeling it, but simply to return to imagining with love once more.

This is why I say there is no pressure, no shame, no fear in this practice. You cannot fail at this because there is nowhere to fall. When you notice yourself imagining from fear, you have become aware. In that awareness, you have the power to choose differently. You can choose to return to loving what you imagine.

It always comes back to love. Fear is merely the forgetting of love. Remembering love is as simple as imagining something, anything, that you genuinely love and loving it. *And when you imagine with love, you become love, for we become what we imagine.*

If you are skeptical, I invite you to test this approach. If you think imagining in love does nothing, try it. Experience what happens when you remove your fears for a bit and love what you imagine.

> *"So you try it tonight, tomorrow night, until it finally becomes a habit and you live by it. If perchance you should forget it, my prayer is that it will not be for long, that you'll come right back to it again...*
>
> *You're here to bear fruit and bear it abundantly. Let no one tell you, "Be satisfied, you have enough, that this is alright...just eke out the days and wait."* ***Don't let anyone tell you that. If you have a hunger, satisfy it. Satisfy it in this simple, simple way. No one will be hurt, because when you do it this way he isn't going to hurt anyone, for he's not going to hurt himself.***
>
> *So, if you say I want this, that and the other for another, alright, he won't be hurt. If you want it for another, ask a very simple question, "Would I want it for myself? If anyone gave it to me would I want it?" Yes. Well then, do it. And whenever you do it lovingly, you're doing the right thing. All day long you can create, create lovely wonderful things for every being in the world. Spend a half-minute, just a few seconds rearranging words."* - ***Neville***

**Artwork Commentary:**

This artwork depicts the same gentleman in two contrasting mental states. On the left, he imagines himself imprisoned; on the right, he envisions his freedom. The crucial insight is not merely that he must imagine freedom, but that without actively imagining it, he inevitably falls back into the prison of his own making, where all he perceives are walls and unanswerable questions.

We must always exist in some state within ourselves, and it appears we are constantly pulled between two fundamental modes of being: One of love and unconditional freedom, or one of bondage that fixates solely on external circumstances. The man on the left imagines with his senses alone, looking only with his physical organs. He sees walls he cannot surpass and mountains he cannot climb, trapped by what his limited perception of Self.

Meanwhile, the same man on the right opens the door to his own imagination from within, and the clouds represent a carefree, nonjudgmental freedom. The key revelation is that both figures are the same gentleman, merely existing in different states of mind, yet this difference changes everything about his experience of reality.

This distinction echoes the two worldviews offered by Neville and Scripture. You are either the man of the senses who sees only with physical organs, or you are the man of imagination who believes in your imaginal eyes. The man of the senses is bound by what appears to be, while the man of imagination creates from what he conceives within.

The reason this matters is that imagination is not mere fantasy or escape, it is the creative force through which we shape our experience of Self. When we rely solely on our senses, we become reactive, interpreting and responding to a world that seems fixed and external to us. But when we engage our imagination, we become proactive, actively participating in the creation of our reality from the inside out.

The prison and the freedom are not two different places; they are two different ways of being. The walls exist only insofar as we perceive them as insurmountable. The moment we shift from sensing to imagining, from reacting to creating, the walls dissolve because we recognize them for what they truly are, constructs of a limited perspective rather than absolute truth.

# Inner Self Must Be Exalted

> *"The world may tell you that you are crazy, but I am telling you from experience that you've got to* ***feel*** *you are God in order to know who God is!"* - **Neville**

IT COMES DOWN TO IDENTITY, who you think you are in your imagination. Who you are identifying yourself with.

In order for these meditations or Neville's ideas to truly work, and in order to feel completely free, you must identify yourself with the one *within* you. This Inner Man of Imagination.

When meditating, close your eyes and set aside the outer-world. You are left with a darkness, a sacred space of creation. In here, you can summon images and words you want (*or do not want*) to hear and see. But it is you who is doing it all.

Now listen to the voice in your imagination, your awareness. Understand this: That is the true you. No, not this outer body. This Inner Man of Imagination is Self! That Self took upon this limitation and it is the only thing that must be changed.

> *"Leave the world just as it is and change Self. No one to change but Self."* - **Neville**

Neville is referring to the Inner Man, the only Self that truly exists. Why should we leave the world alone? Because it merely expresses Self! Why change only Self? Because "Self *must* always be expressed." This is the law that Neville is speaking of. You need not wonder "Will my imaginal act express?" For who is doubting? Self! Who is worrying? Self! And what gets expressed? Self! So a worried, doubtful Self is what is expressed *naturally*.

> *You can always trust Self will be expressed.*

This is why it is important to change Self, by changing the contents and conceptions inside your imagination. Leave the world alone and change Self. When I speak of changing Self, I do not mean in terms of "fixing" Self. Self is the Conceiver behind the conceptions. So the Self, you, are already worthy, and there is nothing to fix. When you hear "change Self" it means to change the conception you hold of Self. Not as something to fix or gain, for there is nothing to fix or gain within, only a change of experience of Self.

To clarify, here is what I mean: that voice within, the one in you that imagines, is you. That is the one who is desiring. That is the one wants to be exalted. That is the one who wants to have their desires fulfilled.

Can you see that? The one who is desiring, is in desire *in imagination.* So that is where you fulfill by rearranging the structure of imagination by imagining fulfillments with love.

Discard the outer-world and that includes your identification with this body. This is all an expression, a symbol of that Self, the Imaginal Man. So identify yourself, not with this outer body, but with the Inner Man, the one who is truly desiring.

So just take a moment and close your eyes and observe the blackness. Then pay attention to your inner voice. That is the one who is desiring. That is the one who is in pain. That is the one who wants to be free from whatever bondage. That is the one who needs to be exalted, the true Self. That is the one who wants to see beauty, to hear good news and who has the ability to! That is the one who desires to live a lovely life. It all starts from within ourselves.

So give it to yourself in your imagination! It is remarkably simple. If you take this seriously, you will change how you see and experience life. For you will change how you experience your imagination and they are one. You will identify yourself from within then you will grant your every wish from within. It does not matter if it is impossible, if your Self wants it, imagine it within. There are no limitations for that Self. If it seeks freedom from guilt, release that guilt in your imagination. Do not ask permission from anything. There are no rules that says you cannot have things in imagination. The beautiful thing is that the inner world can give you anything. Though I dislike separating You and Self because they are not truly separate, I am doing so only for clarity.

If you embarrass yourself in your imagination, or hurt yourself, spark fear into yourself, you are doing that to yourself inside. You worry about what society thinks, what so-so might think? Who is doing the worrying? Self! It is all you inside. When you feel hurt or scared, it is not your body feeling this, it is your Inner Self, the true you, the one capable of shedding its state like a snake sheds its skin. When fear arises, who creates it? Self! Self is imagining it! But that Self does not want to remain in fear; it longs to imagine something new.

When you identify with the outer-world rather than your True Self and the limitless inner world, you remain stuck. Self becomes irritated, fearful etc. The fear in your body, your irritations, that angst will forever remain until you fulfill it within.

> *"So tonight, you take yourself, start with self, and try it. See if you do not in the immediate future actually change your world to conform to these changes that take place within your mind.* ***As I change within, I change it without.*** *"* ***- Neville***

We already do this but we do it in ways that are harmful to Self. We try to eat this and that, and read this and that to save Self but Self cannot be saved by outer means. Self always wants fulfillment in imagination. So identify not with this world, but with your Inner Self, the one who is desiring and has the power to fulfill.

Since you hold the power, why not exalt yourself? You may think you are too old, too lost, too defeated, too broken to change. Forget that! The only reason you think this way is because you are not identifying yourself with the Inner Man of Imagination. You are identifying with the outer, with the body, with past failures, with what others have said about you. But none of that is the true you. You are not bound by what the senses express. The Inner Man is always free to imagine anew, regardless of what the senses report.

If you see that you are that Inner Man, then you realize you can do something. What can you, the Inner Man, do? In spite of the senses screaming otherwise, in spite of reason arguing against you, the Inner Man, can change. You can imagine differently. You can rearrange the structure of your imagination. For better or for worse, but choose life. Imagine a life worthy of remembering. It is all done inside of you.

> *"The great artists of the world, no matter who they are in the world they are on this level. And what I speak of here is an entirely different level–when you experience this separation from this world and that experience I call religion. Religion is the devotion to the most exalted experience that one really has realized in this world.* ***He is simply devoted to this reality that reason may deny, all other things deny, but he knows he has experienced it.*** *" -* ***Neville***

**Artwork Commentary:**

In this artwork, a veil symbolically appears to separate you from seeing that you are the Being behind each state, that you are the Conceiver, not the conception. The Man on the throne of contemplation is you, the steps are your states. You are never the steps but the Being always above them. The ascending stairs represent states of being, not states of fixing what is broken, but enriching experiences of Self. You are inherently worthy of every step, every state, every experience. At the summit of each step, you will discover it is always been you, because everything exists within your own imagination. A veil appears to obscure your vision, preventing you from seeing that you are the being behind each state, you are not the dream itself, but the Dreamer.

When you catch yourself imagining something within your own imagination, you have caught yourself in the act of creation within yourself. You are aware of thoughts forming, images appearing, feelings arising, all within the private theater of your imagination. There is a veil that prevents the mortal eye from seeing what you are doing in there, yet you are intimately aware of what you are doing.

The outside world cannot perceive your inner imaginings, but you can. This proves you exist as the observer behind the veil of physical perception, as the imagination that creates and witnesses simultaneously. Your awareness of your own imagination is direct evidence that you are the Dreamer, not merely the dream, that you are the one behind the veil, looking out through it, not the one trapped on the other side looking in.

# Love What You Imagine

*"You don't have to sit down and burst a blood vessel pounding out the details of your desire. You can imagine as you walk down the street... **A simple assumption is easy and can be lots of fun!"** - **Neville***

A FUNDAMENTAL TRUTH in regards to thoughts and feelings that I discovered is this:

*Thoughts come from your feeling.*

Do you grasp the significance of this? Can you see how this insight transforms everything?

It means that all fearful thoughts, worries about potential problems or doubts such as "What if it never happens?" originate *from* your *feeling*. When you honestly examine your imagination, ask yourself: "Where do these thoughts come from?" Or simply, "What is generating these thoughts?"

When a fear-inducing thought appears, try observing it carefully. Slow down and pay close attention. You will discover that the thought was not first but your *feeling* of fear preceded it. Though subtle and difficult to notice, this sequence becomes clear when you truly pay attention.

Feeling of what specifically? *Feeling of Self.* It is the feeling about myself that causes me to have certain thoughts, motivations, habitual arguments or connection purposed conversations on the inside. A change in feeling of Self, is a change in ones inner life.

This is crucial because if the *feeling of Self* is the cause of the thought, then the thought has no power of its own. It has no truth in itself. The thought is generated. This means that when you change your *feeling of Self*, all the thoughts necessary for your bridge of incidents are already laid out for you. You do not have to worry about having the "right" thoughts or saying the "right" things in your imagination. So there is no more trying to think perfectly. Beautiful thoughts come naturally from beautiful feelings of Self.

*"Now, this is how it works. But you must, above all things, when you carry on this inner conversation with those who will be sincerely thrilled because of your successful transaction in closing the deal to*

*own the thing, but also in the successful running of it, the operation of it, you must* ***capture the feeling! Feeling truly is the secret****. You must* ***feel the reality*** *of what you are doing." -* ***Neville***

Many times I have had fearful or doubtful thoughts and wondered, "What is the underlying belief? What belief do I need to change to stop having these thoughts?" I would find something such as, "I am safe," and repeat it all day in my imagination trying to "change the belief." But a belief is just a *feeling*. It *feels* true. *From* that position, you think in accordance with those feelings.

Replace the word "belief" with *feeling*. Think only in terms of: Creating, feeling and thinking. You create the feeling of Self that you want, and from that, thoughts naturally emerge. That is a state. So let go of the idea that beliefs are difficult to change or that they are blockages in your subconscious that must be conquered. That is making this unnecessarily complicated. It is your imagination, and you can feel whatever you choose. You create your own blockages by feeling blocked, and you create the difficulty of removing them all on the inside.

Now replace the word "belief" with "feeling" because "belief" implies something difficult to change. When you understand that a belief is simply a *feeling (just like desiring is just a feeling)*, the concept of "changing a feeling" becomes much more achievable. This is all that needs to change because *from* your feelings, you generate thoughts that align with the nature of that *feeling*. What you feel to be true is the makeup of your Self, and there is nothing to change but Self.

Fearful feelings give birth to fearful thoughts. When you change your feeling, you will recognize there was no truth in your fearful thoughts. You only "believe" them because you feel them to be true.

Here is an example: say you are lying in bed when a thought about someone breaking into your house enters your imagination. Fear follows, making the thought seem real. You worry about manifesting this fear, then try to identify the underlying belief, randomly selecting one that makes sense. Perhaps you search through childhood or teenage memories. Next, you attempt to replace this belief by repeating the words, *"I am safe in my house"* over and over, trying to convince yourself. You might feel temporary relief, but tomorrow the cycle repeats.

I followed this approach for a long time, and frankly, it is ineffective. It is an ineffective way to change yourself. It is stressful and lacking any true understanding of Self.

Here is a better approach: when you are lying in bed and the thought of a robber appears, followed by fear making the thought seem real, pause immediately. Ask yourself, *"Why am I creating this?"* The answer becomes clear: Because of my *feeling* of fear. I feel fear first, and *from* this feeling, thoughts of robbers emerge.

There is no inherent truth in the thought of being robbed. It is merely created by your feeling. By changing your feeling, these thoughts naturally cease. Just as the thought of the robber arose naturally from that fear, new thoughts will naturally emerge from your new feeling. What is actually happening is that there is an underlying feeling of being unsafe. Recognizing that this belief of being unsafe is simply a feeling of Self which then clarifies what needs to changed.

Remember that this is *all happening in your imagination.* You can feel safe within your imagination. You can feel completely confident and secure in your inner world. Remind yourself of this truth: *"I am safe in here. Within my imagination, I am completely secure."* This is pure *feeling*. Begin to *feel* this safety. Just feel it, and do not question, reason, or analyze you way out of it. Simply feel.

> ***"Anyone can do it. This game is easy to play and can be lots of fun in the doing.*** *Think of an object you would like to hold. Think of a place you would desire to be. Then find an object in that room and feel it until it takes on sensory vividness.*
>
> *Don't make it a lamp, but that lamp; not a table, but that table. Sit in that chair until you feel the chair around you. View the room from that chair and you are there, for you are all imagination and must be wherever you are in your imagination. Now, cast your bread*

*upon the water by feeling the relief of being there, and let your genie (your imagination) build a bridge of incident over which you will cross to sit in that chair, hold that lamp, and touch that table."* - ***Neville***

Why focus solely on *feeling*?

Because we think *from* our feelings. This is how we know we are in a particular state. So immerse yourself completely in feeling the reality. Surrender entirely to the feeling (*because the feeling is your "end"*), and you will naturally think-from that position. There is no effort required because thoughts are the fruit and the feeling is the tree. Just as an orange tree must produce after its own kind, your thoughts will be aligned with your feeling.

Return to your role as Creator in your world of imagination. Stop identifying with your thoughts and understand they originate from what you *feel* your reality to be. From this awareness, simply shift your feeling to what you desire to feel. If you feel that this requires too much effort then there is misunderstanding. Using your imagination to feel what you wish is not a burden or forbidden but a freedom.

This is why Neville says "*Don't make it a lamp, but that lamp; not a table, but that table. Sit in that chair until you feel the chair around you.*" *That* chair implies something concrete about you. Similarly, do not pick a random stranger off the street to congratulate you on your good fortune. You can if you want to but why not choose *that* person, someone specific who would naturally be present in such a moment? A true friend would be there supporting you, wouldn't they? So imagine *that* friend's support, hear their voice, feel their genuine joy for you.

When you make your imaginal acts personal, they become infinitely more real to you. Generic scenarios often lack the reality needed to change your idea of Self. But when you see *that* specific chair in *that* specific room, when you hear *that* particular person's voice saying those *exact* words, this is when your imagination comes alive with feeling. And remember, feeling is the secret.

The people you choose to populate your imaginal scene with should be those who would naturally be part of that reality. If someone in your circle would genuinely be thrilled by your success, include them in your scene. If someone would be shocked at the hearing of your new state, then let them be shocked. If someone else would be envious, and you know they would be, then imagine that envy. It is not about being arrogant. It is about what *feels real* to you. Their envy implies your change in state, for what would they be jealous for? Their curiosity about how you achieved it implies your accomplishment is real.

This anchors your imagination in a feeling of reality. When you imagine random, faceless people, you can feel you are fabricating something artificial. You do not need to imagine the president or Caesar to come and shake your hand in congratulations to change a state. All you need is some response, some motor movement, some honest reaction in those around you on the inside.

But when you imagine *that* person reacting in *that* way, a way that aligns with their actual personality and your relationship with them, you will find yourself losing yourself in the reality of that dream. And when you lose yourself that way in your imagination, you can truly *feel* it.

*That* chair in *that* room means you own or have access to *that* space. *That* friend's congratulations means you have achieved something worthy of celebration. *That* person's jealousy means you have risen above your former state. All of these responses, whether praise or envy, confirm the same thing: you have changed.

A questions comes, what if I do not know anyone around me? What if in my situation I know of no such people? I would say that this way that Neville is speaking of is only *one way* to imagine. If you want to be friends with a different crowd but do not know anyone, *feel* that you do. Start to *feel* that you know people. *Feel* that you are not a stranger anymore but a friend. *Feel* that feeling of comfort knowing you are around people who respect you. Your feeling needs no basis in fact for it to be feel as real.

*The best way to gain a friend is to be become one.*

This does not have to be limited to friends but just notice the pattern of what is being said. The best way to gain something is to become *that* something, and we use feeling to become *that*. Assume you are a friend and the friends will come.

So are scenes not necessary? Not exactly. They can be used to make the feeling of reality more present. And as we know, feeling is the secret. Not scenes are the secret, but feeling. But if you cannot use a scene, then the goal is still the same, *change the feeling*. Start to feel after a new reality within you for reality is within us after all. If you can use a scene, why not use it as a tool? If you do not have a scene, continue changing the feeling.

Personally, I love to feeling after things that are a bit beyond the scope of what I believe I am allowed to feel. Even if it makes no sense me, but it is a feeling I want, a feeling of total awe and wonder, I will feel it. Even if there are no people in the idea, if I love the idea, love the feeling, I will accept it.

*You do not need anything outside of you to change anything within you.*

*"First, feeling is the one and only reality" and the second, "Don't think, feel; feel the reality of."* - ***Neville***

The answer to what you should do and feel is always in your deepest desires. To truly change your *feeling*, it must be something you genuinely, deeply want to *feel*.

I must emphasize this point. When you sincerely feel what you have always wanted to feel, you will naturally think-from that position. This is what it means to be in a state. This is living in the end. It is all about *feeling*. It cannot be something you only "sort of" want to feel. That will never create lasting change. It might work temporarily, but you will not commit to it. It must be a feeling you are truly yearning for.

Example from my own experience:

I used to be harshly self-critical. I would call myself names and constantly put myself down. I felt guilty about past actions and things I might do in the future. I thought this pattern was impossible to break because I tried many things with no lasting results. Any improvements would only last a week before I reverted to feeling terrible and talking down to myself. I would automatically anticipate punishment coming my way and try to change those thoughts to change my feelings. I would spend hours trying to reason my way out of this state, only to find myself trapped in a different mental cave. My gut constantly held this underlying tension. Despite my best efforts to find relief, I could not sustain it for more than a week or maybe a month. I desperately wanted relief, but nothing I did seemed to work long-term. I tried SATs (*state akin to sleep*), replayed scenes over and over, practiced mental diet all day (*flipping thoughts*). But over time I realized I was attacking the "thoughts" not the actual cause.

You may desire to think and feel what you want but the moment you do that, you restrict yourself of that for the sake of the past or fear of the future. You may think of things that you have done that you dislike, or things that were done to you that you dislike, and because of this you cannot imagine what you want. But the questions you should ask yourself are, "Is that what you want? Do you want to restrict yourself? Do you want to guilt yourself or fear the future?" Of course not. Then learn to give yourself what you want in your imagination and what you want is freedom to have what you want. This issue is resolved by *feeling* that you can have what you want.

The truth is, you can think anything in your imagination. But most importantly, you can *feel* anything in your imagination. You can actually feel what you desire.

I do not mean just a basic desire, such as "I am loved." That is good, but don't you want to feel more than that?

> *"Don't tell me what you don't want, tell me what you want."* - ***Neville***

What do you truly want? Just a bit of love? Or do you want to feel like you are the most loved being? Where there is nothing but love in your imagination? Where everyone cherishes you and deeply desires to help you, and you do not have to do anything to receive this abundance of love?

Why not feel that? Because of what? Fear? Are you afraid to *feel* that deeply? Does anyone have to know what you feel in your depths? If you do not allow yourself to feel that way, you are rejecting this inner experience, so do not complain when the world mirrors that rejection. Free yourself entirely in your imagination. Stop worrying about whether it will happen or what will happen. Reality is found in your imagination, which is Self.

Now that I am feeling what I want to feel, I find myself unable to criticize myself when used to do so often. Whenever an old thought surfaces, I neither feel it nor fear it. It no longer seems real to me. That is how I know all that fear was an illusion. It always has been. I cannot sit and talk down to myself anymore. I am exalting my state inside imagination. I am seeing myself how I want to see myself because I can and so can you.

This should be fun as well! A good friend asked me, "So what do you do when you are speaking with someone and you do not want to listen to them?" I said, "I imagine what I want." Now truth is, sometimes I get annoyed, it is only a natural reaction. But I do have an imagination that I must use! Then he said, "So you just hear them say, "You are so awesome! You are the greatest!" And I replied, "If that is what I want to hear, then yes." It takes no time at all to do a lovely imaginal act. It always comes down to my desire in my imagination. I want to fulfill everything in here. That is the goal.

*Feel the reality of already being what you desire.*

It is only fun if you imagine and feel what you want. It is not fun "trying to get" or "trying to manifest" or "checking the world to see if it is growing." Growth, getting what you want, experiencing what you want is all done within!

One day you will look back and see how lowly you once thought of yourself. You will not hate yourself or feel angry with yourself. You will feel detached, almost in disbelief. You will wonder how you lived that way for so long (*I mean live that way in your imagination*). You will extend compassion to yourself, but then you will turn around and continue your walk.

So start walking assuming all the lovely things for yourself. Make it fun and freeing. It does not have to take hours on end. You can imagine a lovely thing and then imagine another one. You can hold onto one for a longer time if you love it, then hold onto it. If you want to love a new idea then love a new idea. Imagination can be most freeing!

> *"If you doubt it tonight, I would only ask you not to deny it to the point of not trying it but hold it in abeyance and try it now. Just try it, even if you want to disprove it. I tell you; you will not disprove it. You will, in the attempt to disprove it, prove it.*
>
> *And then, slowly you will come to completely accept it, and then you will walk in the company of God. You won't have to wait for Sunday morning to meet him in a church, or any time of day. No matter where you are – you could be standing in a bar enjoying a drink, having fun at a dance, and you are in the company of God. It makes no difference where you are once you know God, and God is your own wonderful human Imagination. And you'll become extremely discriminating, because you'll know you can't entertain these ideas with complete acceptance of them and not reap them in your world. And who wants to reap the tears forever?*
>
> *So, you become ever more discriminating.* ***Don't think for one second that you'll live a loose life. No. You'll become a far***

***more wonderful person in the world. You hear a piece of gossip – it doesn't interest you." - Neville***

**Artwork Commentary:**

This artwork presents two figures confronting the same physical reality, walls and closed doors, yet experiencing profoundly different inner worlds. A chair on the left of them symbolizes the contemplative space where perception is formed. The man on the left sees only barriers: walls that confine, doors that remain shut. His gaze is fixed on the limits before him, and these limits become his entire reality.

The man in the middle, however, looks through and beyond these same obstacles. He ignores the closed doors entirely, as if they hold no power over his imagination. Where one perceives entrapment, the other perceives freedom, not as something granted by external circumstances, but as something generated from within.

Our Self is shaped not merely by what exists around us, but by what we choose to see. The man in the middle does not deny the presence of walls and doors; he simply refuses to let them define the boundaries of his imagination. His freedom exists because he has cultivated a love for it so deep that it transcends physical limitation.

The man in the middle imagines freedom because he loves freedom with an intensity that reshapes his perception. He has internalized freedom so completely that even when the world attempts to shut him out, even when doors close and walls rise, his inner vision remains unbothered. His freedom persists not because his circumstances have changed, but because his devotion to freedom itself has become stronger than any external constraint. What we love deeply enough, we will always find a way to perceive, regardless of what reality presents to us.

# Imagination Is Not A Courtroom

There are many rules that a person can follow inside this realm of imagination:

"I *should* do it or else..."

"I *must* do it this way or else..."

"I *have* to do this or else..."

These are rules we create in our imaginations. Why do we follow them? Simply because we are trying to control the world through our physical actions. When we do not do what we "should do," we inflict anxiety, guilt, and shame upon ourselves.

Browse and you will find countless forms of media persuading you on what you "should do," "have to do," or worse, "must do." What if you do not comply? You are labeled with various insults: failure, worthless, lazy and accused of not trying hard enough.

Please remove all these rules from imagination. They fundamentally do not belong in this inner world. This inner world is one of image making, not rule making. You create new images and new words inside this place. You can rearrange existing words such as a recent conversation. Regardless, it is about image making.

How do we remove these rules? The same answer, by doing and *feeling* what you desire to do in your imagination! Simply embrace the thought and feeling in spite of what reasons you have. Once you do that, you have succeeded in surpassing these rules and limitations. You are freeing yourself in your own imagination. This is what eliminates all these rules. When a rule appears, which expresses as a feeling that stops you, ask yourself, "Do I want to follow this rule?" If not, then don't. It is your imagination after all. You created the rule in the first place for rules must have a rule maker.

*Love needs no rules, so love what you imagine.*

When you follow rules in your imagination rather than creating new images, you will eventually encounter a feeling of mental claustrophobia. Since things grow after their own kind, then rules will create more rules. We start with one then there are two, then four, then eight etc. All until we feel confined into our own imaginations, and we lose sight of who we are inside.

Many believe the world exists solely outside of them, so they create all these rules to control it. To them, life is a wild entity that must be controlled. So to keep the fear at bay, rules are created. It usually comes into the form of restrictions and self-denial. One day man thinks they should sacrifice an animal, the next they are kneeling on pews in a cathedral.

A mental maze is formed and trying to leave can make one feel lost. These rules give birth frustration, irritation, guilt, and a poor self-image. They become walls inside and imprison you. When you try to escape while still clinging to these rules, you create a hydra in your imagination. You may kill one thought, but then two more emerge. You continue fighting, and these frustrations multiply.

Our imagination shapes to us. Meaning your imagination becomes a courtroom *only* because you have become guilty! Pardon yourself completely and the courtroom will disappear and the imagination will reflect the freedom. Why?

> *"As in water face answers to face, so the mind of man reflects the man."* - ***Proverbs 27:19***

Because face answers to face but the mind reflects, not the mind but Man! The shaping of imagination is based upon the Man. This is why if Man desires a change in life, they must change themselves. The world will never change if Man doesn't, for the world is created by imagination but imagination reflects Man.

Since the imagination reflects the Man, if the imagination is in chaos, is it because the Man is in chaos. The imagination changes and follows the Man.

The imagination was never meant to be a courtroom where you stand in trial. It was meant to be a garden where you plant seeds. You do not plant seeds by obeying rules, you plant them by imagining the desire fulfilled to their fullest extent.

When you are truly thirsty, do you merely have a sip of water? No, you drink until the thirst ceases to be.

> William Blake once said, "*He who desires, but acts not, breeds pestilence.*"

The meaning of pestilence is a contagious or infectious epidemic disease that is virulent and devastating.

What could be more accurate? When you fail to act, when you are not a doer, you create disease. These are the plagues mentioned in scripture. A true doer looks into the perfect Law of Liberty, the law that frees you.

And what does it mean to act? To do? It does not mean to move your physical body in the world. True movement is not done with the physical feet, but with mental ones. To be a doer is to *feel* a dream real, so real that it is no longer a dream to you, but becomes your present reality. It takes on the tones of reality all inside yourself. When you are a doer, when you practice making dreams real inside you, you are eating from the Tree of Life.

You see, the world does not care what you *intend* to feel or what you *wish* you could imagine. It only responds to what you *are* in imagination. And what you are in imagination is determined by what you feel to be true of Self in your imagination. When you assume the feeling of the wish fulfilled, when you dare to feel it in spite of reason, in spite of senses, you have *acted*. You have moved. You have done the work that matters.

This is why scripture says the doer will be blessed in their deed. Not the one who hears the word, but the one who *does* it. And doing it means daring to feel differently within, regardless of what the senses say. That is the inner movement that begets all outer movement.

William Blake is saying nothing different than what was said in Proverbs:

*"Hope deferred makes the heart sick, but a desire fulfilled is a Tree of Life."* - ***Proverbs 13:12***

So when you eat from the Tree of Life you are fulfilling your desires within. Consequently, you are also healing your heart. There is no healing in the hearts of anyone by following mental orders and inventing new mental rules.

Years ago, I was told by my teacher that I could not handle a more challenging English class. The class required reading several books and writing numerous papers. I was told I did not possess the intelligence to complete those tasks. Yet, I could not stop myself from writing about and reading Neville's work. So what was the difference? I was the same person. The difference was *what* I was reading and writing about.

I share this story as a symbol for your imagination. Use me in the story as a personification of your imagination. You (*The Inner Man of Imagination*) may be told there are rules you must follow, and these rules restrict you from imagining what you truly want. Something convinces you that you are not qualified to imagine such thoughts or feel such feelings. But the issue is not your imagination itself, it is *what* you are choosing to imagine with your imagination.

My teacher's assessment was based on the assumption that I could not engage with complex material. But that was not true. I was deeply engaged with Neville's teachings, reading, analyzing, and writing extensively about these ideas that were just as complex, if not more so, than anything in that English class.

Just as I was the same person capable of deep engagement when the subject matter resonated with me, your imagination is the same powerful imagination regardless of what you are imagining. The question is not whether you *can* imagine something, but whether you will *allow* yourself to imagine it fully, without restriction, without permission from the outside world.

The rules you have been given are not laws of reality, they are suggestions about what you should accept as real about yourself. But you are the operant power. You decide what is real by what you imagine and accept as true within yourself. Do not let external voices convince you that certain thoughts or feelings are off-limits to you. Your imagination is yours, and it responds to what you feed it, not to what others say you should feed it.

Remember:

> *If you are what you want in your imagination, you will do what you "should, have and must do" in the world. For we act from what we are.*

There are many in the world who shout they have morals until they are tested. When a situation arises that requires them to exercise those morals, the morals suddenly vanish like water evaporating on a hot day.

Why does this happen? Because their morals were never *felt* as real within them. They were only *thought about*, only agreed with them intellectually. They were rules imposed from without, not states lived from within. And so when pressure comes, when the moment of truth arrives, there is nothing there to support them. The morals collapse because it was never rooted in their *being*.

The same is true with imagination. Many will say *"imagination creates reality"* and yet they do not imagine. They agree with the principle in theory, but when life presents a challenge, when circumstances press against them, they abandon imagination entirely. They return to worry, to fear, trying to manipulate or force the outer-world with physical effort alone.

But if you truly believe that imagination creates reality, then you must *exercise* it, especially when the pressures come. Not when everything is going well and you feel no need for it, but when the world is shouting "This is impossible!" and your senses are screaming "No!" *That* is when you must imagine! When life comes with a pressure, do not crumble but imagine! Believe in the reality of the imaginal solution! That is the internal work and do not forget what you have done!

*"How sweet are Your words to my taste! Yes, sweeter than honey to my mouth!"* - ***Psalm 119:103***

Just try it for a bit. Taste the word of God if you will. Taste the word and how sweet it is.The sweet taste is the feeling the reality of a mental solution. It will always taste sweet, just as honey.

This may sound repetitive, but some concepts need to be presented multiple times in different ways before they truly resonate. When understanding finally appears, you will experience an internal shift. Embrace that shift and deepen it. That shift will bring you power and freedom because it is the catalyst that opens your imagination to feeling and doing whatever you want in it.

Begin with the simple feeling that "I can have and feel whatever I want in my imagination." Once you accept this, you will start to live upon it by naturally doing what you want in imagination.

*"Now, how do I look into the Law, the perfect Law, which sets me free, the Law of Liberty? I look into my mind. I'm now imprisoned. I've heard the sentence. I know exactly how long I'm supposed to serve. Now, I look into the Law of Liberty in my mind, and I assume that I am free. I'm set free. How? I am not concerned. Who brought it about? I am not concerned. I simply look into the perfect law, the Law of Liberty, and I dare to assume that I am free. If I dare to assume that I am free, I rearrange the structure of my mind, the same mind that heard the sentence that I accepted when I heard it. Now, I do not accept it. I look into the perfect law, the Law of Liberty. And if, as I'm told in Scripture, I persevere, then I will actually receive that which I am doing. I must not forget what I have done and sleep this night as though I am in prison;* ***for if I am now set free, where would I sleep? Let me know exactly where would I sleep? Well, dare to assume that I am sleeping there now****.*

*If I sleep in the assumption that I am free, I am not in jail. Even though the bars are there, I don't see them, close my eyes against them. As Blake tells us, man's perceptions are not bounded by organs of perception: he perceives more than sense, however acute, can discover.*

*And so, reason or the ratio of all that we already know is not the same that it shall be when we know more. If I take this tonight and test it, and it proves itself in the testing until I have added to my knowledge. And so, I know more than before I tested it, and so when I find myself up against something that seems beyond solution, I have found something that can solve it. All I have to do is to rearrange the structure of my mind.* ***So, I dare to assume that I am the man that I would be and sleep as though I am. That's the rearrangement of that structure of the mind. I am the same being. I'm Neville. I know exactly those that I knew before, but now I know them differently. I know them now as a freed man****, but I must not be a hearer of what I heard in Scripture. I must be a doer. I must do it.*

*So be not a doer, only, be a doer in the full sense of the word. So that I actually, I do it and persist, the word is persevere in Scripture: the first chapter, the 22nd to the 25th verses of the Epistle of James. So, I will simply do it. And though tomorrow, I am confronted with the obvious facts of life that I'm still in prison, it still doesn't matter.* ***I did it. I am doing it and I will continue to do it until that which I have done is perfectly externalized within my world. I am telling you this from experience. I know it.*** *" -* ***Neville***

**Artwork Commentary:**

This artwork presents a warped room where perception itself becomes the subject. On the left, a chair sits trapped behind bars, a symbol of blocked contemplation, of thoughts confined and unable to rest. On the right, a door opens with a clock mounted above it, marking time as both passage and prison. Time here is not freedom but another barrier, another way the room constrains the one who perceives it.

Yet the person refuses to be limited by these physical and temporal boundaries. They imagine beyond the room, beyond time, beyond the bars, beyond whatever obstructs them. They see *through* the room and perceive what they want to see, a second room materializing in the center, born from pure imagination.

The room tries to define reality through its walls, its objects, its measured time. But the person refuses this definition. They create their own space, their own reality, overlaying what is given with what is desired. Notice how the room remains exactly the same. It is not the room that is changing but an entirely new one is being formed in imagination.

The perceiver can ask themselves, what does this room say about me and what does the the room I am imagining say about me? For what is truly happening here is a change in Self.

The warping of the room itself reflects this tension between imposed reality and imagined possibility. The distortion suggests that the room was never stable to begin with, that all spaces, all realities, are subject to the force of how we choose to see them. What appears solid can bend. What appears fixed can shift. The bars and the clock are real, but so is the power to see past them.

The second room develops "out of nothing" because imagination does not require material. It requires only the refusal to accept limitation as final. This is the central insight: that imagination has the power to create spaces where none existed, to perceive doorways where there were only walls. The person in this room is both trapped and free, trapped by the physical structure, free through the act of imagining beyond it.

# I Am Not Going To Tell You "You Are Crazy"

SO FAR WE have touched on how we should do everything we want in our imaginations without fear. How doing what we want, which is so simple, truly frees us inside. Since I began doing and feeling what I want in my imagination, I have never felt so normal. Every time I do what I want inside, it all feels wonderfully normal. The moment I have any desire, I fulfill it within. I see and experience its fulfillment in imagination. No questions are asked. I no longer care what the desire it is, how big or small. I do not condition it or wonder if it is possible anymore or if it is going to work. I simply do it. Then it starts to become a normal natural feeling state. So take this simple idea of imagining creating reality, and become serious about it.

When I was trying to abide by all these "rules," that is when I felt crazy. Neville states it clearly: We create our own lack and we need to rise within, and not condition our desires:

> *"Realize that you, yourself brought about this condition of waste and lack and make the decision within yourself to rise to a higher level." -* ***Neville***

> *"The reason most of us fail to realize our desires is because we are constantly conditioning them.* ***Do not condition your desire. Just accept it as it comes to you.*** *" -* ***Neville***

If you have been following along, we have explored how we can do whatever we want in our imagination, changing Self, using metaphors, and now let us focus on an example from Neville's life. This is my favorite story from Neville, when Abdullah called him crazy. This story resonated with me because I was just like Neville. I craved rules to follow so I could feel good about myself. When I was a Christian, I tried my best to follow all the rules: No alcohol, no sex, no smoking weed, no this or that. I just read the Bible and did whatever I could for the church, but deep down, I desired to please God.

Yet, in scripture it says, *"Without faith it is impossible to please God..."* - ***Hebrews 11:6***

Now I feel like both characters in this story. When I first read it, I understood Neville and partially understood Abdullah. Today, I am much closer to fully understanding Abdullah. All these rules seem so pointless. That is all I can feel after doing what I want within my imagination without fear. I see how unnecessary these restrictions are, yet I feel completely normal removing them, even though I once believed following such rules was the only way to live.

For example, I wanted to be freed from guilt. I wanted to stop feeling guilty because from this feeling, I would create all sorts of punishments inside myself. These punishments would mysteriously appear in my world because they reflected my Self. When I began to feel I could do and feel whatever I wanted in my imagination, I simply realized I did not want to feel guilty in here. I do not want it, and that was enough for me to stop it and give myself what I want instead. It truly was that simple. I had spent years trying to reduce these chronic accusatory thoughts but never could. Now I see that I was creating them within me. Nobody but me was creating the fear. *I wanted it gone, and I did not look to anyone to remove it.*

So I began to *feel* I could have what I want. I gave myself the freedom to experience peace instead of guilt. *I allowed myself the freedom to feel whatever I wanted. I stopped feeling scared in my own imagination and felt that I could do anything in there.* I stopped following the rules: "You must feel grateful," "You must make sure you fall asleep perfectly in the feeling," "Make sure you think these thoughts instead of those bad ones."

So now lets dive into my favorite story that Neville told:

*"Let me tell you why I am doing what I am doing today. It was back in 1933 in the city of New York, and my old friend Abdullah, with whom I studied Hebrew for five years, was really the beginning of the eating of all my superstitions. When I went to him I was filled with superstitions. I could not eat meat, I could not eat fish, I could not eat*

> *chicken, I could not eat any of these things that were living in the world. I did not drink, I did not smoke, and I was making a tremendous effort to live a celibate life." -* ***Neville***

We will ignore the tremendous effort part. So here Neville explains why he began using his imagination this way. Neville had imposed all these rules on himself that he must follow. He was trying to be "good." Many people would actually admire his efforts. He was living what appeared to be a moral, honest, and dedicated life. To the outside world, he might have been considered healthy for abstaining from these things.

Many people, myself included, would become fearful at the idea of living without rules. We look at the world and think, "People shouldn't eat and drink whatever they want! They can't just be free! Smoking is harmful and should be avoided! They must go to church! The must be this and they must do that." Notice how the focus of these rules are all about other people. Remember, there no one to change but Self! This is not about other people, it is about you. There is no need to focus on what others "should" do. Other people are not your concern. Your only question should be, "Am I doing and feeling what I want in my imagination right now? Am I who I want to be?" You will naturally find yourself surrounded by people who reflect your inner state. The point is not about whether you drink or engage in these activities. The real message is understanding that there is no one to change but Self.

> Neville continues, ***"Abdullah said to me, "I am not going to tell you 'you are crazy' Neville, but you are you know. All these things are stupid.*** *" But I could not believe they were stupid."*

Neville simply could not understand why his self-imposed restrictions seemed absurd to Abdullah. He followed these rules to feel "good." So then what is the underlying feeling driving this behavior? He felt inherently "wrong or bad," so he created rules to control this perceived wrongness. By following these rules, he could then consider himself "good." He was searching for a way to validate his own goodness. We have all experienced this state of imagination. Neville refers to this state as "John the Baptist" and notes that all religions operate within this rule-based framework.

> Neville once said, "*We must learn to know ourselves as Infinite Love, as good rather than evil. This is not something that we have to become: it is, rather, for us to* ***recognize something that we already are.***"

This principle applies beyond Infinite Love, it applies to everything! So what transformed Neville? He saw something he could not ignore inside and that changed him.

Abdullah called Neville crazy because he truly was. Though the world might view Neville as living a disciplined, structured life, Abdullah saw him as insane. Why? Because when you free your imagination, these arbitrary rules become meaningless. Not drinking alcohol does not make you more worthy nor closer to God. It simply does not make sense to base your worth on such things. Do something if you want to, and don't if you don't want to. But to obsess over these "quibbles" as Abdullah called them is to live in a delusional state. Imposing guilt upon yourself is nothing short of madness. No one can punish you unless you first punish yourself inside.

> *"Others will condemn us only as long as we continue in that for which we condemn ourselves. So: "Happy is the man that condemneth himself not in that which he alloweth."* ***For to life nothing is condemned. All is expressed. Life does not care whether you call yourself rich or poor; strong or weak. It will eternally reward you with that which you claim as true of yourself. The measurements of right and wrong belong to man alone. To life there is nothing right or wrong." - Neville***

> *(Continuing the story)... I remembered what Abdullah had said to me, "***After you have proven this law you will become normal, Neville***. You will come out of that graveyard, you will come out of that dead past where you think you are being holy. For all you are really doing you know, you are being so good, Neville, you are good for nothing."*

Imagine dedicating your life to being good, only to be told you are crazy and good for nothing. Abdullah truly thought this state was not just misguided, but utterly absurd. If you live a life with all these rules, Abdullah would tell you, you are living in a graveyard.

Yet the most fascinating thing he said was, "*After* you have proven this law you will become normal." Normal is way one feels about themselves. Normal is wonderful! To Abdullah, giving yourself what you want in your imagination is normal. It is abnormal to deny yourself what you want. Is that not amazing?

*After* Neville goes out and lives by his imagination, once he *proves* it, he will become normal. Most people believe the opposite, they think they will go crazy for imagining having what they want. The second they decide to do what they want in imagination, their heart races, their gut sinks, fear overwhelms them. Why? Because they have conditioned themselves to believe that fulfilling their desires in imagination is somehow abnormal, dangerous, or delusional.

Because they cannot let go of their fear, because they continue to question and condition their desires, they retreat back to the state they were trying to leave. They return to the rules, to the guilt, to the feeling of being "good for nothing" while trying so desperately to be good. They never give themselves the chance to prove the law because they never truly live by it. They imagine conditionally, fearfully, half-heartedly, and so nothing changes. They remain in the graveyard, convinced that their fear was justified, that imagination does not work, that they must continue following the rules.

This is why Abdullah's statement is so profound. *After* you prove the law, you become normal. Not before. *You do not wait until you feel normal to start.* You start now, you prove it to yourself through your own experience and *then* you become normal. The feeling of normalcy comes from having proven to yourself that you are the operant power, that your imagination creates reality, that there is truly nothing to fear in fulfilling your every desire in imagination. Once you know this through direct experience, the fear dissolves. The rules become absurd, and you realize you have been free all along.

To prove this law, you must first give yourself what you want without conditions in your imagination. Otherwise, you will attribute results to external causes. You will not believe you caused it. For Abdullah, recognizing yourself as the Cause is what makes you normal. If you truly want to prove this law, start by radically changing Self. See yourself entirely differently by feeling what you want to be. Start small if you have to, but change how you typically feel about yourself and things in your day.

*Continuing the story,*

*"It was the year 1933, I was unemployed and had no place to go except a little room on 75th Street. I went straight to my old friend Abdullah and said to him "Ab, the strangest feeling is possessing me.*

*For the first time in 12 years I want to go to Barbados."*

***"If you want to go Neville, you have gone.*** *" he replied.*

*That was very strange language to me. I am in New York City on 72nd Street and he tells me I have gone to Barbados. I said to him, "What do you mean, I have gone, Abdullah?"*

*He said, "Do you really want to go?"*

*I answered "yes."*

*He then said to me, "As you walk through this door now you are not walking on 72nd Street, you are walking on palm lined streets, coconut lined streets; this is Barbados. Do not ask me how you are going to go. You are in Barbados. You do not say 'how' when you 'are there'. You are there. Now you walk as though you were there."*

*I went out of his place in a daze. I am in Barbados. I have no money, I have no job, I am not even well clothed, and yet I am in Barbados.*

*He was not the kind of a person with whom you would argue, not Abdullah. Two weeks later I was no nearer my goal than on the day I first told him I wanted to go to Barbados. I said to him, "Ab, I trust you implicitly but here is one time I cannot see how it is going to work. I have not one penny towards my journey." I began to explain.*

*You know what he did. As I sat in his living room he rose from his chair and went towards his study and slammed the door, which was not an invitation to follow him. As he went through the door he said to me, "I have said all that I have to say."*

*On the 3rd of December I stood before Abdullah and told him again I was no nearer my trip. He repeated his statement, "You are in Barbados."*

*The very last ship sailing for Barbados that would take me there for the reason I wanted to go, which was to be there for Christmas, sailed at noon on December 6th, the old Nerissa.*

*On the morning of December 4th, having no job, having no place to go, I slept late. When I got up there was an air mail letter from Barbados under my door. As I opened the letter a little piece of paper flickered to the floor. I picked it up and it was a draft for $50.00.*

*The letter was from my brother Victor and it read, "I am not asking you to come, Neville, this is a command. We have never had a Christmas when all the members of our family were present at the same time. This Christmas it could be done if you would come."* - ***Neville***

"*If you want to go, you have gone.*" When you have a desire, fulfill it completely in your imagination without conditions. It all happens in the imagination! You go to the end, not because you must, but because that is what you want! You feel that you already have it, not out of obligation, but because that is what you want! You visualize yourself already there, not because it is required, but because that is what you want! Remember what Neville said in the past, that imagination does not work under compulsion. It works when we have imagined the wish-fulfilled. This is the principle.

Abdullah did not tell Neville to *hope* he would go to Barbados. He did not tell him to *try* to go. He told him he *had already gone*. This was not metaphor. This was instructions on what to do in the imagination. Imagination is not just a rehearsal for life, it *is* life. What you accept as true in imagination, you will start to express that truth, because the outer-world is only the shadow drama of inner convictions.

Neville had no money. He had no ticket. He had no visible means. And yet, Abdullah insisted, "You are in Barbados." Why? Because Abdullah was teaching Neville to see with his inner eyes.

This is why Abdullah would not entertain questions of "how?" The "how" is not your concern. Abdullah gave Neville a singular task. To assume the feeling of the wish fulfilled and persist in that assumption regardless of what the senses report.

Neville did not devise a plan. He did not scheme or manipulate. He simply walked in the assumption that he was already in Barbados. And two days before the last possible ship sailed, the letter arrived, the money appeared, and the outer-world rearranged itself to match his inner conviction.

Did Neville waver? Yes. He went to the "how" and said since his senses said, "I have no money," then he could not see how it could work. But Abdullah was telling him to see the present "working" of it with his imaginal eyes. See Barbados, sense it and experience it *now*. Regardless of money, of what reason says, he persisted in *already* being there.

So when the feeling of desire comes upon you as it did Neville, you do what Abdullah says, not because you must, but simply because that is what you genuinely want to do.

Here is a question that was asked to Neville that follows this train of thought:

***Question**: Suppose my wants cannot materialize for six months to a year, do I wait to imagine them?*

***Answer**: When the desire is upon you, that is the time to accept your wish in its fullness. Perhaps there are reasons why the urge is given you at this time. Your three-dimensional being may think it cannot be now, but your fourth dimensional mind knows it already is, so the desire should be accepted by you as a physical fact now.*

*Suppose you wanted to build a house. The urge to have it is now, but it is going to take time for the trees to grow and the carpenter to build the house. Although the urge seems big, do not wait to adjust to it. Claim possession now and let it objectify itself in its own strange way. Do not say it will take six months or a year.* ***The minute the desire comes upon you, assume it is already a fact!*** *You and you alone have given your desire a time interval and time is relative when it comes to this world. Do not wait for anything to come to pass, accept it now as though it were and see what happens. -* ***Neville***

When you have a desire, the deeper you, who men call God, is speaking. He urges you, through the language of desire, to accept that which is not as though that which is. Desire is simply his communion with you, telling you that your desire is yours, now. Your acceptance of this fact is proved by your complete adjustment to it as though it were already true.

What is Neville's answer? When the feeling or desire comes upon you, *that* is the time to *accept in fullness!* Do not wait, do not put it off. Accept in fullness! That is truly what you want to do!

This is not a method you reluctantly perform because some teacher told you to. This should become the natural response to desire itself. When desire arises within you, it is already accompanied by its fulfillment in the mental level.

Most people treat their desires as problems to be solved not as gifts to accept. They look at their desire and immediately begin calculating and conditioning. "How long will this take? What steps must I follow? What conditions must be met first?" By conditioning it, by constantly questioning it, by delaying its acceptance in imagination, they are saying "I do not have it now." And so they do not. This is why Neville says that when the desire comes upon you, ***that*** is the time. Not later, not when conditions are right, not when you feel more worthy or prepared.

Do you see how this will make you become normal? Do you see how wondering if you are worthy of the fulfillment of that inner desire is crazy? Do you see how that would make one go insane? Do you ask someone if you are worthy? No. By simply assuming you have what you want you are implying you are *already* worthy and prepared. Do this and after you prove it, you will become normal.

A common question that is often asked is,

*Do I imagine my desire being fulfilled 24/7?*

The answer is no. Let's take this example again that Neville gave from his own experience.

Think of it like this: Abdullah said, "*Live as though you are and that you shall be.*"

The goal for Neville in that story where Abdullah tells him to see Barbados while he is in New York, is not to visualize being there 24/7. That would make no sense. Because Neville has to interact with people in New York. He is going to have to take the subway or have to eat food in New York or drink a martini. He was living in a basement, and he had mouths to feed. He is going to have to decide things *in* New York.

So imagining being in Barbados 24/7, and neglect everything in New York is *not* the instruction. What Abdullah was teaching him to do, was to no longer think Barbados as somewhere you are *trying* to get to. Instead, to see Barbados as somewhere you *are*. The point is that every time Neville thinks of Barbados, it should not be from the standpoint that he is not there yet. That Barbados is still a desire.

Because if you think that Neville should be forcing himself to imagine being in Barbados 24/7, and neglect everything in his life, then he should not take the money his brother gave him. Because why should he take money from his brother when he is already there? Do you see the issue? So the goal is not to live in this sort of delusion/neglect of your life. The goal is to change *that* section, or *that* desire in imagination and fulfill it.

> *"He said to me, "You are in Barbados."*
>
> *I said, "I am in Barbados?"*
>
> *He said, "Yes. You are now in Barbados. And so... you see Barbados, and you see America from Barbados, and you can smell the tropical land of Barbados, see only the little homes of Barbados, and* ***that's all you do. You just simply sleep this night in Barbados."***
>
> *Well, I thought him insane, really... I mean, at the moment, it seemed so... stupid. Because... 72nd Street, we still had 50- and 60-story buildings. And little Barbados with a little three-story building almost the tallest that you'd find. And narrow little streets and no sidewalks. And I'm walking on a sidewalk that is wider than the widest street in Barbados on 72nd Street.*
>
> *Well, nevertheless, that night I slept in Barbados." -* ***Neville***

So whenever Neville thinks of Barbados he should never think of Barbados as a desire. He should never think, "I want to go. How will I get there?" He should always see himself there when he thinks about it. Then Barbados is not some distant place to the Inner Man, but instead Neville sees palm trees. He feels the sand. Smells the ocean. See's the boats. He takes what appears to the senses as "over there" and brings it "here."

Barbados is the same Barbados, so what changed? Neville, the Inner Man, changed locations! He put himself ***in*** Barbados, rather than thinking about going there, he saw *from* there.

Neville had daily obligations, and duties while in New York. He is going to have to give his attention and focus to these obligations in New York. This is not the issue. The issue is that he desires to go to Barbados, then he must stop wanting to go and BE there when he imagines Barbados. That is what Abdullah is instructing. When Neville does think of Barbados, and continues thinking of Barbados as some desire, as something he cannot go to, then he has not changed anything. That is what Abdullah was saying to start living as though you are there and that you shall become. So every time you think of what you want to be or what you want to have, if every time you think *of* it in your imagination, you are coming at it from a standpoint of still desiring it, you have not moved. You have not brought it "here." You must *think-from* that standpoint. That is the difference.

*"About three times I tried to open up the discussion with my friend Ab between that moment when I first talked to him and the end.* ***He would never discuss it, on the basis: "How could he discuss with me how I am going to Barbados when I am already in Barbados?" That's stupid to discuss how I'm going to go when I am in Barbados! And if I am faithful to my assumption, I can't discuss the "how." I'm already there!***

*Well, this went on... on the morning of the fourth day of December... there's no job, no place to go... and the last boat that will get me there by Christmas is going to sail on the sixth.*

*Under my door is a little letter from my brother Victor. And he said, "As a family we were never around the table at Christmas together. That Cecil"– he's my oldest brother... he left home before the last was born, because we have a large family; there's eight years between my sister Daphne, who was the eighth child, and then my brother Joe. Well, in that interval, my brother Cecil went off to Demerara. So... never as a family were we ever together at Christmas. So in the letter, he justifies why he's asked me to come. "I know you don't have a job, and there's no excuse for not coming. And so I'm enclosing a draft for fifty dollars... you may need a shirt, a pair of shoes, socks or something, and I've notified the Furness Withy Line that you'll come for a ticket. So the ticket is waiting for you at the Furness Line."*

*Well, I was so excited... I rushed on down to the Furness Line and I told– gave them my letter. They said, "Yes, we have a message here from your family in Barbados. We'll give you a ticket, but we haven't any First Class tickets left. You can go Third Class, and use the facilities of the First. But you have to sleep Third Class, until you hit the island of St. Thomas. When you hit St. Thomas, someone disembarks, then you may take a First Class bunk."*

*I said, "I'll take it."*

*I rushed right up to Abdullah, and I said, "Ah, I got my ticket for Barbados, but I have to go Third Class." I'm all elated and happy about it.*

*He said, "Who told you that you are going to Barbados? And who told you that you went to Barbados Third Class? You went to Barbados, and you went First Class."*

*Would say no more.*

*He isn't even happy that I'm going to Barbados now. (audience laughter)*

*So I went down on the morning of the sixth day of December, with my Third Class ticket. Went up to the desk as they're checking in the passengers, and I put my ticket forward, and they said "I've got good news for you, Mr. Goddard. Someone has cancelled, and you're going First Class."*

*And I went First Class all the way down to Barbados. Ten days down; ten days back, with three heavenly months in Barbados."* - ***Neville***

Pay attention to how every time Abdullah spoke about Barbados, it was never about it, but *from* it. Notice how when Neville spoke about it, he was always *trying* to get there. The audience laughed at the persistence of Abdullah, while it is humorous, pay close attention. Why would Abdullah be happy about him going there, when to Abdullah, Neville is *already* there? Every time Abdullah saw Neville, he saw him *in* Barbados and persisted until it became a fact. Even when Neville showed him the ticket and the money to go. Why? Because that is *not* the end! The end is Neville conforming to the image Abdullah had which is that Neville is there, *now*.

> *"So all that I did... I tried to the best of my ability to with his almost insolence... he was rude. But he taught me by his rudeness that I cannot discuss how if I am doing what I'm supposed to do. He tells me right away, "You are in Barbados."* ***Like someone comes to you now, and you would apply this principle toward their request, and they say, "Oh, I would love to be happily married." And you say to her, or him, "You are now happily married." They look at you as though you're insane.***
>
> ***But that's exactly what you're supposed to do. "You are now happily married."*** *Well, if I am now happily married and I'm a lady, I would instantly begin to feel that ring there in my imagination. And I'd let others see that I have my ring– well, that would imply I'm happily married, a wedding ring... and so if I don't wear it from then on, I'm not doing what I'm supposed to do.*
>
> *So in my imagination, I have to go to bed wearing my ring, and actually do all that I would do in that state."* - **Neville**

This is not about neglect or delusion, but changing images and holding faith until they conform. Even when the one you want to change is resisting it, in this case Neville was the resistor. Holding faith is persisting in the image! So you can take a friend, imagine a success for them in a certain area in their life. Do you now neglect your life because you must imagine their success 24/7? No. That is not the instruction. What you must do is every time that friend comes into your imagination, you see them in that new image. Suppose they call you, text you and it is not conforming, do you let go the image and accept the one they are giving? Should Abdullah have just accepted when Neville said, *"Ah, I trust you implicitly but here is one time I cannot see how it is going to work. I have not one penny towards my journey."* Should Abdullah have decided right there to reply with, *"I guess you are right, Neville, you have no penny."* No! If you imagine success for a friend, and they say they failed, do you accept it? No, you still hold onto the image. That is faith in the unseen. The same is true for yourself! Think a realm in life you want to succeed in, either the financial realm, the art realm, the relationship realm, how do you see yourself in them? When you think of that realm are you holding onto the faith, the image that you are who you want to be in that realm? Are you seeing yourself *from* being successful in that realm rather than fantasizing *about* it? What is the difference? The difference is Neville thinking about going, saying *(with feeling)*, *"How nice it would be to be at the beach in Barbados. To see my parents and siblings..."* That is fantasizing. That is not occupying. True occupancy, *IS* being at beach in his imagination. *Seeing* his parents and siblings. Sleeping, not in any bed, but *that* bed in Barbados. So find the answer to how you see yourself and do not duck it. It is far easier to seek familiar comforts than to address how you imagine about yourself. But if you must seek, seek not comforts but fulfillments. So start seeing life from *that* angle of *already* being it. *"That's all you do,"* as Abdullah said.

> *This is how Man creates in life, through faith in the creative power of image-making.*

> *"These are the two outlooks. on the world possessed by every man. I do not care who you are. Every child born of woman, regardless of race, nation, or creed, possesses two distinct outlooks on the world.*
>
> *You are either the natural man who receiveth not the things of the Spirit of God, because to you in the natural focus they are foolishness unto you. Or you are the spiritual man who perceiveth things outside of the limitations of your senses because all things are now realities in a dimensionally larger world.* ***There is no need to wait four months to harvest.***
>
> *You are either the woman of Samaria or Jesus at the well. You are the man waiting on the Five Porches for the disturbance and*

*someone to push him in; or you are the one who can command yourself to rise and walk in spite of others who wait.*

*Are you the man behind the tombstones in the cemetery waiting and begging not to be clean, because you do not want to be cleansed of your prejudices? One of the most difficult things for man to give up is his superstitions, his prejudice. He holds on to these as though they were the treasure of treasures.*

*When you do become cleansed and you are free, then the womb, your own mind is automatically healed. It becomes the prepared ground where seeds, your desires, can take root and grow into manifestation...*

*You can either be attentive to the limitations and feed these and make them mountains, or you can be attentive to your desires; but* ***to become attentive you must assume you are already that which you wanted to be."* - Neville***

**Artwork Commentary:**

The buildings represent the concrete reality of New York City where Neville was physically living. The boats, shore, and sand symbolize the Barbados he was imagining, his desired reality. In this visual metaphor, he is colliding the imaginal Barbados with the physical New York, meshing and blending his imagination with his present reality.

When you read the story of Abdullah telling Neville to imagine himself in Barbados while still in New York, consider it as a parable of the Inner Man of Imagination and the outer-man engaged in dialogue. Abdullah represents the Inner Man, the voice of imagination and faith. He insists that Neville is already in Barbados, urging him to see with his inner eyes, to feel the reality of it now. The outer-man which is Neville who is doubting, sensory-bound, cannot perceive it. He only sees the buildings, feels the cold of the snow, and experiences the physical limitations of New York. Neville, the outer-man, only *feels* the reality of New York. One perspective is spiritual, rooted in imagination; the other is bound by flesh and the five senses.

This story is not just about Neville's experience but about yours. When you engage with this story, you can embody either aspect. You can take Abdullah's part and be the Inner Man who knows with certainty that you are already where you desire to be. Who feels the reality of a new one inside. Or you can play Neville's role, the doubter who only trusts what the senses report. These are two dimensions of your own self, constantly in conversation.

These two cannot coexist indefinitely in equal measure. One must eventually yield to the other. What Neville discovered, and what the story illustrates, is that the outer-man's perspective, the doubting sensory self, must die to the degree that the Inner Man's vision lives. This is not about physical death, but about the death of identification with doubt and limitation. As long as you remain identified with what your senses tell you, you cannot fully trust and accept the reality your imagination.

Imagination cannot serve two masters, two different perceptions. You cannot simultaneously believe you are confined to your current circumstances and also believe you are already living in your desired state. One belief system must be sacrificed for the other to take root and bear fruit. The outer-man, the one who argues for limitations, who presents evidence of lack, who insists on doubting, must be released so that the Inner Man can be resurrected as your living reality.

Abdullah only imagined *from* the assumption that Neville was *already* in Barbados. He never saw Neville as going there some day in the future in imagination. In doing so, Abdullah was inviting Neville to let go of the outer-man, to stop giving it authority over his life and to allow his inner vision to become his only reality. And eventually, that is exactly what happened, the outer yielded to the inner inside of Neville and he found himself on a ship to Barbados on the "outside."

# Feel The Reality Of Self

A COMMON QUESTION that consistently emerges in this series is, "How do I feel?" or "What is this feeling?"

It all starts with desire. Neville says, "We must *want* to change Self." I know I said we should remove "must, should, have to's" from our thinking when it comes to consequences. You do not need punishments if you do not want them. But we must *want* to change. We must *want* to think greater thoughts. We must *want* to feel our best. We must *want* it. We must *want* to feel abundant. We must *want* to feel the best feelings simply for the sake of feeling the best. We must *want* to love our new idea of Self. Not because of consequences if we do not, but because remaining as we are is punishment enough. Do you see the difference?

> *"God, the great artist, created you and falling in love with his creation he gave it the gift of life by giving you the gift of himself and God is love. Greater love has no man than this. Tonight fall in love as God. Imitate him as a dear child.* ***Love any state so much you die to any other****. Live there, as God, and you will live there as man also. Fulfill every desire of your heart, for in time it will all pass away. And always remember who you are, for you are love, the one and only reality of the world, and that, which endureth forever."* - ***Neville***

I have been asked, how many times should I imagine a thing? As if there is a number amount. There is no number of the amount of times you love someone. You would never count such a thing. What many do not understand is that you need to love what you imagine. Because if you fall in love with a new way of seeing yourself, if you fall in love with a new way of feeling about yourself, if you fall in love with it, you will stay committed to it. And when things do not align perfectly in your life outwardly, you will stay committed to it internally because you love it. This is the true definition of persistence.

Think about it from your experience. When you truly love something, do you count how many times you think about it? Do you become a calculator? Are you mechanical? Or does love clear things up? Does love come with freedom and power? Do you need to force yourself to return to it? Of course not. No, you *naturally* gravitate toward what you love, force. You cannot help but return to it again and again, not out of discipline or effort, but out of love for that state.

Persistence is not about forcing yourself to repeat something you find boring or difficult. It is about finding a way of imagining that is so delightful, so satisfying, so aligned with what you truly want, that persistence becomes effortless. When you love the feeling of being the person you desire to be, when you love the vision of your life as you wish it to be, you do not need willpower. You need only to return to what you love.

Remember what Neville said, "*Love any state so much you die to any other.*" Loving a state, loving a reality within, brings the death to the current one. This is not about obsession or desperation. You do not fight the old but you simply love the new.

*"And no one puts new wine into old wineskins."* - ***Matthew 9:17***

So the first step is to *want the feeling*. What feeling? Whatever your heart truly desires. It must be something you deeply, genuinely want to feel. Otherwise, one of two things will happen: either you will remain exactly as you are because you never truly committed to the change, or you will change temporarily but eventually return to your former self because the new state was never truly loved, never truly wanted. Without genuine want, without love for the new state, there is no lasting change of Self in imagination. *Remember this is all happening in imagination only*. You will always drift back to what feels familiar, even if it brings you pain, because at least it is known. But when you love the new feeling of "I", when you deeply want it, you naturally die to the old. The old simply falls away because your attention, your love, your want has shifted entirely to the new.

Once you begin to *feel* the freedom of feeling what you want, you will naturally *want* more of that feeling, more of that freedom. We must cultivate this *want*. Our desire to feel the best feelings must become stronger than our habit of feeling lack. Our desire must become *burning* for more. But we do not leave it burning, we must find some mental fulfillment in imagination. But if you do not genuinely want anything, if you are merely going through the motions because you think you something is off limits to you, then you will always return to your old patterns.

Change in imagination is not always linear. Most times, change is subtle. You may not always find yourself in a lovely state inside. You might have a wonderful morning where you feel completely aligned with your desired state, only to find yourself, by afternoon, slipping back into old patterns of thought. This does not mean you have failed. It is not linear, but subtle changes in the human imagination!

*The key is not to judge nor blame yourself, but to gently return to the state you love as if you never left or fell out of it!* That is the secret! No condemnation at all, just movement. So when you notice yourself drifting, do not condemn yourself. Do not think, "I have ruined everything," or "I am not doing this right." Instead, simply recognize where you are and choose again. Choose not any state, but t*hat* state. Choose the version of yourself you love. This is the practice. This is the art of living consciously, not judgmentally.

And remember, this life is a drama at the end of the day. Just as a drama invites the audience to cry when things are sad or feel joy when they are redemptive, the same is true for this world of imagination. When you imagine yourself being what you wish, enjoy it! Do not think that you are failing simply because you experienced a moment of doubt or feel the old state creeping back in. No, instead without any questions, even if you fell out of it for a year, just jump back into it as if you never left.

This is how reality within works. I did not make up these rules. I found myself in this life just like you. Yet, if you explore that reality within, it is not like the one without. In this inner reality, you can move back into states and it requires *nothing* but your acceptance again.

*"Jesus replied, "No one who puts a hand to the plow and looks back is fit for service in the kingdom of God."* - ***Luke 6:92***

You cannot force your way into a new state in imagination. That does not make sense if you understand that every door in imagination is already opened. I AM is the door and the key to every state inside. Everything comes with its counterpart. If you imagine yourself being imprisoned inside instantly you are put into a symbolic jail cell while also given the key to free yourself. The I AM, the Conceiver is always greater than the conception, even if that conception appears restrictive.

*Are you not greater than the mirror? Is the imagination not also a mirror revealing the Man?*

*"Well,* ***feel after that quality in consciousness until you feel yourself to be it****. When you lose yourself in the feeling of being it, the quality will embody itself in your world."* - ***Neville***

When you know exactly what you want and you love the feeling of having it, the clouds in your imagination disappear and the sight become clear. Do not stay in the edge of a state merely looking at it. In this shadow world, at times we go to grocery stores and we find small concessions that allow you to sample the products. We sample to see if we like it. Or in other words, if you would *commit* to purchasing it. Well, the same is true in imagination. You are not wandering aimlessly through different states, sampling one today and another tomorrow. Eventually you have to say "No" to some samples and "Yes" to others. At some point, you will have to purchase a state. But you do not need any money, the only coin in imagination is I AM. Find the ones you like inside and start committing to them. You are committed, not through force, but through love. And that commitment, that consistent return to the beloved state, is what reshapes imagination. It is what changes Self truly.

This is why Neville emphasized falling in love with a state so much that you die to any other. Death to the old is not a violent act. It is not a struggle. It is simply the natural result of loving something new so completely that the old no longer has any hold on you. Your attention has moved. Your love has moved places. And where your love goes, there you are for we are love.

How to feel the feeling?

> *"You aren't called upon to make the things. All things already are. The whole, vast creation is already finished; I am only becoming aware of it. Any state that I can imagine can be occupied.* ***The whole thing is finished, and all I do is adjust to it and "feel" myself there until it becomes natural.*** *You don't give reality to the unseen; it is loyalty to the unseen reality that gives it objectivity."* - ***Neville***

This is the one most common question I receive. But answer is one that comes from complete honesty. Ask yourself this question, and truly answer as honest as you can. Take a moment and truly think about your response.

> *"How would I feel if it were true?"*

Understand that everything *within* imagination is an assumption. Every thought, every feeling, every state you occupy exists as an assumption you, the Inner Man have accepted in here. *The imagination does not care what you imagine.* It places no restrictions on you. It does not judge your desires or deem them impossible, just as a mirror does not judge. It does not withhold *anything* from you good, bad or indifferent.

Want to release guilt in imagination? Nothing stops you except your own refusal to let it go. Want to rewrite a painful memory and feel differently about it? You can do that. Want to amplify a wonderful feeling you are already experiencing? You can do that. Want to feel excited about tomorrow for absolutely no reason at all? You can do that too. Want to burden yourself with guilt over past mistakes and imagine future punishments that paralyze you with fear? You can have that as well. Want to feel that no one, nothing, can punish you? You can have it. Want to be completely free from embarrassment? The imagination does not withhold it. We withhold it from ourselves.

The imagination is neutral in that sense. If you want to open any door, it will allow it no matter who you are. It is a mirror that reflects whatsoever you feel yourself to be. It does not argue with you. It does not say, "*No, you cannot feel that way.*" We can argue with it, but our imagination will show us being radiant! We may not believe it but it will show us. It simply accepts what you accept.

> *"When I speak of feeling I do not mean emotion, but* ***acceptance of the fact that the desire is fulfilled.*** *"* **- Neville**

So how does one feel? The answer is *acceptance*. Remember what was written in Chapter 7. Neville says that when a desire comes upon you, even if it cannot possibly materialize in six months to a year, **a**ccept in fullness anyway. We are not talking about just any desire here, but desires that genuinely *cannot* materialize in that timeframe. Think about that for a moment. How many of your desires truly cannot materialize in six months to a year? Probably none. And still, Neville instructs us to accept it anyway, *entirely accept it in the imagination*. Neville did not deny himself his wants within his imagination, even when they seemed utterly impossible in the outer-world. Do the same.

Acceptance does not mean you are pretending or lying to yourself. Acceptance in imagination means you stop resisting the feeling of the wish-fulfilled. You stop saying, "But it is not here yet," or "But

I do not see it," or "But how can I feel it when it is not real?" You simply allow yourself to feel as though it were true. You give yourself permission to occupy that state, to rest in it, to love it. This is not self-deception. This is self-permission.

If you accept the desire, it does not matter what it is or whether it can materialize, accept it anyway. Do not fear this acceptance, do not fear the relief or freedom. Embrace it, and feel the acceptance of it being done and let that change you for the better. That is what you desire, a change in Self. Create this wonderful habit of accepting every delightful desire that comes to you. Then you will become normal.

Do not follow the crowd of abnormality, following the shadows of self-denial. They deny themselves in imagination. They believe they must earn the right to feel good, to feel fulfilled, to feel worthy. But in imagination, there is no earning. There is only acceptance. That is normal. That is natural. Anything less is the abnormality we have been conditioned into. So accept your desires. Accept them fully and now. And in doing so, you will return to a normal, natural state of being.

The whole vast world could feel ugly, but *you* decide to feel *(accept)* beautiful. But why restrict this to only beauty and not expand up on it?

~

Self is the key you are seeking.

Like many, I wanted to find the "key" to externalizing the imagination. I searched for the simplest, most pain-free way to make things happen. Initially, I thought making the imagination express was about manipulating and controlling the world. I believed I had to imagine a scene and repeat it mechanically until it materialized, but that was the wrong approach for me.

For when you imagine a scene that does not resonate to you and force yourself to repeat it, you will struggle. You will have days and nights when you do not even want to imagine. Why? Because you are not imagining what truly resonates with you. Do you see the difference? When you feel like you *have to* imagine something a specific way, you destroy the enjoyment. You undermine what you *want* to do. This undermines the change in Self. *Self does not change under compulsion.* Wouldn't you rather imagine your scene with ease and feel love and enjoyment from it? Then do that. It does not have to be complicated, but it can be smooth and natural, normal.

> *"Well, I'll say this much about this power called Imagination:* ***it will do nothing for us until we have assumed the feeling of the wish fulfilled. You can't compel it. It refuses to act under compulsion.*** *I can't compel myself to believe anything. It will only act by persuasion...what would the feeling be like if it were true? I'm trying to persuade myself into that feeling. But to say I will feel it, it will simply bound back. So you cannot compel it, you can't command it. It will only act by persuasion: what would it be like? How would I see the world? What would it be like? What would I feel like if it were true? And so only by persuasion would it respond. So try to persuade yourself. It'll work that way, work like a charm."* - **Neville**

The real discovery is not about control at all. It is about *love*. Do not think love is something only found in a Hollywood script. That is not the love that is being mentioned here. No, this love is creative/transformative power, freedom from all expectation *(sense perception)*. It cannot fail in transforming a man from the bottom of the totem pole to the top! No matter the man, love *always* has the power to transform.

The imagination externalizes not through force or compulsion, but through dwelling in states you genuinely love. When you love a state, you naturally return to it. You do not need discipline or willpower to think about something you adore. You simply do it because we commit to love.

Think about it. When you are in love with someone, do you need to force yourself to think about them? No. They occupy your thoughts *naturally*. You daydream about them without effort. You imagine conversations, scenarios, moments together, all without this sense of labor. The same principle applies to states in imagination. When you truly love the feeling of being who you want to be, you will *naturally* dwell there.

The imagination does not respond to effort. It responds to effortless, honest, curious assumption! What would it feel like were it so? What if I was now who I wanted to me? What if I was not bound to the senses at all and became what I desire? It responds to persuasion which becomes a conviction! Not because you forced it, but because you *became* it.

The most *natural* scenes and imaginings are those that you *want* to imagine. Why? Because when you imagine what you truly want, what feels natural and delightful to you, there is no resistance. There is no inner conflict. You are not fighting yourself as if there are multiple powers at play inside of you. When you imagine something that resonates deeply with you, something that feels like you, *you are not trying to become someone else. You are simply revealing who you* ***already*** *are in imagination. That is why it works. That is why it feels effortless, because it is you.*

So the key is what Neville said: "*No one or nothing to change but Self!*" When you are panicking about what might happen, remember: Only change Self!

Self will forever be your key, and Self is what you *feel* to be true. You can feel what you want to be true. If you find yourself in a position you dislike, use Self to change it and watch your world *naturally* transform. Be patient with yourself, for changes can be gradual. Your world will always reflect Self.

*There is nothing else to change and nobody else to change!*

Changing scenarios around, and rearranging words or going back to the past to recreate is are useless endeavors if it does not change Self! If it does not actually change how you see *(feel)* yourself, it is as if nothing has happened.

Do you want others to see you as respectable? Then start seeing and feeling yourself that way. It will happen *naturally*, because life naturally expresses Self. But you must genuinely want it, not just want it half-heartedly. Perhaps you simply want to relax with a book and be left alone, then feel you have that! It does not matter what it is, simply make it lovely. To hurt people in your imagination is to hurt yourself, for there is no one else in it. Your life inside imagination will become hell, I assure you, if you hurt yourself in it.

You do not need to manipulate circumstances, convince people, or force outcomes. You simply need to occupy the state of being the person who *already* has what you desire. When you do this consistently, the outer-world *must* conform. The outer-world, reason, logic, are *effects*, not the *cause*. Self is cause, not this little outer shell, but the Self within!

So Self is the true way to influence your world. Self is who you think you are and what you believe you have within imagination. This is a feeling of being and having. Now, why does giving your imagination ease matter so much? Because when you make your imaginal acts lovely, natural, and irresistible, you are not forcing yourself into a state, you are *becoming* it.

Start giving your imagination ease by doing what you wish in it. Make it so lovely you cannot resist it. Make it so grand and great, you feel engulfed by it. Why? Because when you love the state you occupy in imagination, you will naturally dwell there. You will return to it again and again, not out of discipline, but out of delight. And the more you dwell in that state, the more it becomes your natural state of being.

Here is an example:

Let's say you are prone to think about past actions or failures that trigger guilt or shame. Remember, the only reason these guilt/shame-inducing memories surface is because you were already feeling guilty/shame about Self. Without consistently feeling guilt/shame about Self, these thoughts would not even arise. So the thoughts are more confirming what you believe you are.

When these memories emerge, guilt/shame follows, and you

might start envisioning future scenarios where punishment awaits. In your cleverness, you create a scene that fulfills this guilt. You are doing *exactly* what Neville teaches, just in the wrong direction. In order to supersede your anxiety inside, you must start creating new things inside. Anxiety is directionless imagination.

So you hate the feeling that "something bad awaits" in the distant future and cannot access the feelings you want. Instead, this dread lingers in your imagination, and you fear letting it go. You wonder, "What if, though...? What if it is true? What if that actually happens? What if someone brings it up?" But consider what is really happening: you fear someone making you feel guilty for past wrongs, yet in this moment, only you are creating this guilt! You are judging yourself, creating the punishment, and feeling the fear. You are afraid of someone doing exactly what you are currently doing to yourself. This is why it is crucial you understand that there is no one to change but Self!

How do you break this cycle? First, recognize that you are *not* doing what you *want*. You are *not* feeling what you *want*. Remember the crucial first step: you must *want* to feel something better. Your *want* must be stronger than this feeling of guilt.

Then ask yourself, "What do I actually *want* to feel?" Do not be ashamed of it, do not dismiss it as impossible. Do not worry whether it will work. Do not duck it, but look at it. Then *simply want it and accept it in fullness.*

Is it that simple? Well, do you ask anyone's permission to feel chronic guilt? Do you seek others to see if you should feel shame? Do you go to some authority figure? Of course not. You accept the guilt without question! The same is true for the wonderful things inside of you.

For example, you might want to deeply feel, "Nobody can embarrass me in my world. Nobody can punish me. People around me naturally praise me. I feel completely safe in my world. It always reflects my Self."

I do not care what feeling you choose. It could seem embarrassing or impossible to others, but that makes no difference to imagination. If I want to feel something, I refuse to fear it. Instead, I accept it completely. I do not even bring up the "outer-world" to myself. That is not my concern. I do not look at my shadow to tell me how to move. It moves when I move.

Perhaps I struggle to feel it immediately. Perhaps fear pulls me back. That is fine, but I still want it, I cannot deny that. I will not let my own fear overcome me. I want this feeling so much that I will persist until I am overwhelmed by its beauty and cannot help but accept it. I want it to be so compelling that it removes my resistance. Then it becomes easier with each attempt.

Do you want the world to stop punishing you? Then stop punishing yourself within. Feel that nobody can punish you anymore, not even yourself. Want to stop hearing bad news? Then imagine hearing wonderful news instead. Why not? If you can experience anything in your imagination, why not choose what you truly want?

Self is the only thing that you need to change, because it is the *only* thing in imagination. There is nothing else. That why Neville Said, "No one to change but Self!"

This question and answer asked to Neville encapsulates what I am trying to convey:

> ***Question:*** *What must I do to inspire creative thoughts such as those needed for writing?*
>
> ***Answer:*** *What must you do? Assume the story has already been written and accepted by a great publishing house. Reduce the idea of being a writer to the sensation of satisfaction.*
>
> *Repeat the phrase, "Isn't it wonderful!" or "Thank you, thank you, thank you," over and over again until you feel successful. Or, imagine a friend congratulating you. There are unnumbered ways of implying success,* ***but always go to the end. Your acceptance of the end wills its fulfillment.*** *Do not think about getting in the mood to write, but live and act as though you are now the author you desire to be. Assume you have the talent for writing.*

*Think of the pattern you want displayed on the outside. If you write a book and no one is willing to buy it, there is no satisfaction. Act as though people are hungry for your work. Live as though you cannot produce stories, or books fast enough to meet the demand. Persist in this assumption and all that is necessary to achieve your goal will quickly burst into bloom and you will express it. -* ***Neville***

Why does Neville suggest repeating the phrase? To evoke the *feeling* of success. That is simply it. To change Self only. The specific words are not important. The words are not the key. What matters is the transformation of Self, shifting from feeling unsuccessful to feeling successful, if that is what the person desires to be.

Notice all the imaginative scenarios Neville suggests. He approaches imagination with childlike enthusiasm, adding one delightful layer after another. He instructs, "Assume it is done! A great publisher has accepted it! Live as though you are already the author you aspire to be! Believe you possess the talent to write! Visualize your book displayed prominently! See people eagerly awaiting your work! Imagine yourself unable to meet the overwhelming demand! Persist in this vision!" *But always go to the end.*

Now consider this honestly, would persisting in such imaginal acts be difficult? If this truly resonates with someone's desires, would they struggle to maintain it? Would they ever think, "Forget it. I do not feel like imagining that tonight. I will go back to my old ways?" Of course not! It is lovely to become something you desire! Who wouldn't want to persist in such a vision? It is a vision in sense for it is currently unseen by mortal eye, but the immortal ones, they see it! Only someone working against their own interests would resist this. This wonderful possibility is yours for the taking.

Neville is not just giving you a technique, but he is showing you *how* to imagine. The details are important to a degree, but it is more important you see the pattern of *how* to imagine. When you find out *how* to imagine, you can build upon it and not be restricted too all these methods and techniques and if they are the cause!

*This is what transforms Self, and that transformation of Self is all you need.*

> *"Now, most of us have this great weakness.* ***We know what we want or we think we know what we want, and we construct it in our mind's eye, but we never occupy it.*** *We never move into it and make it natural. I call that perpetual construction, deferred occupancy. We don't occupy it. I can have a lovely place where I think one day I am going to go, but I keep on postponing the day, postponing the day, and I don't occupy it."* - **Neville**
>
> ***"Well, I say to everyone, dream nobly, I don't care what it is. And you can start as I did behind the eight-ball, completely behind the eight-ball. Then go as far as you can dream:. You have no limit outside of your own ability to dream and occupy the dream...and that is foreknowledge. If I know exactly what I'm dwelling in, I can foretell. If I don't realize what I'm imagining, I can't foretell.*** *There is no astrology, no teacup leaves, nothing on the outside that can tell me. Oh, they will confirm it if I am persuaded. Because I read unnumbered charts and to the degree that I was absolutely convinced of the truth of what I said, it came to pass. Yet it wasn't there; it was my own conviction. So I say to everyone, dream nobly, imagine the wish fulfilled, for he will do little if anything that we wish until we have imagined the wish fulfilled. And after we have done it, no power in the world can stop it from coming to pass."* - **Neville**

~

## Artwork Commentary:

> *"So here, the voice said to me, and it has never lied, "It is for hatching" and the hatching is to bring forth God. Where, outside? No, can't be brought forth on the outside; brought forth in you as you, that's the hatching. Well, if he's brought forth within me as me, this must be just like a big egg; and when the egg is broken I come out and*

> *I am he.* ***So the whole world is for hatching. But while we're playing our parts in the world of Caesar, we can hatch out success, hatch out health, hatch out better relationships, hatch out anything.*** *But first of all, you must want to. It starts with a desire, it starts with the urge."* - **Neville**

In this image, we see a communion between two persons whose heads are eggs, symbolizing the imagination that hatches the conceptions we hold of ourselves. This communion represents what constantly unfolds within us. We are always in dialogue with ourselves, speaking back and forth in an endless internal conversation. If you observe your thoughts and feelings throughout the day, you will notice this inward voice is always active, speaking from and feeling into certain conceptions of who you are.

When you decide to change yourself, you engage in a communion within yourself. The wine in this image represents the conversion of water into wine, the transformation of the physical into the mental realm. It is the shift from perceiving ourselves through external circumstances to recognizing ourselves through imagination. In this inner communion, we can hatch new conceptions of who we want to be. But we must agree within ourselves that we *are* the thing we wish to become. This is self done unto self.

Our imagination is an egg that hatches not what we wish to be, but what we *are*. It consistently hatches our current conception of ourselves. This is why merely wishing for a new identity is not enough, you must actually embody the feeling of that conception as real and present. Only then will it begin to externalize in your experience.

The two persons in communion are really one person. This is an internal action, a conversation between different conceptions within the same being. One aspect of your consciousness speaks to another. The fact is that both voices emerge from imagination, both are you, speaking from different states of consciousness.

When we engage in this inner communion, we are performing an act of creation. We are taking the raw material of our current self-concept and reshaping it through imagination and feeling. The wine, transformed from water, symbolizes this alchemical process. Water is the undifferentiated substance of imagination; wine is that same substance given flavor, intention, identity and feeling. We move from passively experiencing life to actively authoring our identity from within.

The image teaches us that all change is self-initiated and self-sustained. Just as nobody can eat and digest your food for you, no one else can hatch you out of your current conception. No external event, however dramatic, can do it for you. Only you, in communion with yourself, can agree to become something new. And once that agreement is made, once you feel yourself to be what you desire, the hatching begins, and a new you emerges from the shell of the old.

# If I Am Then I Will Be

*"So this night if I would be healthy, I must assume that I am. If I would be wealthy, I must assume that I am. Don't ask anyone in this world for permission. If I would be anything, I must assume that I am; for that is asking in the only name that really responds.*

*When things seemed so black, I couldn't turn for light, I didn't know where to turn. Had no money, had none of this, none of that, and I dare to assume that I was the man that I wanted to be, and I was where I wanted to be---which would have taken quite a fortune. And strangely enough it came out of the nowhere. I didn't have to put my hand in the pocket of another to get it.* ***I did nothing of which I was ashamed of to get it.*** *It just happened.*

*So tonight, you take this wonderful name and you try it. It won't fail you! I promise you, it won't fail you, just "I am."* ***Forget what you've done in this world, forget what people think you are; forget all the little tags to go put on you.*** *Do take off everything and simply dwell on "I am." Then in that I-Amness clothe it with your wish fulfilled.. Just try it. I'm telling you what I've experienced. This is not any theory, this is not speculation, this is pure experience. It comes that way in an ultimate bliss."* - **Neville**

The Self, the true you within, the only you, seeks *feeling* to change above all else. This is what it hungers for. Repeating a scene mechanically, burdened with worry and doubt, only breeds frustration and exhaustion. But when we truly understand that the Self desires *feeling*, we can confidently achieve change.

This is why Neville says both, "nothing to change but Self" and "feeling is the secret." At first, these statements might seem separate, but they are intimately connected. If there is nothing to change but Self, then how does Self change? It changes through *feeling*. This insight is crucial because many of us, myself included, have spent countless hours repeating affirmations with little to no results. We recite them thousands of times, hoping they will somehow "stick in the subconscious." Then we discover the importance of feeling, so we attempt to force feeling into our practice. It works briefly, but soon becomes utterly exhausting because we believe we *must* generate a specific feeling or else.

Remember this gently, there is no *have to* in imagination, only *want to*. Feel what you want to feel, not what you think you must feel. Discover what you truly want to feel by asking yourself, "What do I want to feel? That I am great and my past cannot hold me back? That I am loved beyond measure? That I am free?" *Feel* that to be completely true. It does not matter what it is. It simply has to be something you have always wanted to feel. This is what transforms us, and as Neville says, it feels like "ultimate bliss" and it truly does.

Your body opens up and your imagination eases. It is like quenching a deep thirst within you, finally nourishing and saving yourself from starvation. You feel almost euphoric. Life becomes beautiful and relaxing. But this state only comes to those who are not afraid to let go of what they think they are and feel what they want. Those who are not afraid to embrace even the feelings they fear. If you can, just for a moment, set aside that fear and feel what you want, you will experience that "ultimate bliss" Neville describes.

So when Neville says "assume," or "dare to assume," he is talking about feeling. All of this centers on feeling. Forcing affirmations or feelings is not the answer. Perhaps you are trying to force the feeling of being wanted, which is genuinely what you desire. But because you are forcing it, because you are trying to manufacture it rather than simply dwelling in it, you are simultaneously holding in imagination the opposite. You are affirming through your very effort that you are *not* wanted, and that you must work to change this. The effort itself contradicts the assumption.

If you simply changed your intention to feeling it because you *want* to feel it, because you want to fulfill your desires within yourself through feeling, because it brings you joy and peace, you would be far happier.

Why does Neville say it will not fail you?

He says this because it cannot fail! How can I say this, when I myself have failed in the past? It is because I did *not* change Self! *Self cannot fail at expressing*. How could that fail if you have to express you? *The only failure is the failure to change oneself.*

If you were to remove the feeling of being unwanted and assumed *(felt/accepted with no conditions)* you were entirely wanted, all the experiences of that unwanted Self would cease! If you stopped feeling guilty, all punishments would cease in imagination! You do not need permission or someone to tell you it is okay to feel what you want. Asking how to release guilt or fear is to misunderstand that you are creating these feelings inside. In your imagination, allow yourself to not feel afraid of anything in it. Bring up a beautiful, wonderful feeling and intensify it. If fear stops you, understand that you are the only one stopping yourself. Then allow yourself the freedom of feeling what you want without worry. You are allowed to feel bliss to its extreme and if you want or peace and stillness to its depth. The choice is truly yours for there is no one else in you but you.

If we are honest with ourselves, most of us imagine what we want but we do not feel the reality *(feeling of it being real to you)* of what we want. The Self is starving for that feeling of reality, for that freedom and change. If you want to be wanted and loved, do not just dip your toes in those waters. Dive in and *feel*, not just that you are "wanted" but that you are the most wanted, that you are loved. That you deserve more love than you are giving yourself. That your presence is wanted, and you are so great and loving you always find yourself surrounded by brilliant people. Just watch what happens inside you.

Many people wonder why their imaginal acts seem to fail, why they visualize and affirm yet see no change. The answer is always the same: they did not change Self. They performed a technique, they went through motions, but the *feeling (feeling it real)* of being what they desired was never fully accepted. They never allowed themselves to accept in that state, to dwell there without reservation or doubt. Instead, they touched it briefly, then immediately returned to their habitual feelings of Self.

Start in here, start within. Learn not to be afraid of feeling the reality of what you want. Just as a seed must express the fruit it contains, Self must express the feeling it holds of itself. When you change the feeling, you change what is expressed. When you assume the feeling of your wish fulfilled and persist in that assumption, Self has no option but to harden that assumption into fact. *The Self is what hardens into fact.* This is why you cannot go wrong with freeing yourself, with seeing yourself as the greatest, the highest, most lovely and excellent, with hearing wonderful things.

*You are not trying to change the world, you are changing Self, and the world must reflect that change. So leave the world exactly as is, change nothing about it, just Self!* Have complete confidence in this: *self cannot fail!* It will express whatever you consistently feel to be, without exception, without failure, without delay beyond what your own doubt creates.

So Self cannot fail you. There is no other creator, no other dreamer inside yourself. None. You are doing it all in your imagination. You either fear yourself or love yourself. You give *and* you take. There is no other God in the imagination but you. So make your life easier by releasing the need to be validated by anyone. Live as though you already are validated and you will be, for we are what we live by. The "will be" part is not about the future. You are not focusing on the "will be" part. Your focus should be solely on the I AM, present tense awareness of being. "Will be" is a natural consequence of being it.

> ***"Don't take something little, take something big, something wonderful, for yourself and for the seeming other.*** *There really is no other, but for the seeming other. Lift everyone up to the height in your own mind's eye, and, may I tell you, everyone will realize your every imaginal act for them. When you sit quietly and assume a certain state for another, you are literally mediating God*

*to that other. Really! Because your imaginal act is God in action, that's God."* - ***Neville***

Here are certain phrases that express the fundamental principle: you must change *in* your imagination first to see change in your world.

If I am safe in my imagination, I will be safe in the world.
If I am loved in my imagination, I will be loved in the world.
If I am wealthy in my imagination, I will be wealthy in the world.
If I am praised in my imagination, I will be praised in the world.
If I am treated wonderfully in my imagination, I will be treated that way in the world.
If I am guiltless in my imagination, I will be guiltless in the world.

These are not empty words or wishful thinking. It is *not* about words, for anyone could say these words. It is about the principle and feeling of reality behind them. Can you understand this and feel it to be real to you? The world you experience is not separate from your imagination. You are not trying to manipulate a world "out there," you are changing the one "in here."

Your refusal to feel the reality of a new state in your imagination is the only thing preventing you from experiencing it. Not circumstances, not other people, not lack of resources or time. It is simply that you will not allow yourself to feel the reality of what you desire.

We are what we feel *(feel to be real)* to be and have in imagination and this dream world shapes to us. Your refusal to have it in your imagination, is the only reason why you do not *feel* it.

*"Now let us go into the Silence, and let us believe that what seems to be, is, to those to whom it seems to be. And may I suggest that this night you take the most glorious concept of yourself, I don't care what it is, make it bigger than you now even hoped to realize, because all things are possible to God.* ***Whatever is your present ambition***

***make it a noble ambition but make it bigger; and then try to persuade yourself, as we go into the silence, that it is true.*** *Assume the feeling of the wish fulfilled, and then view the world from that assumption—that you can see reflected on the faces of these imaginary friends that expression which implies that they see in you the man that you are assuming that you are. Now let us go into the silence."* - ***Neville***

**Artwork Commentary:**

In this artwork, a man sits in a chair with pen and paper, deep in contemplation as he decides which conception to assume. This moment of reflection is crucial, he is weighing his options, considering who he wants to become. The empty chair in front of him represents the state of thinking-*from* the conception, the vantage point of *already* being what he desires to be.

The eggs to the left symbolize his old conceptions, the outdated versions of himself he has outgrown or wishes to leave behind. The egg in the middle represents the new conception he wants to hatch out, the identity he wishes to embody. However, contemplation alone will not bring this conception to life. He must do more than merely think about what he wants to become.

He must assume that he *already* is that conception, place himself mentally in that empty chair, and the mirrors of life will begin to reflect this new identity back to him. For the only way to become something is by assuming you *already* are that thing. Sitting in his current chair and endlessly contemplating will never cause the egg to hatch. Action, or rather, the imaginative act of assumption, is required.

When he sits in the middle chair through assumption, he shifts his state of consciousness. He is no longer the person who wishes to become something; he is the person who already is that thing. From this new vantage point, his thoughts, feelings, and actions naturally align with this assumed identity. The external world, which is always a reflection of our inner states, begins to conform to this new assumption.

It is important to understand that this entire process happens within the imagination. The imagination is not mere fantasy, it is the creative power through which we shape ourselves. The physical act of moving from one chair to another is symbolic of an inner movement. We cannot remain in the old chair of our current self-concept while hoping for change. We must inhabit the new chair, the new assumption, fully and faithfully in our imagination.

# Fearful Of Magnificence?

> *"If you keep your mind on the end, dwell on the end...the end is where we begin; "In my end is my beginning." So tell me what you want and don't tell me the means, for I don't know the means and you don't know the means.* ***Just tell me what you want that I may hear that you have it. But don't tell me what you are so I have to rub that out first to know what you want to be. Man insists on telling me all the complex things about the problem,*** *"Listen to me first...give me one hour." If you give him five minutes, he'll take five hours, because he wants to talk about his problems and he just simply wallows in the problems. They will not believe you for one moment that when you say, "Tell me what you want and that is all you need do." So, if they only believed for one moment that imagining creates reality, they couldn't go over that old, old record and play it all over again as to what they are as against what they want to be. But they'll play it over and over...that's the whole vast world."* - **Neville**

Why do we fear the feelings that would liberate us in imagination? Why do we insist on holding onto what we do not want as if it is a treasure? Why do fight for states of lack?

For those well-versed in this discourse, you understand this is about giving yourself *exactly* what you want *in your imagination*. This mirrors what Neville taught: we fulfill our wishes *within* ourselves. But we must go beyond mere wish-fulfillment and elevate our entire self-concept. We should become absolutely grand and magnificent for the sole purpose that we can and we want to.

Yet time and again, we imagine wonderful things, attempt to feel what we desire, and then retreat in fear. This fear prevents the glorious feeling from expanding within us. Doubts creep in, and if we entertain it, that glorious feeling fades. We feel trapped, incapable of experiencing true freedom inside ourselves. Sounds insane, does it not? Do you see how Abdullah was correct that a person trapped in their own imagination is crazy, not normal? Stuck in a nightmare conjure up by the dreamer themself? So we surrender to fear and retreat to our psychological caves, all while still yearning for the freedom we denied ourselves.

But why? Why do we do this to ourselves? The answer lies in our conditioning. We have been taught that good things require struggle, that we must earn our worthiness, that feeling magnificent without external validation is somehow wrong or delusional. We fear that if we allow ourselves to feel wonderful without "proof," we will be disappointed when reality does not immediately reflect it back to us.

We wait and wait and wait for permission from an outer-world to feel good within ourselves, when the truth is the exact opposite: *we must feel it within first, without basis in fact!* The fear arises because we are attempting to break away and become normal for once.

The reason we retreat to our psychological caves is because we have not yet fully grasped that we are always safe in our imagination. Nothing bad can happen to you when you feel wonderful within yourself. The only "danger" is that you might actually succeed in changing your self-concept, and then your outer-world would have to rearrange itself to match. And perhaps, on some level, we fear that change, even when it is the change we claim to want.

*"Let the weak say 'I AM strong.'"* - ***Joel 3:10***

Who retreats to the cave? Who resists the freedom? Who limits thoughts of glory and splendor? Are you not desiring *within* yourself? You can change the words of Joel to declare, *"Let the desiring say 'I am fulfilled.'"* You need no qualifications to feel what you want. Forget the past and your worries about the future. There is no price to pay to *feel* what you want in your imagination. No condition that must be met. You are always *safe* to feel what you want in your imagination.

This safety is absolute. Nothing in the outer-world can prevent you from feeling magnificent within yourself. No circumstance, no person, no past failure has any power over what you choose to feel in your imagination right now. The only barrier is the one you construct yourself, the fear that whispers, "What if this doesn't work? What if I feel this wonderful feeling and nothing changes?"

But what is actually at risk? If you allow yourself to feel fulfilled, loved, powerful, or free within your imagination, have you lost anything? No. You have gained the inner experience of that feeling. You stopped the repetitive song of feeling that you reply daily and touched a new dream inside of you. You have proven to yourself that you *can* feel it. And in that moment of feeling, you have changed your Inner Self, which *is* the only change that matters.

The real danger lies not in feeling too magnificent, but in continuing to deny yourself that feeling. Every time you retreat to the cave of fear, every time you stop yourself from experiencing the fulfillment you desire, you are choosing to remain in the state of desire rather than the state of having. You are choosing fear over freedom. And what does that fear protect you from? From the very thing you claim to want.

Understand that your imagination is the one place where you have complete sovereignty. No one can enter there without your permission. *No external authority can dictate what you feel within yourself.* When you realize this, truly realize it, you understand why there is nothing to fear. The worst that can happen is that you feel wonderful for a moment and retreat. And the best that can happen is that you change your entire self-concept and, consequently, your life.

The reason there is no price to pay is because there is nothing you need to bring in from outside of you. You do not need Caesar's coin *(money)*. The only price to pay is releasing your current state of Self for a new one. It is quite literally an exchange of clothing for the Inner Man. States are the clothes the Inner Man wears. Sometimes when shopping the labels can read different things but you try it on and it fits. So when something feels "too big," I always think of what Neville says, "*Try it on for size.*" Just try the state on for size. Do not question it, do not duck it but try it on. You have nothing to lose inside. It may be something you want but feel a bit scared of but just try it on. Maybe it will feel authentic eventually, and maybe you will love it.

So when fear arises and it will arise because you have conditioned yourself to fear freedom remind yourself: "I am safe here. In here, I am safe to feel this. Nothing bad can happen to me when I allow myself to feel fulfilled within my imagination. For it is all me in here. This is my right, my power, and my natural state. I need no permission, no qualification, no proof. I am free to feel what I desire, simply because I desire it."

> *"My old friend Abdullah said, "Neville, if anyone tries to upstage you in his world, but anyone..." He was very down to earth, a brilliant, wonderful mystic, who spoke and wrote Hebrew and he understood all the great mysteries. He said to me one day,* ***"Neville, if anyone ever tries to upstage you to make you feel little and he is big, make a mental image of him sitting on the toilet and you'll bring him right down to earth...for that cannot be any lower."*** *So make a mental image of him, sitting just there performing the normal, natural functions and taking care of himself too. Well, that is the most marvelous thing. You meet someone who thinks he's so important or she is so important—she is the most fashionable person in the world and she's numbered among the three and a half billion in the world as one of the ten best dressed women in the world—make the mental image if she ever tries to upstage you and see how well-dressed she is!"* - **Neville**

Is there anything the Inner Man cannot do? Can the Inner Man not take any king of this world and make them get a glass of water for them? Can anyone stop the Inner Man from imagining? Try it, take any leader in man's world and make them give you a glass of water. If that is possible to the Inner Man, then who is he? What else can the Inner Man do?

When all you see are beings more powerful than you in your imagination, it is not because they are, but because you have made yourself weak. *Remember, the imagination mirrors the Man.* So not do try to fight them, leave them just as they are, and make yourself powerful inside. What once appeared as a giant, dwindles into an ant, through the mirroring of the powerful man.

When we get used to being small in the imagination, largeness becomes scary. So you accept all the treatment that confirms your smallness in imagination. But do exactly what Abdullah told Neville. Take anyone you feel is greater than you and put them on the toilet. Why? Because no matter how great anyone appears in the world of shadows, they are servant to the body just like you. Nobody escapes this, not matter how rich and powerful. All have to succumb to serving their body. So let no one try to bring you low.

And you do not need anything outside of yourself to begin imagining yourself stronger. There is no law that states you must possess something external to Self in order to feel something about Self. Even if such a law existed, the Inner Man of Imagination would be able to break it. Scripture does not say let the weak do a million things, it says to assume you are strong without anything outside yourself. *Take the weakest of the bunch, make them assume they are strong and the will become it. Not matter how weak. That is the mystery.* It is a mystery that whatever causes one to believe they are weak that comes from without, it does not hold the strength to keep the Man Within weak forever. The Man Within, not matter what the shadows reveal, it can never hold the strength to defeat that Man. It is quite the mystery.

> *"Now let me share with you an experience which happened to me many years ago. Back in the early 1930's I suddenly found myself confronted with two characters. Above me and to my right stood a beautiful angelic being, while below stood a monstrous hairy animal which looked like an orangutan. Speaking in a guttural voice he looked up at this heavenly being and said: "She's my mommy." Repelled by the thought, I struck him and with each blow, he grew in strength. Then, from the depth of my own being I realized that these two were my creations. Speaking with a human voice and looking like an animal covered with hair, this monstrous being was the*

*embodiment and personification of all of my misspent energies. Every unlovely thought, every cruel, thoughtless act aided its growth.* ***Whispering in my ear, influencing my decisions in order to feed its hunger, it fed on violence, while the angelic being was the embodiment of every kind and lovely thought I ever possessed." - Neville***

When you attempt to feel what you have been yearning for and fear blocks you, remember, it is not a separate entity stopping you. The monstrous being is your creation, and you defeat it *not* by fighting it but by not fearing it. You overcome fear of wonderful feelings by recognizing that you are holding yourself back in your imagination. Sample the feeling briefly and see there is nothing to fear. The fear gradually diminishes when you open yourself to it. Once you break through this self-imposed barrier, you will realize it was you all along. All fears are mental constructs you create within yourself. With this awareness, you reclaim the power of creation back to yourself.

When you attempt to feel what you have been yearning for and fear blocks you, remember: *there is not a separate entity stopping you from within.* The monstrous being that Neville saw, is your creation, and you defeat it *not* by fighting it but by *not fearing it.* You overcome fear of wonderful feelings by recognizing that you are holding yourself back in your imagination. Sample the feeling briefly and see there is nothing to fear. The fear gradually diminishes when you open yourself to it. Once you break through this self-imposed barrier, you will realize it was you all along. For the war between you and the feeling of "I" that you want, is an illusion. Because the war implies multiple powers at play. There is only you inside.

Consider how this works in practice. When you imagine something wonderful for yourself and then feel fear, what is actually happening? You are simultaneously holding two contradictory imaginal acts: the wish fulfilled and the fear of its fulfillment. The fear says, "This is too good for me," or "This won't last," or "Something bad will happen if I allow this." But who is speaking? *You are.* You are both the one granting the wish and the one denying it.

The beauty of this recognition is that it returns *all* power to you. If you are the one creating the fear, then you are also the one who can stop creating it. You do not need to battle it, analyze it until it is unrecognizable, or put massive amounts of effort into it. You simply need to stop giving it your imaginal attention and instead give your attention fully to the feeling you desire.

This is why sampling the feeling briefly is so powerful. When you dip into the desired state, even for just a moment, without retreating in fear, you prove to yourself that nothing bad happens. The world does not crumble. You do not lose yourself. In fact, you find yourself more fully than before. Now you can use that same power deliberately, consciously, to feel exactly what you want to feel, knowing that in imagination, you are always safe, always free, and always the operant power.

**'For Once' Meditation:**

For practical application, this 'For Once' Meditation *(this technique helped me overcome the fear of beautiful feelings)*:

1. Lie down and relax. The purpose of this meditation is to experience, just *once*, what you have been wanting to feel. Commit to freeing yourself from within for once. This is not about changing the external world, but transforming yourself from within.

2. Identify something within you that you have always wanted to feel. Let go of any desire to manipulate your surroundings. Allow the world to remain as it is and focus on changing yourself. We transform when we genuinely feel what we want to feel.

3. When you begin to experience this feeling and fear arises, do not resist it. Just this *once*, refuse to be intimidated by that feeling.

4. Instead, bring understanding to yourself about why there is no reason to fear. Tell yourself, "*I will allow myself to experience this wonderful feeling for once. I will free myself just for this moment. I*

*am willing to set aside the fear I usually feel and accept this beautiful feeling. I am ready to free myself for once."*

5. *For once,* permit yourself the freedom to feel what you desire. I promise, if you try it just once, that is all it takes. After experiencing this feeling, you will not want to return to your former state.

~

Here is an example of performing this meditation: Say I want to become more confident, see myself in a higher light, and receive praise beyond my wildest dreams.

1. I lie down to feel this.

2. I begin seeing myself in a higher light. I see myself as wonderful. I walk with confidence I never knew I had. I see myself on a throne. Then I envision myself as a glorious, beautiful being of light. I hear praises directed at me. All because I want to.

3. Next, I go deeper to feel this *(This happens almost simultaneously, but I am breaking it down for clarity).* Suddenly, I start to fear this feeling. It seems unreal. "What if nothing comes from this? What is the point?" Memories of past insecurities and mistakes resurface. The beautiful, freeing feeling begins to fade. I feel stuck, uncertain what to do next.

4. Then I bring understanding and purpose back to myself *(imagination).* I remind myself, "The whole purpose was to feel that beautiful feeling, not to fear it. I want to give my inner self what it truly desires, to feel that amazing sense of ecstasy. This changes Self, and that Self is always reflected in my reality. I am creating the fear and I am the one stopping myself anyway. So *for once* I will allow myself to feel this."

5. The desired feeling begins to return, opening up my body. Anxiety dissolves into ease as I embrace the feeling and the natural high it provides. I want to intensify it, to feel this to my core because it feels so wonderful. I want this to become my fundamental state. As I feel this wonderful sensation, I simply allow it to grow. There is

no need to force anything. I just feel it expand and allow it to free me unconditionally.

6. Once I reach that state of ecstasy, I remind myself how much better this feeling is than fear. I recognize how living in that lower state of fear has only brought unwanted results. I understand that allowing myself *for once* to feel this beautiful sensation will must reflect in my world because I am changing my Inner Self.

7. There is nothing and no one to change but Self. When you see yourself internally as you wish to be, that Self will be reflected externally. Changing Inner Self is the key.

8. Make a commitment that you will fulfill every desire you have within yourself, regardless of whether your outer-self thinks it is impossible.

9. You will know you have done this correctly when the feeling begins to open your body. Ease emerges, and from this state, you naturally think-from that feeling. We are always thinking-from our feelings, so it is our feelings we must change.

Understand desire is a feeling that is held within and the inner you wants this to be fulfilled. It wants to change the feeling of desire to the feeling of fulfillment.

And as Neville says,

*"A change in* ***feeling****, is a change in destiny."* - **Neville**

**Artwork Commentary:**

*"It is my aim to raise you to a confident faith in imagining. That's my purpose.* ***If one could only lift himself up to believe in the reality of that unseen imaginal act, it's done****. But the average person will say, "What, little me? I couldn't be that powerful. I don't have the background, intellectual, social, the financial, none of these." You don't need any background."* - **Neville**

This artwork, we see multiple figures gathered around a table, some dressed in white, others in black. Those in white have begun to awaken to a profound truth that they are the very pearl they surround. Those in black remain asleep to this realization, though their presence at the table suggests a stirring curiosity. The wine that fills this scene represents a mental realm, a space of imagination where awareness begins to dawn.

Within this mental realm, these figures are coming to acknowledge that they are far more magnificent than they ever imagined. For so long, humanity walks through the world believing itself small and insignificant, unaware of the self within. Yet the truth is that each person is the one they seek, the answer to their longing lies not outside, but within. In this reflective mental space, truths are revealed and illusions dissolve. These people surrounding the table are being shown their true nature that they are the magnificent one they have searched for all along.

Some accept this revelation with joy, ready to claim their birthright. Others hesitate, preferring to remain in the shadow of their former self-conception. This hesitation is understandable, to accept one's magnificence is to accept responsibility, to step out of the comfort of smallness and into the vastness of true being. The shadow feels safe because it demands nothing; magnificence requires your prejudices and your ideas of smallness.

Regardless the imaginal magnificence stands tall regardless of whether one accepts it or not. This is not a truth that depends on belief or acknowledgment. It simply is. The pearl does not become a pearl because someone recognizes it, it is the pearl of great price by its nature. Similarly, our imaginal nature is not contingent upon our awakening to it. We are that which we seek, whether we know it or not. The white-robed figures have simply recognized what was always true; the black-robed figures are surrounded by the same truth, even in their sleep.

The mental realm depicted here, symbolized by the wine and the gathering, is the space where the Imaginal Man meets itself. It is where the external search ends and the internal discovery begins.

The table serves as an altar of recognition, a threshold between ignorance and knowing. Those who dress in white have crossed that threshold; those in black stand at its edge, perhaps sensing something profound but not yet willing to fully embrace it. Both groups, however, are held within the same sacred space, surrounded by the same truth, bathed in the same potential for awakening.

# The Feeling Of Identity

*We are told, "God is in heaven and does whatever He pleases." -* ***Psalm 115:3***

*God speaks and says, "If I were hungry I would not tell you, for the world is mine, and all that is in it." -* ***Psalm 50:12***

WHO IS this God described in the Psalms? How can I be free like them? How can I *be* what I want? How can I do what I please? How can I, a mere mortal, feel myself as a magnificent, glorious being? How can I be hungry, tell no one, and yet be fed?

It comes down to our identification of Self. Do not be afraid, but identify yourself fully with the Inner Man of Imagination, the immortal you. The one who is made of ALL IMAGINATION. The one who can do anything they want to do. The one who owns the world and all that is in it. I am serious when I say this; I am not using hyperbole. If you identify yourself with the Inner Man, you will be free.

This identification is not merely an intellectual exercise or a philosophical concept to entertain. It is a *lived experience*, a shift in your very sense of being. When you truly identify with the Inner Man, you are no longer subject to the tyranny of circumstances. At one point in your life, you let circumstances decide who you are. Then at some other point, you, the Inner Man, do not let them decide. You are no longer at the mercy of what the world tells you is possible or impossible. The Inner Man exists in a realm where all things already are, where your desire fulfilled is not a future event but a present reality.

Think about it! When you imagine something, where does that imaginal something exist? It exists within you, in your imagination. And in that imagination, is your imagined something not *already* real? When you see yourself as wealthy within, are you not wealthy in that moment in imagination? When you feel yourself loved and admired within, are you not experiencing that love and admiration *now*? The Inner Man simply *is* what it claims to be.

But when you *first* identify with the Inner Man, everything changes. You are no longer trying to force yourself to believe something that feels contradictory. Instead, you, the Inner Man, are simply claiming what is *already* yours. *The Inner Man needs no convincing because imagination has already made it real.* Your only task is to remain faithful to this inner reality, to refuse to let the evidence of the senses pull you back into identification with limitation.

> *"You can't see the mystery that way. It's either you see it in the depths of your soul between your own being;* ***it's a dialogue between the outer-man and the inner man****. And when you really believe in this inner man, your own wonderful I-am-ness, nothing is impossible, and then things are revealed to you that startle the reasoning mind."* - **Neville**

The outer-man sees nothing but limitations, the walls and mountains. They live in perpetual desire, constantly needing another piece of bread to eat, another validation, another achievement to feel whole. But too many of us have identified ourselves with what the outer-man *has* and *is*, not recognizing that it is merely a reflection of the Inner Man.

Some look at their accounts, their relationships, their circumstances, and declare, "This is who I am." They have made the grave error of identifying with the reflection rather than the person. It is like looking in a mirror and believing that the image you see is the real you, forgetting entirely about the person standing in front of the mirror. The outer-man is simply the mirror image of what you have not only claimed yourself to be, but are holding continuous faith in.

When you identify with the outer-man, you are at the mercy of conditions. You wait for permission from the world to feel differently about yourself. You wait for evidence before you believe. But the Inner Man needs no such permission, no such evidence. The

Inner Man *creates* the evidence by first imagining being what it desires to be.

So if you want to understand who and what you truly are, not what the world tells you, but what you *actually* are, then close your eyes and pay attention. Observe the inner dialogue. Listen to how you speak to yourself about yourself. Notice what you assume to be true, what you assume to be real, when no one is watching or listening. See what you have claimed yourself to be within, what you feel yourself to possess in your imagination. *That* inner state, that inner claim, that inner conviction, *that* is what is always, without exception, being expressed.

> ***"Stop trying to change the world since it is only the mirror.*** *Man's attempt to change the world by force is as fruitless as breaking a mirror in the hope of changing his face. Leave the mirror and change your face. Leave the world alone and change your conceptions of yourself."* - **Neville**

> *"You do not have to persuade others to help you; all you need do is believe you are what you want to be and then let the world (which is nothing more than yourself pushed out) go to work to make your assumption possible."* - ***Neville***

But how? How can you "believe you are what you want to be" when the world is screaming the opposite at you? When your world tells one story, your imagination another, and your circumstances yet another?

When Neville says, "*change the conceptions of yourself,*" he is not speaking of superficial affirmations or vain mental exercises. He means to *identify yourself with the one within and give yourself to that state with feeling of identifying with it.* Our self-conceptions are not what we think about ourselves intellectually as if need to debated for, they are what we *feel* ourselves, our Inner Man, to be. And the Inner Man has complete freedom to see and feel whatever it wishes to be, regardless of what the outer-world presents.

This is not about convincing yourself of something false. It is about recognizing that the Inner Man is not bound by the same rules as the outer-man. When you identify with this Inner Man, you are no longer trying to force belief against contradictory evidence. Instead, you are simply *being* what you desire to be within, and allowing that inner state to naturally express itself outwardly.

Listen carefully to the words you speak within your imagination. Pay attention to the inner dialogue that runs constantly beneath the surface of your awareness. The premise from which you speak, the assumptions you hold about yourself in that inner conversation, dictates where you live inside. The Inner Man exists in its own world, just as your outer-self lives in the physical world. However, this Inner Man does not have to bow down to the thoughts you have consistently held. You are not a prisoner of your habitual feeling about yourself.

> ***"If you could only persuade yourself that what you have imagined is true.*** *So you walk as though it were true, and if you could only walk as though it were true, it would become a reality in your world."* - ***Neville***

The outer-man argues from evidence. He says, "Show me proof, and then I will believe." But the Inner Man works from an entirely different principle. He says, "I will assume it to be true within, and the evidence will follow."

So who are you identifying yourself with? Are you identifying with the outer-man of limitations, the one who sees only what is, who waits for conditions to change before feeling differently, who accepts the verdict of the senses as final? Or are you identifying with the Inner Man, the one who men call God, the one who does whatever pleases him, the one who owns the world and all that is in it, the one who is free to imagine and feel himself to be anything he desires?

This is the pearl of great price. The pearl is the Inner Man. Identify yourself with the Inner Man, and you will be free.

*"Your inner being is he who men call God."* - **Neville**

To the Inner Man everything is already true, not to the outer-man. It already is so, to the Inner Man. There is no need for endless convincing, countless affirmations, or repetitive hoping if you identify yourself with the Inner Man of imagination. When you claim to be the the Inner Man, you will find it incredibly easy, I would say *natural,* to *feel and accept the reality* of what you want.

Pay close attention: When you imagine your "end," is not it already so in that inner moment? You do not imagine "how" to get there; you are already there in imagination. Your challenge is *not* in imagining the end, your issue lies in who you are identifying yourself with.

If you imagine yourself at the end but then identify with the outer-man, you will create nothing but frustration. However, if you first identify with the Inner Man Within and then imagine your end, you will not question if you "are going to get it" for *you* have it! The Inner Man already possesses everything. This is why you must imagine fulfillments because they are in you and are already so. They see the end with inner eyes and it creates their own fate. The Inner Man is both their own destroyer and redeemer.

Identify yourself with the Inner Man, the immortal you, not this body or outer-life. The Inner Man can fulfill all these desires because imagination is infinite in its resources.

***"Disregard appearances, conditions, in fact all evidence of your senses that deny the fulfillment of your desire. Rest in the assumption that you are already what you want to be,*** *for in that determined assumption you and your Infinite Being are merged in creative unity, and with your Infinite Being all things are possible."* - **Neville**

***"You are already that which you want to be, and your refusal to believe this is the only reason you do not see it."* - Neville**

"Your refusal to believe," change this to "Your refusal to *feel (feel it to be real)* yourself to Be," is why you do not see it. For what we feel ourselves to be within will reflect outwardly. How are you already what you want to be? How can you be if you are limited? The answer is that you are always what you want to be when you identify yourself with the Inner Man! Stop limiting yourself within! You create the dreams within you and you draw all people to you to fulfill what you have done and are within! Within is the only place you can be what you want when the world tells you "You cannot." Leave the world as it is, with all its denials, and change yourself within, then watch how everything around you reveals itself as yourself pushed out. Why? Because everyone inside of you is yourself pushed out. Are you not the putting words in their mouths? Do they get a choice? If Neville imagines someone who is trying to upstage him in life on the toilet, do they have a choice? No, of course not.

> *"Sit quietly and ask yourself who you are, where you are and what you are. Your answers will reveal your state of consciousness: your body of belief. Paul said, "We do not look to the outer things, but to the things unseen, for the outer things are transient, but the unseen things are eternal."* ***Your beliefs, seen by the mystic, are personified****. They form a state, which completely controls your behavior. Any modification within your body of belief will result in a change in your outer world."* - ***Neville***

> *Everyone in your imagination is yourself pushed out. People in your imagination are just messengers revealing to you who you are through personifications.*

So in imagination we are interacting with ourselves and the people in it are parts of ourselves personified. *Change not them but you.*

For example, if you enter yourself and you find someone inside and you feel defeated by them, ashamed for seeing them or arguing with them. Those people are not doing that. The Inner Man thinks they are separate and becomes confused. *People in your imagination are just messengers revealing to you who you are through personifications.*

You feel ashamed of yourself? You feel you cannot have something in here? Then hear comes one who appears to confirm your shame, the forbidden desire, and this part of you will take the form of a person. If you dislike this, do not change them but yourself. Leave feeling ashamed behind, feel free and a new personification comes to mirror that freedom. The same person might be used or leave, or new people will come. Either way it must mirror you. *Because it is not what we are looking at that matters but what we see.* What we look at inside ourselves IS ourselves, parts personified. Leave the symbols, the people alone, and change yourself and watch your imagination change with you.

> ***"There is nothing more important than developing your imagination to transform your life from the inside world*** *of your thoughts and feelings to the outside world of your results and manifestations."* - ***Neville***

There is nothing more important than your relationship with your Imagination and Self for they are one and a mirror. Identify yourself with the Inner Man and use the Imagination to create what you want within. Let the Imagination work for you. Is not that what you truly desire? Wouldn't it be wonderful to sit with friends and instead of insecurities surfacing in your imagination, you experienced praise? How to experience praise? You hear it! You feel it. You accept it all within you, and that is all you do. You do not sit around trying to figure out if you are worthy of these thoughts. No, you think them without wondering that, for the wonder implies you are not worthy. If you imagined what you wanted without any question, that behavior implies worth is already there. Let the imagination serve you when you identify with the Inner Man. I am completely serious about this. You will no longer feel inferior to anyone because everything exists as states, and you draw the states necessary to fulfill you, the Inner Man, whether good, bad, or indifferent.

> *"Whenever your feeling is in conflict with your wish,* ***feeling*** *will be the victor."* - ***Neville***

*Whenever there is a conflict between a wish and a feeling,* ***feeling will always be the victor***. If you are imagining your desired outcome while simultaneously feeling worried, doubtful, or concerned, that feeling, not your wish, will express itself in your world. You do not receive what you wish for, you receive what you *feel* yourself to be within.

This is why so many fail despite their persistent efforts at visualization or affirmation. They imagine one thing but feel another. They picture success while feeling like a failure. They visualize wealth while feeling poor. They imagine love while feeling unworthy of it. And then they wonder why their imaginal acts seem powerless.

They have not changed their inner feeling of Self. They have not identified with the state they wish to occupy. Instead, they remain identified with the outer-man, who argues from the evidence of the senses, who feels bound by conditions, who waits for the world to change before daring to feel differently. Your conception of yourself is not what you think about yourself on the surface, it is what you *feel* yourself to be at the deeper levels, and from there you imagine and act from that feeling.

> *The Inner Man exists in a realm where all things are possible, where you can be and have anything you can imagine and feel to be true.*

> *"Far greater is he that is in you than he that is in the world"* - ***1 John 4:4***

*"Do not continue in blindness, following after the mirage of masters. I assure you your search can end only in disappointment."* - ***Neville***

Discard all beliefs about what you think you are or what others have called you. Release every label, every limitation, every identity that has been imposed upon you by the world or accepted by you through habit. When you identify yourself with the Inner Man, you will be free. This freedom is not earned through struggle or worthiness, it is inherent in the very nature of the Inner Man.

This freedom exists because the Inner Man can do whatever pleases them. Notice that word carefully: *pleases*. The Inner Man does what they find pleasurable, what brings them joy, what feels natural and right within. What pleases you? Do that within. Relish in the pleasure accept the pleasurable gift you have given yourself. Pleasure it meant to be honored by enjoying without any reservations. Give yourself what you desire in imagination, and feel the pleasure of already being it. The Inner Man finds pleasure in the act of creation itself, in the freedom to imagine and feel themselves to be anything they desires. The who identified with the Inner Man knows that all things exist within them, and they freely claim whatever state they wishes to occupy.

When you identify with the Inner Man, you are not trying to become something you are not. You are simply recognizing what you have always been. You are claiming your inheritance, which is the freedom to be and have whatever you can imagine and feel to be true. Identifying yourself with the Inner Man is simply a shift in *feeling and awareness* from outward to inward. It is not a complicated technique. It seeing reality from their inner eyes rather than just or organ eyes.

When you fully identify yourself with the Inner Man, you will understand how to apply everything that has been said. Why? Because understanding does not come from intellectual analysis or studying more teachings. Understanding comes from *experience*. When you actually identify with the Inner Man, when you actually feel yourself to be the operant power, when you actually give yourself what you desire within and rest in that assumption, you will *know* the truth of these words. You will know it not as theory but as living reality. The application becomes effortless because you are no longer trying to manipulate conditions from the outside. You are simply being what you desire to be within, and watching as the outer-world conforms to that inner state that you are holding with faith. *Faith is not trying to be, faith is accepting the image of already being.* This is why no amount of reading or studying can substitute for the actual practice of identifying with the Inner Man. The moment you do it, everything starts to make sense.

> *"So you conceive it. Alright, know that you conceived it and say within yourself,* ***"I've imagined it so to be, I'm still imagining it so to be, and I will continue to imagine it so to be until what I have imagined is perfectly expressed.****" Then you will know what foreknowledge is."* - ***Neville***
>
> Say within, with the Inner Man's Divine voice.

**Artwork Commentary:**

In this artwork, we see a woman from her vantage point of looking into her imagination. We witness one scene where she imagines herself in the kitchen, observing herself from this perspective. Then, to her right, she envisions herself relaxing in an entirely different scene. We do not see precisely what she is imagining in the scene to her right. However, each vision symbolizes a different idea of herself.

The dual imagery represents the multiplicity of self-perception and the various roles we embody throughout our lives. The kitchen scene might represent domesticity, routine, or nurturing aspects of her identity, while the relaxing scene suggests aspirations for peace, leisure, or escape from daily responsibilities. These parallel visions exist simultaneously in her mind, neither one more real or valid than the other.

What makes this composition particularly compelling is how it captures the fluid nature of imagination and self-concept. We are not confined to a single identity or a single moment in time. Instead, we constantly reimagine ourselves in different contexts, different environments, and different states of being. The woman in the artwork embodies this truth, she is both the observer and the observed, the dreamer and the dream.

# Subjective, Free Imagination

*"First of all, we think that reality is confined to this Earth and it ends where our senses cease to register it. It doesn't. The world into which I go often and meet people who are supposedly dead, they are just as real and just as bigoted and just as limited as they were when they were here. I meet people...there is no transforming power in death, what we call death. You're going to meet people dreaming—you dream there as you dream here. We think this is not a dream, but that may be a dream. This doesn't seem to be a dream because the dream is so vivid it becomes objective. But when you are in a dream, and the dream is real, it's objective too. And when you return and contemplate the dream, you say, well, it was subjective because now it isn't objective. But while in it when you thought of this world, this would be subjective and that objective.* ***Subjectivity and objectivity are wholly determined for the individual by the level on which his consciousness is focused." - Neville***

REALITY IS NOT CONFINED to Earth but extends into the imagination. Reality is not confined to physical organs but extends its reach into divine inner organs. With divine eyes that see a subjective, free reality bound to no restrictions!

The inner world of imagination is not less real than the outer-world, it simply operates on a different level of focus of consciousness. When we are fully immersed in our imagination, it becomes our present reality. The vividness of our inner experience determines its objectivity to us in that moment.

The Inner Man, your imaginative self, can do, see, hear, and be whatever it desires. You are not merely a physical creature but an imaginative one. Your true nature is imagination itself and that nature is free.

How do we harness this power?

When you meditate or imagine, it is essential to release the outer world completely. Let it go entirely as it is. Instead, *feel* that your inner world is your *only* reality, your own personal, subjective, free reality. Within this space, you can do, have, and be anything you desire. You can make people say what you want them to say. You can embody fearlessness. You can receive gifts. You can transport yourself anywhere. You can receive praise. You can possess whatever you wish. You can possess any items you want.

We are not trying to "make something happen" or "hope it manifests." Release these concerns, for they only obstruct the wonderful feelings and experiences you seek within. We not going "out-there" to do anything yet, we are going "in here" to become free inside. This changes you entirely and by that your life changes. For you and your life are one.

Remember: This is your own personal, subjective, free reality.

Now here's where the profound realization comes in: You already do this.

You already create within your imagination constantly. You already put words in people's mouths in this inner realm. You already imagine scenarios where you are punished, hurt, or denied. You already hear bad news in your imagination before it arrives. You already create fearful situations and play them out internally. You are already the author of your inner world.

*You are creating your own personal, subjective nightmares freely.*

If you are already creating these nightmares, then you have always had the power to create beautiful dreams instead. The mechanism is identical. The only difference is the direction of your attention. When you imagine fearful outcomes, you are not using some "negative imagination" that is different from "positive imagination" you are using the same creative imagination. What is different is *you*. You decide what to dream, what you fancy. You feel free, and all of a sudden imagination adjusts to free you.

When you replay a conversation in your imagination where someone criticizes you, you are actively creating that experience within yourself. You give them the words. You supply the tone. You generate the feeling of hurt. You are the scriptwriter, director, and actor in this inner drama. No one else is doing this to you. The person you imagine criticizing you is not actually present, you are representing them there, and you are deciding what they say and how they say it. Everything they do is not a reflecting of them but of you! Remember, if you see a giant in your imagination, it is not about the giant but about how small you made yourself! A giant is anything that you feel is bigger than you is it not? It does not have to be a person, but an idea, a desire, a circumstance, these are all giants. Change not the giants, leave them alone for they only reflect you. Make yourself larger and giants becomes smaller.

This means that every time you have imagined the worst, you were exercising the exact same creative power that you can now use to imagine the best. The faculty itself is neutral, it is your awareness and direction of Self that determines what it creates. You do not need to learn a new skill or acquire a special ability. You simply need to redirect the imagination you already use every single day.

When you worry, you imagine vividly. When you fear, you create detailed inner scenarios. When you feel anxious about the future, you are already living in your imagination, experiencing events that have not happened in the physical world. This is proof that you are already capable of making your inner world feel completely real. The challenge is not capability, it is choice. Will you continue to use this power to create inner nightmares, or will you finally direct it toward the beauty, love, and fulfillment you desire?

*Always remember, you are free to creative new things, not just rearrange old things. This understanding will be paramount to your inner growth.*

*"He who creates the evil, creates the good, the weal and the woe, the light and the darkness. He who kills is he who makes alive, and he who wounds is he who heals and there is no other God.* ***If you really believe you are the one spoken of here - that it is you who create the evil, the good, the weal and the woe; that none can deliver out of your hand - then you are set free.*** *You will never again believe in another, but know that your life is SELF-CREATED. That you create the storms, as well as the peace and the calm. No*

*longer will you believe he, she, or they, did it, for you will recognize them as reflections mirroring either the storm or the peace and calm within you." -* ***Neville***

Recognize that you are the creator of both your inner storms and your inner peace. It means that no external circumstance, no other person, no past event has the power to determine what you experience within your imagination right now. The person who hurt you yesterday cannot hurt you today unless you bring them into your imagination and give them the power to hurt you again. The circumstance that troubled you last week cannot trouble you now unless you resurrect it in your imagination and give it life.

Consider how often we replay painful memories or rehearse fearful futures. We bring people into our inner world and have them criticize us, reject us, or harm us, over and over again. We create elaborate scenarios of failure, loss, and disappointment. These inner experiences take on the tones of reality. They generate real emotions, real stress, real suffering. What we often miss is that none of it is happening except in our own imagination. We are doing it *to* ourselves, *by* ourselves, through the creative power of our own imagination.

The question then becomes: how do we stop blaming others for what is happening within us? How do we stop giving our power away to external circumstances and reclaim our role as the creator of our inner experience?

The answer is to *begin to finally do what you want in your imagination.* Instead of automatically replaying that painful conversation where someone criticized you, rewrite it. Make them say something kind, something encouraging, something wonderful. Why? Just because you want to. Instead of imagining the worst possible outcome for that situation you are worried about, create an entire new outcome born out of creativity not fear. Change everything if you need to because you want to out of your own freedom. Dwell upon what interests you and learn to love to imagine.

> *"So I think if I had so much money I could live beautifully and then all of a sudden it doesn't work, it doesn't fit, because something penetrates it, inflation or this, that or the other, and all of sudden the whole thing is disturbed forcing me now to use my Imagination, my creative power, to construct some imaginal solution to this new problem. This synthetic problem is defined in the dictionary as "the compiling of separate elements which produces a new form."* ***So something penetrates my form, and then it forces me with this new form to conceive a new solution to that form. Now this is how we do it. I'm confronted with any problem I don't care what it is. I look at the problem, I don't duck it I see it.*** *Now, what is the solution to that problem? Suppose I were in jail, well, the solution would be to be out of jail, to have someone simply discharge me for reasons I need not know, but I am out of jail. I'm sleeping at home and I'm not listening to anyone knocking at the door to re-arrest me. If I were not in jail and I were free, where would I sleep? I would sleep at home. Well then, while in jail sleeping, I assume I am at home sleeping. I construct a scene implying the fulfillment of my desire."* - **Neville**

This is not about denial or pretending that outer challenges do not exist. It is about recognizing that the war is within, not without. The outer-world will always present situations, some pleasant, some challenging. *The world penetrates creating synthetic, artificial problems but must submit to the imaginal solution.* Your experience to these problems is determined by what you do with them *in* your imagination. Two people can face the same circumstance and have completely different inner experiences of it, because they are imagining it differently but truly they are imagining *themselves* differently.

You begin to consciously create a personal, subjective, free reality where everything unfolds beautifully, where people speak kindly to you, where circumstances work in your favor, where you embody the qualities you admire. You will start to realize there is no one to blame for what you were previously imagining in here. You see with absolute clarity that fear does not exist "out there" in the world, but within you, and you are its creator.

This realization is wonderful news, not terrible news. For if nightmares are created by you, then so are beautiful dreams for their root, their essence is made of the same substance, imagination. The power that creates your suffering is the exact same power that can create your joy. You do not need to acquire this power, you already have it and use it every day. You simply need to redirect it consciously. By taking full responsibility for what happens within us, not in a guilty, self-blaming way, but in an empowered, creative way, we gain the power to change what we experience *within* ourselves.

This is not magical thinking, or neglecting external problems, it is a profound shift in identity. You literally become a different person when you change what you consistently imagine. And a different person, walking through the same world, will have an entirely different experience of it. The world has not changed. *you* have changed, and therefore your relationship to everything in it has changed, even your relationship with your own imagination that you are one with.

Use that creative power, which you *already* possess and use constantly, to create the inner experiences you truly desire. Create humor, art, poetry, meaning, fulfillment, freedom! Just create! Make your imagination a sanctuary of beauty, love, and fulfillment. Do this not to manipulate the outer-world, but to free yourself within. For when you are free within, you will discover that you were never truly bound by anything external. You were only ever bound by what you imagined to be true.

> ***"That which you think about with feeling, that which you believe (feel) to be true and that which you imagine yourself to be or to have is the cause of everything in your personal world (inner world).*** *You may believe that there is some other cause; you may blame others for your problems; you may believe that the events were wrought by fate or chance, but if you are objective and*

*observe your own beliefs and thought patterns, you will see that your world accurately reflects all that you believe (feel) to be true of yourself and others. There is no one and nothing to change but the ideas from which you think (What we feel, we think-from). We think from ideas that we consent to as true and we imagine situations that match our beliefs (If we have fear, we think-from fear). Consciousness is the only reality. It is the creative principle that brings into your experience the exact duplicate or reflection of that which you imagine to be true. The world in which we live mirrors all that we believe and imagine to be true, be it good, bad, or indifferent. The sooner that man rids himself of the belief in a second cause, the sooner will he realize that nothing happens to him except that which originates in his own consciousness."* - ***Neville***

Tonight, allow yourself to hear someone speak lovely words to you. Receive good news about someone else. Give yourself that item you have always wanted. Share love with others. Witness the beauty you wish to see. Feel what you have longed to feel. Let people express wonderful things to you in this space. This is your own personal, subjective, free reality. There is no need to hurt anyone, and doing so only hurts yourself and creates another mental nightmare. This would merely return you to the cycle you are trying to escape. Instead, elevate others and yourself. Become the savior, the redeemer in your own imagination.

You take a subjective dream, a state within your imagination, and then you make that state of imagination *real* to you. However, you do, it I do not care, but you make it *feel real* to you. You believe in the *reality* of that imaginal act. Without this belief, it will produce little in you and in your life. But always remember: everything you imagine is about *you*, not about the other person in your imagination. They are symbols representing something about you. That is why you want to make it *real*, so that you feel the *reality* of being different than what you are now.

> *"In your meditation allow others to see you as they would see you were this new concept of self a concrete fact. You always seem to others an embodiment of the ideal you inspire. Therefore, in meditation,* ***when you contemplate others, you must be seen by them mentally as you would be seen by them physically were your concept of self an objective fact;*** *that is, in meditation you imagine that they see you expressing that which you desire to be." - Neville*

Notice how in Neville's meditation is not about other people. It is about them seeing *you* the way you want to be. They do not have a choice but to see you expressing your ideal. When you bring someone into your imagination, you are not actually bringing them in. You are bringing in your own conception of yourself, your own version of you that exists nowhere but within your own imagination. The person walking around in the outer-world appears independent of your perception, but the person you imagine, the person you speak to in your imagination, the person you rehearse conversations with, that person is you. They are a part of you taking on personhood form, speaking with their voice, but expressing something about your own inner state.

This is why when you imagine someone criticizing you, you feel hurt. Not because they actually criticized you, but because you used your own creative power to construct an experience of criticism within yourself. You became both the critic and the criticized. You played both roles in the theater of your own imagination. Similarly, when you imagine someone praising you, loving you, or supporting you, you feel uplifted not because they actually did those things, but because you gave yourself that experience through your imagination.

Suppose you feel trapped inside and you imagine someone who represents your entrapment, perhaps an authority figure, a person, a circumstance personified. This person in your imagination seems to be the source of your bondage. They say "No" to you. They limit you. They control you. But truly they are only doing this because you are experiencing yourself as trapped, and your imagination is simply expressing that inner state through their image.

Now, suppose you decide to imagine being free. You shift your inner state from bondage to freedom. As you dwell in this new state, you may notice that another version of that same person appears in your imagination, or perhaps the same person begins to behave differently or they fade away. They now say "Yes." They support you. They release you. Did your freedom come from them changing? No. Your freedom came from *you* changing, and because you changed, your imagination automatically began to reflect that change through the images and symbols it presents to you, including the image of that person.

The people in your imagination is not the source of your state; they are the expression of your state. They are the mirror, not the face. When you change your face, the mirror must reflect that change. This is why it is always about *you*, not about them. Your imagination can only show you what you are, what you believe yourself to be, what you are currently embodying in imagination.

Remember, *"It is not what you are looking at but what you see."* It not what you are looking at but what you see, and what you see if from your state. So before you manipulate what you are looking at physically, change your state, to change what you see. If you still see yourself the same, then you have not changed your state!

The world did not change but you did. So when you go into yourself to change but you come out seeing yourself and everything the same, you did not change. This is merely feedback not a punishment. When you change, you see yourself differently and feel differently about you. The world remains the world but you changed.

> *"You know exactly what to do whenever you are confronted with any problem.* ***You see the problem, you don't duck, you look at it, and then you construct some imaginal scene which would imply the solution, the fulfillment.*** *Having activated it, you simply drop it and let it come into this world. And it does! If you are so sure of that then you can tell it and share it with others."*- **Neville**

**Artwork Commentary:**

In this artwork, I wanted to depict the feeling of subjectiveness, the deeply personal nature of perception and meaning. The composition features seemingly random objects: a vase, an altar, a pyramid, a tree. Long shadows cast by a strong light source evoke profundity and mysticism. Though the objects appear randomly placed with no particular order, the image maintains a sense of harmony and balance. The arches frame the room with a feeling of royalty and importance, suggesting a sacred space that exists beyond ordinary reality.

What I am trying to capture is an imaginal royal place, a sanctuary of the imagination where you are free to play, explore, and create meaning. You can run over to the tree and gaze upon it, seeing whatever resonates with your inner world. You can approach the vase and transform how you perceive it, shifting its meaning to you. Or you can sit on the stairs in quiet contemplation, simply being present in this imaginal space.

This is a sanctuary where you, the dreamer, are free to do whatever you wish. And in that freedom, the freedom to perceive, interpret, and create your own meaning, you discover peace. The peace does not come from the objects themselves, but from recognizing your own agency in how you experience them.

The reason I emphasize this freedom leading to peace is because so much of our suffering comes from feeling trapped by fixed interpretations of ourselves. We believe things must be one way, that meaning is objective and unchanging. But when we recognize the subjective nature of experience, when we see that we have the power to shift our perception, to find new meaning, to reimagine what we are looking at, we liberate ourselves from that rigidity. You remember that you are not bound by any single interpretation of Self.

# No Permission Needed

*"As man I must become conscious of being wealthy if that is what I want, conscious of being healthy if that's what I want, conscious of being famous if that is what I want, I don't care what it is.* ***Ask no man his permission to be anything in this world****...you simply go right into the state desired. It came out of you, but you've got to occupy it and actually become it in the same way that God had to become you to make you God. So you have to become the state to make that state yourself. So what do you desire in this world? You name it and ask no one in this world if it's possible. All things are possible to God and God dwells in you: your own wonderful human Imagination that's God. There never was another God and there never will be another God."* - ***Neville***

HOW CAN we truly know that we are operant power, the cause of our worlds, if we do not test it? I mean testing it radically, without reservation or hesitation. Remember, the outer-world is a reflection of what the Inner Man has, is, and does in their own personal, free, subjective reality and that Inner Man is you.

If we wish to create radical change in our outer circumstances, we must first radically change the Inner Man. We must give the Inner Man what they want. In other words, we must radically transform our own personal, free, subjective reality. How do we accomplish this change? Through feeling.

We do not change until we change within. This is the fundamental principle that most people overlook. They wait for circumstances to shift before they allow themselves to feel differently. But this is backward.

When I speak of radical change, I mean giving yourself permission to feel *exactly* what you would feel if your desire were already fulfilled, not partially, not conditionally, but completely. This requires courage because it means abandoning the evidence of your senses and your current circumstances. It means choosing to dwell in the feeling of the wish fulfilled, even when nothing in your outer world supports it yet.

This is why Neville constantly emphasizes *feeling*. Feeling is the secret because feeling is the language of the Inner Man. What feeling again? The feeling reality. It feels *real* to the Inner Man.

Read Neville's words here,

> *"Arise! Go down to the potter's house and there I will let you hear my words. So I went down to the potter's house and there he was working at his wheel, but the vessel in his hand which he was making of clay was spoiled, so he reworked it into another vessel as it seemed good to the potter to do..."* - ***Jeremiah 18:2-4***

> *"He didn't discard it!* ***So someone seems beyond repair don't discard it, test this power this creative power****. There is nothing more wonderful in this world, nothing more creative in man than to believe a thing into existence! I can't conceive anything more wonderful than that."* - ***Neville***

He did not discard it! He reworked it into what pleased him. That is you. You are the potter within. Notice how Neville uses the phrase "someone *beyond* repair." Do not discard them, but instead reworked them as it seems good to *you*! Test this principle on those who appear beyond redemption, even if you believe that person is yourself. This is how we discover whether this truly works.

Neville does not merely suggest "assuming something nice occasionally." Instead, he challenges us to "dare to assume." Remember that an assumption is a feeling. So dare to feel what you want. Without this action, you remain unchanged. The word "dare" implies risk, boldness, audacity. It suggests that most people will not do this because they are afraid. Afraid of disappointment, afraid of looking foolish to themselves, afraid of hoping for something that may not come to pass. But this fear is exactly what keeps them trapped in their current state of imagination.

When you *dare* to assume, you are not timidly hoping or wishing. You are boldly claiming what you desire as already yours. You are not asking permission from the outer-world or waiting for evidence to support your claim. You are decreeing it from within, as the operant power that you are. This is why testing it radically matters.

This is how you become the potter who shapes your reality according to what pleases you. But what clay are we truly reworking? Self! Self is the clay that we mold! We change ourselves into our ideals and we start to live from being that before than happens outside of us.

Do you want respect from others? Then you must first receive it entirely within your imagination. Do not wait for someone else to offer it to you. Do not wait for circumstances to change so that you *then* feel respected. This is backward. Go to the potter's house, your own imagination, and rework the clay, yourself.

This is the recognition that you are operant power, and that your imagination is the only true cause in your world. No matter how far you think you have fallen from grace, never discard yourself. Go within, into your own personal, free, subjective reality, and transform what troubles you into what pleases you. Rework the vessel as it seems good to you to do.

> *"Now a lady wrote, saying: "This dream disturbs me greatly. In the dream I entered an exquisite jewelry store, [and] picked up many items, among which was a beautiful green gem. Then I left without paying for the articles I took. On this level I would never do such a thing and cannot understand why I would do it there." My dear, you should be thrilled because you did it. On this level you are eating of the tree of knowledge of good and evil, but you are way beyond this tree, for you are now eating of the Tree of Life by fulfilling the 50th Psalm: "If I were hungry I would not tell you for the world is mine and all within it." If everything is yours, whose permission do you need to take it? As an in-current eyewitness, you do not function here save when you open your mortal eyes. In this world of Good and Evil you would never go to Tiffany's and walk out without paying for your purchases, but as the Spirit of truth, you are feasting upon the Tree of Truth and error in the world that is yours.* ***In that world there is no need to ask***

***permission of anyone to take anything you desire." - Neville***

*"Everyone who thirsts come ... he who has no money, come, buy and eat! Come, buy wine, buy milk, without money, without price." -* ***Isaiah 55:1***

*"In that world there is no need to ask permission..."* What world is Neville speaking of? The personal, subjective, free reality within. The Inner Man needs no permission! The Inner Man does not care whether or not it is possible!

In your subjective reality, understand that you need no permission to feel what you want to feel. No permission to decide whether something is "possible." No permission to feel deeply all the time. No permission to experience what you desire. Identify yourself with the Inner Man who is free to do, feel, and be whatever they want. You can go anywhere and take what pleases you. It is all yours.

You will never understand this if you identify with the outer-man, the man of limitation. The outer-man is bound by the laws of the physical world, by time, by space. The outer-man asks, "How is this possible? Where will it come from? What must I do first?" But the Inner Man is infinite and can feel whatever he wants, whenever he wants! The Inner Man recognizes no barriers, no prerequisites, no conditions that must be met before he can experience what he desires.

This is why the woman in Neville's example could enter the jewelry store in her dream and take whatever pleased her without paying. She was operating from the perception of the Inner Man, where everything already belongs to her. She needed no one's permission because in that state of imagination, there is no separation between desire and fulfillment. There is no lack, no insufficiency, no need to earn or deserve what is already yours by imaginal right.

Most people live their entire lives waiting for permission. Permission from their circumstances. Permission from other people.

Permission from their past failures or successes. Permission from their bank account, their education, their social status, their age, their appearance. They believe they must first change something in the outer-world before they are allowed to feel differently within. But this is bondage, not freedom.

The Inner Man does not wait for the outer-world to grant permission. The Inner Man claims what they desires now, ***in*** imagination, and dwells in that state until the outer-world has no choice but to conform.

*You do not need permission to feel that your imagination is real!*

If you only partially accept that you are the Inner Man, if you only occasionally permit yourself to feel what you desire, if you compromise between the feeling of the wish-fulfilled and the evidence of your senses, then you remain divided against yourself. A house divided cannot stand.

The change must be radical because the principle itself is radical. You are not attempting to modify your circumstances through external action. You are claiming that imagination is the only reality, that imagination creates reality, and that your subjective experience is the actual cause of your objective world. This is not a timid claim. This is not something you can test half-heartedly and expect conclusive results.

When you identify with the Inner Man, you are experiencing the *now* in imagination. There is no need to wait. As Neville says, "*I may not have a dime but **in** imagination I have much!*" This statement reveals the specific reasoning: the Inner Man exists in a dimension where having and being are not separated by time or circumstance. In your imagination, you can be wealthy *now*. You can be respected *now*. You can be loved *now*. You can be healed *now*.

Do not just apply this principle to money. Apply it to whatever you want. Never limit yourself to one thing or else desperation grows. We all have different desires, so discover what you truly want and experience it fully in your subjective, free reality. Give yourself permission to feel it completely, without reservation, without conditions, without waiting for the outer-world to change first.

> *"My imagination puts me in touch inwardly with that state. I imagine that I am actually where I desire to be. How can I tell that I am there? There is one way to prove that I am there, for what a man sees when he describes his world is, as he describes it, relative to himself. So what the world looks like depends entirely upon where I stand when I make my observation. So, if as I describe my world it is related to that point in space I imagine that I am occupying, then I must be there. I am not there physically, no, but I AM there in my imagination, and* ***my imagination is my real self!*** *And where I go in imagination and make it real, there I shall go in the flesh, also. When in that state I fall asleep, it is done. I have never seen it fail. So this is the simple technique upon how to use your imagination to realize your every objective. -* ***Neville***

Pay careful attention to Neville's bold statement: "*My imagination is my Real Self!*" Neville is being completely sincere and feels no embarrassment for stating this truth. The Inner Man is your True Self. This is the Self you should exalt, without shame or hesitation.

Why does Neville identify imagination as the Real Self rather than the physical body or the reasoning mind? Because imagination is where you actually experience being. When you imagine yourself in a state, you are not pretending to be there, you are actually there in imagination, can you believe that? And imagination is the only place where you truly exist.

The physical world is merely a reflection, a shadow cast by the light of imagination. The outer-man, the physical body with its limitations, its history, its circumstances, is not the real you. It is the result of who you have been in imagination. It is the hardened clay that was shaped by the potter, which is the Inner Man.

This is why you need no permission to occupy any state in imagination. You are not asking reality to let you in. You are not petitioning circumstances to allow you to feel differently. You are recognizing that imagination is the actual creative power, and that within it, you are free to be, do, and have whatever you desire.

When you go to a place in imagination and describe your world from that vantage point, when you see yourself as already respected, already loved, already successful, you are proving to yourself that you occupy that state. Not physically yet, but imaginatively. And since imagination is your Real Self, that is where the true change occurs. The physical follows the spirit (*imagination*).

> *Imagination puts us in touch with larger dimension of reality, but in truth, it puts us in touch with a larger dimension of ourselves.*

> *"Here is a very healthy and productive exercise for the imagination, something that you should do daily:* ***Daily relive the day as you wish you had lived it, revising the scenes to make them conform to your ideals****. For instance, suppose today's mail brought disappointing news. Revise the letter. Mentally rewrite it and make it conform to the news you wish you had received. Or, suppose you didn't get the letter you wish you had received. Write yourself the letter and imagine that you received such a letter." -* ***Neville***

Your subjective reality is not bound by the facts of life. Within your imagination, you possess complete freedom to go back in memory and change what you want. It is *yours* to reshape! Do not revise according to what you "think you should" want, but according to what genuinely *pleases* you.

When Neville speaks about revision, he is instructing you to recreate experiences as you wish they had been. This is the true essence of revision: changing experiences into what is loving and pleasing to you. You are not correcting history for moral purposes or to align with some external standard of how things "should" be. You are claiming your authority as the Inner Man to determine what your past means and what emotional tone it carries.

Many people misunderstand revision as a technique to "fix" mistakes or erase regrets. But this perspective still operates from the outer-man's viewpoint, where you are subject to what has happened. The Inner Man does not fix the past because the Inner Man was never broken by it. Instead, revision is the recognition that your memory of an event is more real than the event itself, because memory exists in imagination, and imagination is your Real Self.

If you remember a conversation where someone rejected you, that memory lives in your imagination now. The actual event is gone, it exists nowhere except in your subjective reality. And since your subjective reality is the cause of your objective world, that memory continues to create your present experience. It continues to shape how you feel about yourself, how you expect to be treated, and what you believe is possible for you.

But you have complete authority over your subjective reality. You can return to that memory and reshape it to reflect what would have pleased you. Not because you are denying what happened, but because you are recognizing that the meaning you assign to what happened is yours to determine. The outer-man says, "This is what occurred, and I must accept it." The Inner Man says, "This is what I choose, and I will experience it as I desire."

Every moment, you are choosing what to dwell upon, what to remember, what to feel about yourself and your world. These choices are not passive observations; they are active creations. Your imagination asks only one question: "What do you want?" Not what do you deserve, not what is reasonable, not what others will approve of, simply, *what do you want?*

When you understand this, revision becomes far more than a technique to improve your mood. It becomes a declaration of your identity as the Inner Man. It becomes proof that you need no permission from the past to feel differently in the present. The facts of your life do not determine your subjective reality unless you allow them to.

> *"There are those who are depressed all day long and remain that way all of their life. I remember back in New York City, when I would see certain people walking in my direction I would want to cross the*

*street, because I did not want to hear their depressing stories. They would spend hours telling about their wife or husband, their children or grandchildren, and each story geared to depression. Never changing their mood, their world never changed. Seeing no change, they would not recognize a law between the inner world they maintain and the outer world of response.*

*But if you apply this law you can predict your future.* ***Feel a new mood rise within you. Sustain it and soon you will meet people who embody this new state. Even inanimate objects are under the sway of these affinities.*** *In a certain mood I have gone to my library and removed a book I have not touched in years. And when I casually open it, I find confirmation of my mood. A table, though remaining the same, will be seen differently based upon your momentary mood, for everything reflects it. It is your mood which decides your fortune, not your fortune that decides your mood. People feeling poor attract poverty, not knowing that if they felt rich they would attract wealth." -* ***Neville***

When people never change their inner world through the medium of feeling, they see no change in their outer-world. This is not a mystery. If the Inner Man remains depressed, anxious, or poor in imagination, the outer-man will continue to express those states perfectly.

We do not truly believe this imagination of ours until we experience a radical change within ourselves. Without such change, we dismiss results as mere "coincidence" or inevitable occurrences. We say, "Things just happened that way," never recognizing the causal relationship between our inner state and outer circumstances. But when we deliberately transform our inner world to align with our desires and identify with the Inner Man who *already has* what we want, something profound occurs, our desire dissolves into the experience of *possession*. Possession feels wonderful and grows into a greater joy and peace.

> *"Now, in order to play the game of life, you must know what you want to replace what you have. When you know what it is, you must assume the feeling that you have it. Although your reason and senses will deny its existence, persistence will cause your assumption to harden into fact and objectify itself upon your screen of space.* ***Play the game this way. You may think it doesn't work, but that's because you have not tried it. You may believe the idea is stupid, but I tell you: the mood decides your fortune. Believe me, for I have proved this principle over and over again in my life." - Neville***

*"You may think it does not work, but that's because you have not tried it."* This statement rings true to me. I thought this approach worked occasionally but not consistently. I found it silly at times and even wanted to quit, but I simply cannot deny my experiences. Those moments when I see myself reflected so beautifully, so exactly in this world, there is no denying it.

I never understood this until I started doing exactly what I wanted in my imagination. Once I identified with the Inner Man, I discovered many things I did not wish to experience. I realized I was imagining not what pleased me but what frightened me! When I frighten myself, I am actually giving myself exactly what I do not want to receive.

But within that fear lies what I truly want, and from there I can give it to myself. In that terrible nightmare lies a a freedom, my desire. I use my fear to show me what I want so I stopped fearing fear itself. Once I accepted that I create everything within me, I gained the power to redeem my world within me! I transformed the unlovely into lovely. I lifted up those I had looked down on. I am, and continue to be, the savior in my own imagination. Then I started to see change. But I did not wait to do it, I had to do it *now*.

> *Do not be afraid to give yourself the greatest feelings and imaginings.*

*"He calls upon us to* ***test him (the Inner Man) every moment of time.*** *But you can't buy him unless you pay the price, and the price, it takes everything that you have to buy it.* ***Everything, not a few things." - Neville***

*"The average person would say, "Well, after all, I know that's all well and good, but Sanka [decaf coffee] does keep me in a state of sleep when normal coffee keeps me awake. And I know that an extra martini does so and so to me, and I'll take none. Or maybe, I should take vodka because it's good for my breath and not the martini."* ***And a thousand things in the world people have concerning what they should do." - Neville***

Imagine waking up in a dream where you realize you have complete creative control. You can dream anything you wish into being. In this lucid state, who would you consult with? Who would you approach for permission to create what you desire?

Would you seek out other people in the dream? Couldn't you simply imagine them saying "yes"? Couldn't you put those very words of approval in their mouths? And if you can do that, then whose permission are you truly seeking? It is your own permission, dressed up as someone else's voice. You are the dreamer asking yourself for permission from your dream.

Why ask at all then? Why not simply create directly? Why introduce this unnecessary step of seeking external validation when you are the source of everything within that dream? Every authority you seek outside yourself is ultimately your own authority projected outward.

So why not just create, instead of seek? It cuts through all the elaborate mental gymnastics, all the seeking, all the waiting, all the doubt. The Inner Man does not need permission. The Inner Man does not need to overcome obstacles. The Inner Man does not need to prove worthiness. The Inner Man simply creates by imagining and feeling it to be so. They assume the state they desire, they feel themselves to be what they wish to be.

So why question these things at all? Why ask "Can I have this?" or "Am I worthy?" or "Will this work?" when you are the power by which all things come into being in your inner experience? These questions only arise when you forget who you are. This is why so much advice does not work well. For the advice is *trying* to make you worthy, instead of coming at life, knowing you *already* are. There is no trying to become worthy. You assume you already are it not by doing things, but by living *FROM* already being it.

The Inner Man has inherent worth because you can imagine whatever you want without needing external permission from anyone or anything. This means *you* have inherent worth, a worth that can never be taken away. It exists independent of circumstances, independent of approval, independent of achievement. Your worth is not conditional. It is foundational to your nature as the Inner Man.

You cannot come at life trying to tweeze out these feelings of unworthiness, shame, and bondage forever, or else you will waste your time. Instead, you must come at life from this understanding: *I am already worthy, unashamed, and free, because that is my true nature as the Inner Man.* This is not something you earn. This is not something you prove. This is what you *are*. And the moment you accept this, you stop trying to become it. You stop striving for worth and start *living from* worth. You stop fighting shame and start *occupying* the state of freedom.

If you are always trying to remove unworthiness, you are assuming it is there to begin with. If you are always trying to escape shame, you are assuming you are trapped in it. But assumption creates reality. So the act of "trying to fix" these things keeps you identified with them. It keeps you in the state of the problem, not the solution.

*The one who imagines trying to be worthy, will continue to imagine trying. The one who imagines FROM already being worthy, creates whatever their loving hearts desire without any self-doubt.*

This is the freedom that comes with identification. You stop seeking permission from a world that exists within you. You stop waiting for conditions to change before you dare to feel differently. You stop looking outside for validation of what you already are within. You simply create, because that is your nature as the Inner Man. And in that recognition, you find the pearl of great price.

*Do not be afraid, instead of being nervous, enjoy your imaginal acts. Enjoy being new, free!*

> *"So were I hungry, I would slay and eat.* ***Why would I ask permission of another to take my own?*** *And so, the whole is yours, for he became you. So appropriate...appropriate the security that you want in this world and feel that you are secure. Appropriate anything in this world just as though it were true and walk as though it is true. In a way that you do not know it will suddenly appear in your world. That suddenness had its beginning that maybe you will forget. But do it now, assume it's coming in the immediate future, that it is here. And see if you cannot relate it to that night that you really imagined. When these lovely things begin to happen in your world, you will find that memory will return and you will know the time that you did imagine it."* - ***Neville***

~

**Artwork Commentary:**

In this artwork it shows a cluster of identical chairs represents the unoriginal, repetitive narratives handed down to us, predetermined patterns of thought we are expected to contemplate for the rest of our lives. Meanwhile, the solitary chair positioned apart signifies a fundamentally different state of contemplation.

This is not merely about being different or embracing an outsider identity. It is about no longer seeking external approval or validation to imagine what one wishes to imagine. It is about choosing what one *wants* to contemplate, on one's own terms. It is an of heroic defiance to use one's imagination they way one wants to.

The uniformity of the grouped chairs symbolizes a truth that the majority prefer to have their imaginations shaped by others rather than shaping their own imaginations. Man, unfortunately, gravitates toward being told what to think, what to feel. If the news tells Man to be afraid, then Man becomes afraid. If the world tells Man to worship a deity, Man will start bowing. The comfort of consensus, the safety of accepted narratives, these are forces that keep people seated in those identical chairs.

Very few, symbolized by that single, separate chair, decide to take initiative and mold their imagination according to their own vision. These rare individuals do not wait for permission or for someone else to shape their imagination. They understand that true contemplation requires autonomy, that genuine thought cannot be outsourced.

When we wait for permission to imagine ourselves differently, we have already surrendered our mental sovereignty. The act of waiting itself is the problem mentally. By seeking permission before we allow ourselves to contemplate freely, we are acknowledging that our thoughts require external authorization. This is precisely the trap the grouped chairs represent, not just conformity in what we imagine, but conformity in believing we need permission to imagine at all. The single chair does not reject the group out of rebelliousness; it simply exists in a space where the question of permission never arises. It has moved beyond the entire framework of seeking approval, into a realm where the Inner Man operates as its own authority.

# God Of The World Of Imagination

*"...Now is nothing more than a blind man confined only to his five senses.* ***Nothing beyond what the eyes, what the ears, what the nostrils, what the tongue and what the sense of touch will reveal as true can be accepted as true.*** *He is limited to the limit of opacity and contraction...*

*Now, we are called upon to exercise this power that actually sacrificed itself and became us, actually became me, became you. Well, how do I exercise it? Blake stated quite clearly: "I know of no other Christianity, no other gospel than the freedom both of body and mind to exercise the divine arts of Imagination."* ***Well, can I actually exercise the divine art of Imagination and prove I can go beyond my senses, what my eyes dictate, what reason dictates, what all my senses dictate?*** *I know from experience I can. So here, I start exercising the divine arts of Imagination and I dare to assume that I am at the moment what at the moment reason denies and my senses deny. And to the degree that I am self-persuaded that what I am assuming to be true is true, to that degree the outer world changes to conform to this change of belief within me. I am working on this body of belief based upon all that reason has dictated, all that my senses have dictated. And so, to the degree I can bring about modifications and sometimes radical changes within this body of belief, when I do it changes in my outer world."* - **Neville**

There is only one Being, though this Being creates the illusion of duality, appearing as both the Inner Man and the outer-man. In truth, there is only one world and one Man experiencing that world: The Inner Man.

There exists the world of the senses, solid, tangible, governed by laws, and then there exists the World of Imagination, boundless and unlimited. The man who experiences the world of the senses is what we call the outer-man, constrained by what their five senses reveal. The Man who experiences the World of Imagination is the Inner Man, free to create and shape this reality according to their desires.

Yet when you examine your own experience, you discover that

the outer-man is merely the Inner Man's dream of limitation. Just as in sleep you dream yourself into various scenarios and believe yourself bound by the dream's rules until you awaken, so too does the Inner Man dream itself into the experience of the outer-man. The physical world is Imagination pushed out, it is the Inner Man's beliefs and assumptions crystallized into sensory experience. The world appears literal to the outer-man but is symbolic to the Inner Man.

*"Your inner being is he who men call God."* - ***Neville***

The outer-man perceives only limitations and restrictions in the world of the senses. They feel bound by the "facts" of life, imprisoned by what appears to be unchangeable reality. The outer-man lives fully convinced that this world of the senses is happening *to* them, not *interpreting* them. They rely solely on their five senses to navigate this world, accepting only what their eyes see, what their ears hear, and their hands can touch as truth. Naturally, they feel like a victim of circumstances attempting to control their environment through force, manipulation, and endless strategizing. The outer-man fears that life will throw situations at them that they are unprepared for. Since they feel powerless against the tide of events, they dread the future. Unable to change the past, they carry guilt and regret like chains. This is how they remain confined within self-imposed limitations.

Then there is the Inner Man who dwells in the World of Imagination. In this realm, they are unlimited and can create whatever they wish. They is free beyond measure, and everything they can conceive of is theirs, everything.

*Can you truly separate yourself from imagination?*

The answer is no, you cannot. You may attempt to push certain imaginal acts aside, dismiss them as mere fantasy, or try to return to the reality of your senses. But do those imaginal experiences ever truly disappear? They do not. They continue to exist in imagination.

When you imagine something vividly, it becomes part of your experience. You cannot un-experience it. You cannot truly separate yourself from what you have imagined because imagination is not something you *do,* it is what you *are*. The Inner Man *is* imagination itself. Every thought, every feeling, every assumption you hold exists within the World of Imagination, including your current sense of being the outer-man limited by circumstances.

This is why you cannot escape imagination, you can only choose what you will imagine. Will you imagine yourself as the powerless outer-man at the mercy of circumstances? Or will you imagine yourself as the Inner Man, the creative power who shapes reality through assumption? Both are imaginal acts that you believe the reality in, but one creates bondage while the other creates freedom. You are always imagining. The question is: are you imagining consciously or unconsciously? Are you imagining what you want, or are you passively imagining what you fear?

> *"If you want another in your world to be important, treat him as though he were. If you want someone in your world to be known and be important, treat them as though they were, and in your own mind's eye build them up and they'll all be lifted up. Do it without their knowledge, without their consent. You love them enough to want to do it, do it. Don't ask them if it's possible or permissible, do it.* ***Treat everyone with respect if you want them to be respected in this world, and they will respond, everyone will.*** *So you live as though things were as you desire them to be and they'll become that way."* - **Neville**

In the World of Imagination, the Inner Man possesses absolute creative freedom. If they wish to walk into a store and take what they desire without paying, they can do so, and they can also imagine the cashier waving and smiling at them warmly. Everything is permissible in the World of Imagination (*1 Corinthians 10:23*). "Permissible" means you can change anything within this realm without asking anyone's permission.

If the Inner Man becomes frightened within this world, or begins to feel guilty and fears punishment, they can rest assured that they are always the one creating these experiences. There is no other God, no other Creator in the World of Imagination. Every feeling of fear, every sensation of guilt, every imagined punishment, all of it originates from the Inner Man's own creative power turned against itself.

However, here is where crucial understanding is needed. Without grasping this point, everything I write, and everything Neville wrote, becomes confusing and seemingly contradictory. The outer-man is simply an expression, a manifestation, a symbol of the Inner Man. The only Man that truly exists is the Inner Man. This world is the imagination in the flesh, imagination made seemingly tangible.

You are never *not* the Inner Man. You cannot stop being the Inner Man. There is no other Man. There is only One Being, and that Being is you, the Inner Man, the Dreamer, the Creator, the on made of ALL IMAGINATION. That Being took upon the flesh.

Think of it this way: when you dream at night, you might dream yourself into a scenario where you are a poor person struggling to survive, or a prisoner trapped in a cell. In that dream, you fully believe you are that limited character. You feel their fears, their restrictions, their helplessness. But upon awakening, you realize that you were never actually that limited character, you were always the Dreamer dreaming that character into existence. The prisoner was never real; it was always you, the Dreamer, imagining yourself as imprisoned.

The same principle applies to your waking life. The Inner Man may convince themselves that they are merely this physical outer body living in this unpredictable, dangerous world, but they are still the Inner Man who can dream a new thing.

*"This is the battle within me, the battle between the outer man of the senses and the Inner Man of Imagination."* - ***Neville***

So God is the Cause. Yet, if I say "I am God," you might think I am claiming, "I, this little body of mine, this limited man is God." But that is not what I am saying, nor what Neville is saying. God is the Inner Man, the awareness itself.

*You walk on concrete, tiles or carpet in the physical world, and you are also walking in an imaginal world. Who is walking? The Inner Man who is God of that world of thought!*

When you become fearful of your world or dislike what it shows you, many of us try to change it by forcing physical changes upon it. We "move the furniture," so to speak. We rearrange a few things, thinking that will suffice, only to find ourselves facing the same mental patterns again. If you fear something in on country, you will fear it in another if you move there. Rearranging the physical world does not change the Inner Man, the only one there is! When someone wants to escape their problems by changing locations, who is "thinking" about moving? The Inner Man of imagination. There is no other God (*Cause*). There is no escapism for we cannot escape ourselves. There is only a change in Self!

Consider how futile it would be to try changing your reflection in a mirror by reaching toward the glass and attempting to rearrange the reflected image. Yet this is precisely what we do when we try to change our circumstances without changing our inner state. We are trying to manipulate the reflection instead of turning around and changing ourselves, the source of the reflection.

The Inner Man can convince themselves that they are this outer-man. Let's say this outer-man desires respect. The Inner Man, forgetting their true nature, believes they are this outer-man who lacks respect and decides to pursue money to buy respect. However, true respect exists only in the World of Imagination! It cannot be bought or found in this world of the senses.

So you might buy the appearance of respect temporarily through money, status, or power, but they do not truly respect you, they respect your money, your position, your ability to benefit them. Remove the money, and you will see they never respected *you*.

Who is the "you" that lacks respect? The Inner Man! Why does this happen? Because the Inner Man, who lives in the World of Imagination is dwelling there in a state of no respect! The Inner Man has not given themselves respect in imagination, so no amount of outer manipulation can produce genuine respect in their world.

So instead of reconnecting with their true identity as the Inner Man, which they always are and have always been, the Inner Man tries to force changes upon this world of effects. They exhaust themselves manipulating circumstances, controlling people, accumulating things, all while not understanding that the outer-man merely reflects who they are being and what they are assuming in the World of Imagination. The world cannot give you what you have not first given yourself in imagination. It can only reflect back to you what you already are in imagination.

> *"In my own case, here is a man...never saw him until I was drafted. I didn't now who he was, but he was, in Caesar's world, my commanding officer. He was a colonel and I was a private and his word was law. He could order me to do anything, and under the rules I had to do it. When he said no to my request that was final. It could not be appealed to any higher echelon in the world of Caesar. To whom did I go? I went to my own wonderful human Imagination. That's the one to whom I went. "I know whom I believe in," said Paul. Yes, to me, I personify it because I'm a person, and so I commune with myself.* ***The Inner Man walked all around the place, but no one present could see him, and walking around all this place dressed not as a soldier on furlough but as a civilian, honorably discharged.*** *Then comes this wonderful confirmation of the screen, the hand, the pen, the writing, and now comes, the vision breaks into speech. When vision breaks into speech, the presence of Deity is confirmed. The voice said, "That which I have done I have done! Do nothing!" I did nothing but wait patiently for nine days. Then the same man had a change of heart, and to this day he knows he had the authority to keep me there, and he believes*

*he initiated that change of heart. He had no choice in the matter." -* ***Neville***

Notice how Neville points the fact the although the outer-man was in the army, having to serve a duty, the Inner Man was walking around as an honorably discharged civilian. Although, *nobody* could see the Inner Man with mortal eyes. So what pair of eyes was Neville looking with? The inner eyes of imagination. He let go to the position of the outer-man in exchange for the position of the Inner Man. Neville is the Inner Man, but for clarity he explains it as if he is separate. While the world saw Neville as a solider, Neville saw *himself* as the Inner Man of Imagination walking around in *that* inner world as a lovely free man.

The Inner Man, who is the "I am," only experiences things in the present moment. The "past" and "future" are not different time periods in the World of Imagination, they are, in fact, happening "*now*" to the Inner Man. When you truly identify as the Inner Man, you do not wait for your desire, you recognize that in the World of Imagination where you actually live, it already exists and you already possess it *now*. But you the Inner Man, must simply persist in that mental space until you occupy it as your own possession.

You might ask, "So what if I identify with the Inner Man and live in the World of Imagination? Why does it matter?" It matters because you express what the Inner Man feels they are and have in that inner world. Everything around you, the clothes you wear, the laptop you type on, the books you read, the movies you watch, were once only imagined. All these things existed first in the World of Imagination where you are God.

The question itself, "What difference does it make if I live in the World of Imagination?" reveals a fundamental misunderstanding. You are *already* living in the World of Imagination! You cannot *not* live there. Even when you deny the power of imagination, you are using imagination to make that denial. Even when you claim imagination is meaningless, you are imagining that position to be true.

The act of questioning imagination's importance is itself an act of imagination.

This world of the senses is not separate from or opposed to the World of Imagination, it is the *expression* of that inner world. It is the invisible imagination made visible, made flesh, made sensory. You are always in the World of Imagination, and you are always the Inner Man living in that world where you possess infinite creative freedom. So what are you imagining yourself to be? What are you accepting as true of yourself in that inner world? What do you want to create from imaginary scratch?

Now take this understanding and read Neville again. You are the one *within*, and you are *not* just this body moving through space and time. You are living in the World of Imagination where you need no permission to be, feel, and have what you desire. Not because you are trying to gain something you lack, but because in that inner world where you truly exist, you can simply assume you already are and have what you desire, and that assumption, when persisted in, must become flesh.

> *"Seated here tonight you believe you are a man or a woman. You believe you are here, but are you willing to believe you can go beyond what your reason and senses dictate? You do not have to limit your power of belief to what your reasonable mind dictates. The choice and its limitations are entirely up to you, for all things exist in the human imagination and it is from your imagination that your belief stems. If you go beyond the dictates of reason, it must be via your imagination, and since all things now exist there, you can at any moment go beyond what your reason and senses dictate.*
>
> *When you leave here tonight, you expect to find your home where you left it. You will go to sleep there and believe you will wake up in your bed tomorrow morning. You believe you are clothed right now. I tell you:* ***your capacity to believe is the human imagination, which is the only God. All imagination, you have restricted yourself by the body of sense and reason you wear.*** *Reason says you are in this room, that you have a certain amount of money*

*and can have no more unless you make a physical effort to get it. But you would wish you had more wouldn't you?*

*Assume your wish through the sense of feeling. That assumption, subjectively appropriated and believed to be true, is faith. Can you believe in its reality? Knowing all things are possible to him who believes, can you persuade yourself that, although your reason and senses deny it, your assumption will make it so?*

*Everything here was once only a desire, believed. This building, the clothes you wear or the car you drive were first a desire, then believed into being.*

*Yes, I believe there is a man named Neville. He may work for you to aid the fulfillment of your desire, if you believe you have it. Many men can and will come to aid you, even without knowing they are doing it, if you believe. You do not have to persuade others to help you; all you need do is believe you are what you want to be and then let the world (which is nothing more than yourself pushed out) go to work to make your assumption possible. I promise you: your desire will be fulfilled, for all things are possible to him who believes.*

*Let us say you would like to be in San Francisco now, but you don't have the time or the money to make the trip. What do you do? You ignore the present moment and subjectively appropriate your objective hope by sleeping in San Francisco tonight. As you lie on your bed, look at your world through the eyes of one who is sleeping in San Francisco. You may wake in the morning to find you are still physically in Los Angeles, but while you slept changes were taking place which will compel you to make the journey. I tell you: you will always go physically to the subjective state you have appropriated.*

*Remember: all things are possible to him who believes, and with God all things are possible. Man believes that God created the world and all within it, but he does not equate God with himself, the believer. But the Bible equates God, the creator of everything, with one who believes. And belief need not be restricted, but can go beyond the evidence of sense and reason." -* ***Neville***

In Neville's story, who is imagining themselves in San Francisco? The Inner Man is! So when Neville says, *"If as I describe my world it is related to that point in space I imagine that I am occupying, then I must be there. I am not there physically, no, but I am there in my imagination, and my* ***imagination is my real self!*** *And where I go in imagination and make it real, there I shall go in the flesh, also."* Neville said that Imagination, the Inner Man, is his Real Self! This means he does not have to force or pound ideas into his imagination, because everything already ***is*** so in imagination! Just as everything in this world of the senses with all its limitations already exists, so too does everything exist in the World of Imagination. When he asks, *"Can you believe in its reality?"* How can you? By identifying yourself with the Inner Man! For the Inner Man to believe, they must feel it to be theirs! And you can do this when you feel yourself to be the Inner Man in the world within!

The truth is you have always lived in Imagination. You always do. When you worry, who is doing the worrying and where is this happening? It is the Inner Man who worries, and they do so in the World of Imagination. Understanding this reveals that the Inner Man, who you always are, is creating worry in the World of Imagination where all things are possible! Yes, this is a complete waste of time, but it is merely habit. If you lived in a world where anything is possible and you could create whatever you want, would you choose to create situations just to worry about them? Of course not.

This is why Neville emphasized that imagination is not some mystical force separate from you, *it is you*. Your True Self. The Inner Man who imagines is not a part of you; it is the totality of what you are. Everything else, this body, these circumstances, this physical world, is the *expression* of what the Inner Man has imagined and accepted as true.

I am saying this because this is the truth I have discovered from Neville's work and verified through my own experience. When I identify with the Inner Man, I have never felt more free. Every day I see how I have been creating a limited world within the limitless World of Imagination, not because I lack power, but because I have been unconsciously using my power to imagine limitation inside.

When I begin to feel afraid, worried, or anxious, I pause and recognize, "I am the Inner Man experiencing these feelings in the World of Imagination. If I am experiencing fear in imagination, then I am also capable of experiencing peace, abundance, and fulfillment in imagination." The same "I am," the same awareness, that feels fear can feel joy. The same imagination that imagines lack can imagine abundance. There is no external force preventing this shift.

> *"See, I am doing something new! Now it springs up; do you not see it? I am making a way in the wilderness and streams in the wasteland."*
> ***- Isaiah 43:19***

Who is the one who is making something new? Who is speaking here? The Inner Man of Imagination! So there is no need to go off of some broken foundation. If you wish to have creative freedom and you wish to create something new from scratch, you can! You can just create and create and create new things ***in*** you! It now springs up within you! Do you not see it?

~

**Imaginal Experiment:**

1. Imagine you are in a beautiful field of flowers with the sun shining and everything is perfect.
2. Now shift the scene: Imagine yourself trapped inside a cage with thick iron bars. There is no key, no door handle, no visible way out. You can see that beautiful field through the bars, but you cannot reach it. Feel the frustration, the longing, the sense of being confined and powerless.
3. While still inside the cage, look down at your hands. Now, simply imagine a golden key materializing in your palm. Feel its weight, see its shape. Use that key to unlock the cage door and step out into freedom.
4. Pause and recognize what just happened: You created the beautiful field. You created the cage and the bars that imprisoned

you. You created the key that freed you. It was all you. You were the Dreamer the entire time, and there was never anyone or anything else controlling your imaginal experience. You had complete creative freedom in every moment, even when you were imagining yourself as trapped.

The reason this exercise is so powerful is that it demonstrates your complete creative freedom within imagination. You did not need anyone's permission to imagine the cage, and you did not need anyone's permission to imagine the key. You did not need to wait for external conditions to change, you did not need to "earn" the right to be free, you did not need to figure out the mechanics of how a key would appear. You simply imagined it, and it was so.

This is what Neville meant when he said you live in the World of Imagination where all things are possible. In that world, you are not subject to physical laws, time, space, or external conditions. You are the Dreamer, and whatever you imagine is immediately real in that world. The cage is as real as the key, the imprisonment is as real as the freedom, but they are all equally imaginary, which means they are all equally under your control.

This is similar to what Neville wrote in *Power of Awareness*:

> *"How can this feeling of naturalness be achieved?*
>
> *The secret lies in one word – imagination. For example, this is a very simple illustration: assume that you are securely chained to a large heavy iron bench. You could not possibly run, in fact you could not even walk. In these circumstances, it would not be natural for you to run. You could not even feel that it was natural for you to run. But you could easily imagine yourself running. In that instant, while your consciousness is filled with your imagined running, you have forgotten that you are bound. In imagination, your running was completely natural."* - ***Neville***

> *"You are already that which you want to be, and your refusal to believe it is the only reason you do not see it."* - ***Neville***

Who already is the one they want to be? The Inner Man within the World of Imagination! When I fully identify with the Inner Man and enter the World of Imagination, something profound shifts within me. In this realm, I realize the extent of my creative power. I can possess anything, interact with any object, hear whatever I wish to hear, and create whatever I desire.

I can receive words that I wish to hear. I can halt people's movements and redirect their actions. I can feel any emotion I want and create from these feelings. I can experience the sensation of being without fault and beyond punishment in my inner world. I can elevate myself or humble myself to a peasant's status. I can inflict guilt and punishment upon myself, or convince myself that my fearful creations are "real" and that I am powerless against them.

I can embrace my beloved and express all my tender thoughts. I can live in my dream house and wear whatever clothes I desire. I can tame wild beasts without fear. I can place myself in a cage, then simply imagine a key appearing in my hand to escape. I can meet Neville at an orchestra and share a conversation with him at a bar. Or I can be in completely stillness. I can recognize that I have everything I want because I am the Dreamer!

Learn to put your trust in *that* world. When you trust *that* world, when you give yourself everything you desire in *that* world and accept yourself as the one you wish to be in *that* world, you are exercising your true nature as the creator of your experience. You are recognizing that the cage was never real, the limitations were never imposed from without, and you have always had the freedom to imagine yourself as you choose.

> *"So I'll believe in him (the Inner Man) 100 percent. Go to bed this night...and I need x-number of dollars. Alright, there's no one to whom I can turn, no collateral, nothing, but I have to have it.* ***Can I believe in him...knowing that all things are possible to him? Can I turn to him in absolute confidence and trust and assume the feeling of the wish fulfilled, and for a moment mentally act***

***as I would act were it true? And sleep regardless of all the people in the world who are dunning me to pay off...ignore it completely?*** *I cannot devise the means, I do not know how it's going to work, but I must actually trust his power and his wisdom, and sleep as though it were true. Then in a way no one knows and I could not have devised it works. Well then, I must always remember whom and not what...this is a person. I'm a person, I am trusting myself, but in the depths of my own being, for I know whom not what I have trusted. I know whom I have believed and that is now assured knowledge. Here, the present knowledge indicates my past trust and all of a sudden it happens. This is how this wonderful principle works."* - ***Neville***

**Artwork Commentary:**

In this artwork, I sought to capture an atmosphere that exists in a liminal state, a present yet intangible, solid yet permeable. A gentleman sits in contemplation within the landscape of his own imagination, gradually awakening to its fundamental fluidity. He is discovering that the walls before him are not true barriers but mere constructs within imagination, transparent boundaries he can see beyond. The eight ball, which moments ago appeared dense and heavy, now stretches and warps before his inner eyes, demonstrating the malleable nature of what we perceive as a fixed inner reality. The floating images around him are not random, they are invitations, representing a potential state of being, worlds he can inhabit simply by making them real to him. Each one awaiting for him to step into a different version of himself, a different timeline, a different way of being.

This inward man is experiencing a profound awakening. That the obstacles reveal themselves as illusions, limitations as false beliefs, and seemingly solid structures as pliable forms awaiting an imaginal reshaping. This inner world bends under the gentle pressure of imaginal fingertips, reshaping itself according to the conviction of inner awareness.

When we hold an image in our imagination and we make it real to us, we are not merely daydreaming but we are sculpting the fabric of our inner experience. The gentleman in this artwork represents each of us at the threshold of this realization. He is learning that the difference between his current state and any desired state is not a matter of external circumstance, but of internal conviction.

# Fulfill Inside Imagination

*"So I have a desire. How am I going to move towards the fulfillment of it? How will I get near? Suppose my desire this night would take me to the East, how would I get near 3,000 miles away?* ***Because I am all Imagination, it's easy.*** *"Man is all Imagination and God is Man and exists in us and we in him. The eternal body of Man is the Imagination, and that is God himself" (Blake, Annotations to Berkeley). All things are possible to God. Is there something you can't imagine? You may not believe it, but don't tell me you can't imagine it!"* - ***Neville***

RIGHT NOW, as you read this, you are living in this outer-world. You own things, you have possessions. Based on what you have in this outer-world, you create identities for yourself. If you have no money, you claim to be poor. If you lack love, freedom, or face punishments, you claim you are unloved, trapped, and guilty. *Remember, we claim we are things based on what we have and receive.*

Let's say you desire money, love, or peace, it does not matter what it is. But say you do not have it in this outer-world, and because you do not have it, you claim that you are "broke, unwanted, at war, etc." But what if instead you identified yourself with the Inner Man who lives in the World of Imagination?

Close your eyes and enter the world within. Bring your desire to your imagination. *Understand that you must fulfill it in this world. Let the outer-world remain as it is, leave it entirely alone.* Now imagine whatever desire you wish to fulfill. Do not limit yourself to material things. Many of my own desires were not physical at all! I wanted to *feel* that nothing would go wrong. I wanted to *feel* tomorrow could bring more connection and more freedom! I wanted to *feel* free from punishment. I wanted to *feel* able to show love without fear. I wanted to *feel* relief from self-sabotage. I wanted to *feel* that everything I do is excellent and marvelous. I wanted to *feel* brilliant. I wanted to *feel* immune to embarrassment. I wanted to *feel* relaxed for once. I *wanted to feel things too, not just imagine material possessions. I wanted to free myself in my own Imaginative*

*World within me!* I wanted to *feel* these things as true in my own inner world. I stopped concerning myself with the outer-world. I realized the world within me, what we call the imagination, is completely safe, entirely giving, and wholly loving. There is no judgement here, only self-judgement and you can remove that if you love yourself. Remember there is no shame in imagination, only freedom to choose change.

This is why I emphasize *feeling* so strongly. It is not enough to merely visualize or think about what you want. You must actually feel that it is yours in your imagination. Feel the possession of such a wonderful things. Feel the relief it give *for* having it. Feel the joy of having it. Feel the satisfaction. These are secondary feeling *from* having it. So the goal is not to force relief, joy or satisfaction. This comes *after* you feel the reality of possessing that which you desire. When you truly feel it, the desire dissolves because desire only exists when you feel you lack something. But when you feel you have it in your imagination, there is nothing left to desire, only to experience!

> *By feeling, we mean feeling the reality. Can you feel it real to you? Can you accept it is real to you? Regardless of what is, can you feel the possession of it being real to you? That is what is meant by feeling.*

For material desires, see yourself with what you want. If you cannot visualize it, hear it instead, hear the congratulations, hear the confirmation, hear the evidence of your fulfilled desire. Remember, you are only changing you *(Self)* and your World of Imagination. In this outer-world, we form our identities based on what we think *(feel)* we have. *We can choose which world to identify with.* By identifying with the Inner Man and possessing what we desire in that inner world, we create a new identity, a new Self.

You can only truly experience this freedom if you actually feel what you are imagining is real. This is the shift Neville speaks of: *treating the imaginal act as equal to the external confirmation of that act.* Can you imagine having your desire and feel it is actually yours, not pretend, not "act as if," but genuinely *feel* it belongs to you?

Can you feel someone loving you and actually *feel* their love washing over you in your imagination?

When I feel anxiety or unwanted thoughts, I no longer see them as forces I must overcome. Instead, I recognize that I am creating them in my Inner World, and in this Inner World, I can do anything! When I fear something bad might happen and see it going south in my imagination, I accept that I am creating that scenario. From there, I can create what I want in my imagination, and since it is my imagination, I need no one's permission to *feel* what I want to be true instead. If I have a thought I dislike, I know I can transform it into something lovely, and I can *feel* this new lovely thought to be equally true. If I want to move on from anything, let go of anything, I need no permission, I just do it!

Do you know what happens when you do this? *You stop desiring and start possessing and being*. The desire completely vanishes for what you were wanting. The Inner Man who feels desire is automatically expressing this desire, which is a proclamation that you do not have it within. But this same Inner Man can imagine himself with what he wants and feel he has it when he removes the outer-world; then, desire transforms into fulfillment.

> *Thoughts are meant to be thought, feelings are meant to be felt, and desires are meant to be fulfilled.*

So when you actually feel it, you no longer wonder how or when. You are not waiting anymore. You are not hoping it will happen. You are actually *experiencing* it right now in the only place that matters: within yourself, where all creation begins.

Start thinking this is who you are. Do not focus on desire so much but rather the one who possesses it, *you*.

Now listen *carefully* to the words of Neville in the lecture, "*Our Real Beliefs*":

> *"Real Belief and Knowing are one. When a man really believes it is just as though he knows it. It is tantamount to knowing. So when I*

> *tell you belief, I call it faith, I call it belief. It is not complete until it becomes experienced. One must experience it and then they know it. You will hear the same thing tonight, everyone present hears exactly the same thing, but no 2 will hear it in the same depth. Some will hear it on the surface, others will hear it below the surface, and others will hear down in the very depths of their Being. It is where you hear it... Tonight I hope you do not reject what I am here to tell you. You can accept it or reject it. But I tell you, if I get through tonight and you apply it because you are the operant power. I can tell you but it does not operate itself.*
>
> *If at this very moment I ask you to think of a friend, just think of a friend. And now hear him tell you something lovely. Something lovely about himself, a mutual friend or you. Just hear it.*
>
> ***Do you believe (feel) that actually took place?*** *You may say, "Well... I imagined it, but it didn't REALLY take place." I will tell you that the day will come and I hope now, that when you imagine a State before you have external confirmation of that State, to you it is as though you heard it externally. You know it.* ***That this internal act is equal to the external confirmation of that act.*** *You get to that point..because the difference between God and Man is measured only in terms of this imaginative power."* - ***Neville***

If you fulfill your heart's desire within, because that is where desire originates and resides, can you *actually feel* it is fulfilled? Not pretend it is fulfilled, not hope it will be fulfilled, but genuinely *feel* the fulfillment as a present reality? Once you do this, you naturally walk in the state of the wish-fulfilled. It is all beautifully natural, but you must try it. You must actually *feel* your desire taking place *now*. It is beautiful because it changes you in lovelier version of yourself! No anxiety but loveliness. You love feeling you have it!

The key here is understanding that feeling is not emotional excitement or forced belief. Feeling, in this context, means acceptance, accepting as true, as *real*, within yourself that you *already* possess what you desire. When you see yourself in imagination with what you want and accept it as real in that inner world, you are no longer desiring it. You are experiencing it.

Many continue to desire from a place of lack rather than experience from a place of fulfillment. They repeat over and over trying to be fulfilled rather than feeling and think *from* already being fulfilled. This is the difference between success and failure, between occupancy or failure to occupy to the Inner Man. The Inner Man must occupy it!

It is my sincere hope that you hear this in the depths of your Being. Not merely with your intellect, but in that deep place where knowing resides. Because when you truly grasp this, w*hen an internal act becomes equal to external confirmation of that act*, you will stop waiting for the outer-world to change before you feel fulfilled. You will realize that you can feel fulfilled now, within, and that this inner fulfillment is the cause of our outer changes, not the other way around.

**Practice the shift in *feeling it real*:**

1. Follow Neville's guidance by imagining someone you know. Bring this person clearly before your imagination's eye.

2. Listen as they tell you something wonderful about yourself or share wonderful, fulfilled news about their life.

3. Now practice making the crucial shirt in your *feeling*. Experience the sensation that "*This is real. They are actually telling me this.*"

*4. Feel* yourself losing yourself into this new reality where you truly hear what you want to hear. This is no longer merely "imaginary." Can you genuinely feel that what you just heard was as real as if you heard it in this physical world?

5. This feeling is precisely what Neville wants you to experience when you imagine. So you stop worrying about how or when your desire will manifest and instead simply experience it now. Release all that anxiety and fully experience what you desire.

6. When you begin to feel your Inner World as real, you discover true freedom because you can imagine anything you desire! You can feel that liberation you have always longed for.

Remember, the Inner Man cannot desire and possess simultaneously. You must choose a space in imagination. When you shift into *feeling* you have it within, when you accept it as real in your imagination, completely trusting in it until you feel you possess it, the Inner Man is no longer desiring. The Inner Man is now *possessing, experiencing, having*. Once you realize your Inner World is real and responds to your acceptance, you understand that nothing in the outer-world needs to change for you to feel free, fulfilled, and complete. You are no longer at the mercy of circumstances. You are no longer waiting for permission from the external world to feel what you want to feel.

> *"**You are as free as the wind** if you believe these principles in scripture, not based upon anything on the outside at all, all based upon you. Can you believe?" - **Neville***

**Artwork Commentary:**

This artwork reveals a room that appears enclosed to the mortal eye, solid, bounded, impenetrable. Yet to one who perceives with their inner eye, the walls dissolve. What seems impermeable becomes like curtains drawn back, revealing what lies beyond. The inner eye of imagination does not merely look at surfaces; it sees through them.

The black and white tiles on the floor represent the outer-world, the realm of the knowledge of good and evil. When you exercise your imagination by seeing through the walls, you step beyond the tree of knowledge of good and evil and feast instead on the tree of life. To feast on the tree of life means to fulfill your imagination, not to remain in the state of wanting or desiring, but to actually possess that which you desire in imagination.

The senses constantly presents obstacles, walls you cannot see past, limitations that appear insurmountable, ideas you cannot think your way through using logic alone. Most people respond to these barriers in one of two ways, they either debate endlessly, trying to reason their way through the impossibility, or they bang against the walls in frustration, demanding they open. Neither approach works because both remain trapped in the same state inside.

But when you use your imagination wisely, you do not argue with the wall or try to force it down. You simply see through it. You assume the state of *already* being on the other side. The chairs represents the states you feel you cannot see because of the walls, or the senses. The wall was never real except as a belief in limitation. By fulfilling your desire in imagination, by living from the end rather than toward it, you dissolve the obstacle. The moment you possess something in imagination, you have already overcame the barrier that seemed to separate you from it. You exercise the Inner Man of Imagination, not through force but through making what their inner eyes see as real.

# What Else Do I Want?

*"If you are at a crossroads as to what you should do, remember: one aspect wants to be fed and it can only feed on violence. The other can only feed on the noble thoughts of man, and man creates them. You see your own creation, and it is all the same power of your own wonderful human imagination.*

*From then on, you know where you are.* ***You are a creative power****, and you go out to change everything in your world to make it conform to something lovely. You don't do it on the outside. You do it on the inside. You do it all in your imagination.*

*Imagination is God. There is no other God. His name is I AM forever and forever and forever. That's God. So here in this wonderful world of ours, you have the power. You don't need financial power; that won't do it. You can't buy health. You can't buy respect. Or you can buy it for a little while, but they don't really respect you. Let the money go, and they don't respect you. You don't need anything in the world of Caesar to buy what you want..."*

*"Come, all you who are thirsty, come to the waters; and you who have no money, come, buy and eat! Come, buy wine and milk without money and without cost." -* ***Isaiah 55:1***

*Neville continuing... "Come, you are told, buy it, without price, without money. And you say, "Buy it without price?" You see it's not Caesar's coin that you use, you use your own wonderful human imagination.*

*So I ask everyone here to try it. Don't just listen to it and not try it. You are the operant power. It doesn't operate itself.* ***And so when I know what I should, then do it. Go to sleep tonight, all right, how am I sleeping and what state of consciousness and I sleeping in? Am I sleeping as someone that is unwanted?***

***Well then, I will rise tomorrow to find myself unwanted. Ignore the facts of life and assume that you are wanted. Ignore the facts of life and assume that you are affluent, and see how things work in your world." - Neville***

SUPPOSE you want to hear something or experience something in your imagination. The moment you decide to imagine it, you might start questioning: "Will this work? What will the bridge be? When will it happen? Is this whole concept fake?" You try to devise the means, not knowing that your desire has its own way of expressing itself. The instant these questions arise, you are no longer entering into the state of your desire fulfilled. You are still dwelling in the old state, bringing its doubts and limitations with you.

You cannot bring these worries and questions with you if you want to truly fulfill a desire in your imagination. You must be willing to die to the old state *completely*. What does "to die to it" mean? When you imagine having exactly what you want, you do not question anything. You do not worry. You do not wonder "What if...?" You do not entertain the old state and its limitations for even a second. You die to it entirely.

Think of it this way: the old state is a set of beliefs, feelings, and assumptions about yourself and your world. These form a complete identity, a state of consciousness. When you try to imagine something new while still identifying with the old, you are attempting to serve two masters. You are trying to be both the person who lacks and the person who has. You are trying to feel both unfulfilled and fulfilled. This is impossible. Consciousness cannot be divided against itself and produce anything but confusion. Remember when wish and feeling are in conflict, feeling wins. If I feel a certain way about myself, but wish to be different, I do not get my wish but what I feel myself to be!

The reason you must die completely to the old state is because states are total. A state is not just a thought or a feeling, it is an entire framework through which you experience yourself. When you occupy a state, you think *from* it, feel *from* it, and perceive *from* it. Everything you see in yourself is filtered through that state. To enter a new state means to adopt a completely new framework of Self, and this requires letting go of the old one entirely.

Let's reiterate again: If you go into prayer, meaning you to go to feel the possession of what you desire. If you come out of that prayer, and you see yourself the exact same way. You did not move anywhere. You did not die and resurrect because you did not die yet. Dying is ceasing to be. An entirely new, clean person comes out of that prayer. Once you see this, you see how wonderful this is. Why? Because you have held yourself captive to the past thinking it is who you are. Once you see you can die and rise anew, everyday, you will feel so free and inspired! No need for approval, no need to tell anyone, you do it all inside!

Think about what happens when you truly imagine your desire fulfilled. If you are genuinely in that state, if you have truly died to the old and been reborn into the new, then the questions and worries of the old state simply cannot exist. They are incompatible with the new state. A person who *has* their desire does not wonder *if* they will get it. A person who is loved does not question *whether* they are loved. A person who is secure does not fear insecurity. These concerns belong to a different state entirely. You are not your worries or your states that reveals them. You are the being *behind* them, always.

This is why the shift feels so dramatic when it happens. When you truly surrender to the new state, when you allow yourself to *be* the person who already has what you desire, everything changes. The old questions dissolve. The old fears vanish. You realize you were clinging to them, and in releasing them, you discover a freedom and lightness you had forgotten was possible. This is what it means to die and be reborn, to shed one identity and assume another, completely and without reservation.

*You cannot bring your current limitations, worries, questions and feelings with you to your new state.*

The states or self-concepts you hold in your imagination are simply things you "hold." That is all they are. Do you think the concept you are holding becomes more "real" because it is reflecting in your world? I assure you it does not. Whether it is being reflected does not truly matter. These conceptions we hold of ourselves are merely what we *(the Inner Self)* have appropriated in the Inner World of Imagination. Appropriate something new and literally *take (possess)* it in imagination, whatsoever you desire. But to truly take it, you must shed the old state with all its worries and limitations when imagining something new.

When you die to the old state, you enter the new state the consciousness of having your desire. In this new state, you experience your desire in the *present moment* within your imagination. Your feeling shifts from longing to fulfillment. You actually experience your desire and think-*from* the perspective of the desire being fulfilled. This transformation happens entirely *naturally*.

Why naturally? Because you are not forcing anything or manufacturing a feeling. You simply are aware of being the new state. When you truly occupy a state, the feelings, thoughts, and perceptions that belong to that state arise automatically. A person who is loved does not have to *try* to feel loved, they simply do, because that is what it means to occupy that state. A person who is successful does not have to convince themselves of their success, they know it, feel it, and are self-convinced.

This naturalness comes from *surrender*. When you stop resisting, when you stop holding onto the old state "just in case," when you allow yourself to fully die to what was and be reborn into what is, the new state embraces you completely. The shift is effortless because you are no longer divided against yourself. You are no longer trying to be two people at once. You have chosen, and in that choice, you have become whole.

This is why trust is so essential. You must trust that the work you have done in imagination is enough. You must trust that by occupying the state of the wish fulfilled, you have set everything in motion. You do not need to know the bridge. You do not need to control the how or the when. You simply need to remain faithful to the state you have entered, to continue thinking-*from* it rather than *of* it.

And when doubts arise, because they will at times, recognize them for what they are: echoes of the old state. Do not fight them.

Do not resist them. Simply observe them, acknowledge that they belong to a state you have left behind, and return to the naturalness of the new. Each time you do this, the new state becomes more familiar, more established, until one day you realize you are no longer returning to it, you are simply *in* it, you have become it.

> *"When you go into your imagination, make sure that you are actually performing the action, hearing the words, touching the object, or smelling the aroma in your self-conceived drama. What you do in your imagination is not merely a daydreaming which you see events in your mind's eye. You must enter the dream as if you were actually there.* ***You must make "then" now and make "there" here****. To make this perfectly clear, imagine that you would experience driving a new car after you have achieved your goal. In that case, you would not merely see a new car in your mind's eye. You must actually enter the dream. Feel yourself seated behind the steering wheel. Smell the newness of the interior. Feel yourself enjoying a comfortable ride. Feel the happiness that would be yours after accomplishing your dream."* - ***Neville***

Here is what I mean by present moment: When you imagine something you want, being present requires you to stop all questioning and wondering. To *be present* means releasing every question, worry, and wonder. Being present is *experiencing* your imaginal act as though it is happening to you right now, as if it were happening to you externally.

When something is actually happening to you in the physical world, you do not question whether it is real. You do not wonder if it will work out. You do not worry about the mechanism by which it came to be. You simply *experience* it. You are fully immersed in the sensory reality of the moment. This is the state you must enter in imagination in regards to your desires. This simply means you want to feel real to you because we experience that which feels real.

*"Therefore, the individual who can summon that will whatever imaginal activity he pleases and to whom the visions of his imagination are as real as the forms of nature, is the master of his fate." -* ***Neville***

Now here is something I enjoy doing in my imagination. After feeling present in my fulfilled desire, I ask myself a simple question: "What else do I want?" I ask this to demonstrate how unlimited I am. I want to prove that my imagination cannot be exhausted, that it will keep giving and giving regardless of the request or its "impossibility." This practice teaches you that in the World Of Imagination, *you* are limitless for imagination is limitless and you are one with it! The Inner Man can have and feel anything they desire. This also shows you that you can intensify your wonderful feelings to degrees you never knew existed.

I repeatedly ask myself this question: "What else do I want?" When I want to hear good news, I simply hear it as if it is happening to me right now, in the present moment. If I want to change what someone said to me in the past, I revise it. I hear exactly what I wanted to hear, as though it is coming to me externally.

After these experiences stir up amazing feelings, I ask again, "What else?" Perhaps I want to feel completely secure, so I allow myself to surrender to that security as deeply as I desire. "What else?" Maybe I want to be shown love in the way I personally conceive it, so I experience that love. "What else?" I might want to see myself in a certain position in life, so I visualize it as my only reality. "What else?" Perhaps I want to hear a specific compliment, so I hear it, effortlessly. "What else?" I might want to intensify these wonderful feelings beyond what I thought possible, so I intensify them. "What else?" Maybe I want to see someone succeeding in life, so I hear them share their wonderful experiences. "What else?" I might recall a memory that sparks joy, so I relive it. "What else?" I might want to imagine something seemingly impossible, so I do exactly that. "What else?" When my imagination wanders upon a beautiful scene, I allow myself to fully indulge in it. "What else?" I might wonder how it feels to live without fear, so I release all fear and experience pure ecstasy. "What else?" Perhaps I want to taste a specific food or drink, so I savor it completely. "What else?" Maybe instead of guilt, I want to feel amazing, so I choose that feeling instead."What else?" And so on...

*The entire point is that to do what you want within. Your desires will be different, so simply fulfill them. Think of this process as ascending a staircase of exaltation. Remember there is no fear in imagination, only exploration.*

I need no one's permission. I do not have to consult a council or fear decadence. Nothing in my imagination should frighten me! Fear alone drives you down unwanted paths. Go directly to the "end" in everything. Do not concern yourself with the middle, that is not your, the Inner Man's goal. You want to fulfill your desires. When you fulfill your heart's desires in your imagination, to heal yourself. You show love to yourself and everyone within your Inner World. Have doubtless love about yourself. I urge you to fulfill all your desires daily. Set the external world aside and create an inner subjective reality that is perfect for you. Remember, "perfect" varies for everyone, so do not pressure yourself into thinking it must conform to any particular standard. This is *deeply* personal, if it ever needs modification, ask no one, just non-judgmentally modify.

To me, this is not merely imaginary or "just in my imagination." I feel the reality that it is actually happening to me. I do not care if people call it insane or if society deems it irrational. I do not worry about what I "should" think. The world overflows with rules about what you should and should not do, but where is the freedom in that?

*You walk in an imaginal world as well, not just a physical one. In this world, it not so much about what you do in here but **who** you are in here. Are you free?*

Find God and worship only God and God is your own Imagination, the Cause. Test God in all things. If God, the Inner Man, proves itself in reflection, why worry about others' opinions? Take whatever you want in imagination, without cost or permission. Your imagination will never deny you anything.

When you enter the present moment, when you shift into *feeling* that it is *actually happening* to you, that is where true freedom exists. Once you experience that shift of "this is real," apply it to everything in your Imagination. You make the new state seem real to you. You actually make imagination real to you. You will know you have shifted states, when the limitations and questions of the old state disappear.

> *"Don't be concerned about what you've accumulated as things in the world. Find God and worship only God, and God is not on the outside. You'll never see God on the outside; you will see it within. Because can you see "I am"? You can see "I am a man" - you see the man reflected. You can say "I'm a poor man" - see the man reflected in the eyes of those who know he's poor. And* ***you can see every concept you hold of Self, but the conceiving Being you don't see. That's God.***
>
> *My concept of myself could this, that or the other. The concepts will be reflected in society, and men will tell me who I am conceiving myself to be. But no man knows who I really am. I the Conceiver, they don't know. But they know what I have conceived myself to be. My bank balance will tell the banker what I have conceive myself to be in the financial world. And all these concepts, Man will see concepts. But they can't see* ***me****, the Conceiver.* ***Well, don't forget the Conceiver, that's God.****" -* ***Neville***

~

**Artwork Commentary:**

In this artwork, we observe figures confined to dark rooms, one woman even faces a shadowy wall. These images symbolize the limiting beliefs that trap people within narratives that diminish their sense of Self.

Yet one woman gazes into the distance, away from the others. Above her head, a bird soars, a symbol of free thought. She has awakened to curiosity about what else exists within the boundless World of Imagination. She recognizes that remaining fixed in one mental place is madness when infinite landscapes await exploration.

Tragically, most people prefer their enclosures. They find comfort in their small rooms of imagination, even when darkness engulfs them. The familiar prison feels safer than the unknown expanse. Yet every single one of us is that woman, wondering what else exists within this vast mental plane. We all carry that seed of curiosity, that longing to see beyond our current walls.

This is why willpower fails in imagination, it is the wrong tool entirely. Willpower tries to force, to fight, to muscle through resistance. But imagination does not respond to force; it responds to curiosity, to surrender. When you become curious about a different version of yourself, you naturally move toward it. When you surrender to new ideas of Self instead of battling them or forcing yourself to believe them, you create space for genuine change.

Willpower operates by creating an adversarial relationship between you and your desired state. It positions your current state as something to overcome, your habits as enemies to defeat. This generates internal conflict and resistance. The act of forcing creates the friction that makes change exhausting.

Curiosity and surrender, by contrast, removes resistance. When you approach a new state of being with genuine curiosity, "What would it feel like to be different?" You are not fighting your current reality. You are exploring a new one. You are not declaring war on who you are; you are investigating what else you are within.

The woman staring into the distance is not straining or struggling; she is simply allowing her attention to wander toward what calls to her. That gentle, curious attention is what opens doors that willpower can only pound against.

# Changes In The Dreamer, Changes The Dream

*"We agreed to dream in concert, and we will not violate that covenant.* ***All of us agreed to dream in concert. But within the dream I can change and modify certain states.*** *But I am called upon to tell every person in this world that they can change anything within the framework of this little field in which we now operate." -* ***Neville***

You lay down, turn your lamp off, and pull your blankets toward your chin. A deep breath escapes from your lips and your body relaxes just enough for a feeling of comfort to overtake you. You close your eyes and drift into sleep.

Moments later, you awaken. You look down at your hands and find yourself in a world just like this one. Something feels slightly off, but you cannot quite place it. After contemplating a bit longer, you realize what is happening: you have become aware that you are awake inside a dream. You understand your physical body is back home on your bed while you are conscious within this dream.

With this knowledge, you decide to test your power. You close your eyes and imagine something, anything, and the moment you open your eyes, there it is, materialized right before you. You come to the profound realization that *everything* here is under the control of your imagination. Everything is in subjection to it.

Knowing that you have this power, the question then becomes: "What are you going to create?" This is your own dream, and you can dream anything. What would you choose? If you could control everyone and everything, what would you do? If imagining creates instantly in this dream world, what would you imagine? There are no mistakes here because you can always correct them. You are entirely free to create anything. What would you create? What would you see? What would you choose to hear? How would you be treated? What things would you give yourself? How would you create the perfect dream? Would you let go and be free?

This is precisely how I approach my imagination. When I imagine, I think of it as I have just awakened inside a dream and can bring anything I want before me. I can hear someone, anyone, it does not matter who, say exactly what I want them to say. I can see what I want to see. *Everything* is under the control of my imagination. I mean this literally. Everything in your imagination, no matter what it is, is under your control. In the dream world, there are no "facts." Everything can be manipulated and transformed to your liking.

Anyone who has experienced awakening inside a dream understands the feeling I am describing. You feel you can do and create anything! Knowing your body is asleep on the bed, you can leave the surface world entirely alone. There is nothing to do in the physical world because your body is asleep. Instead, you can do anything you like in imagination, and you can feel that freedom to let the surface world go. There is nothing to control in the world because the surface world does not matter in that moment. All that matters is: "What are you going to dream in your depths?"

The beauty of this understanding is that it frees you from the burden of manipulation. You are not trying to force anything into existence through sheer willpower or repetitive affirmations. You are simply recognizing that the inner world is the only world you can truly control. And more importantly, it is the only world you *need* to control, because changes there naturally express themselves outwardly.

This is the attitude I carried with me after experiences of lucid dreaming. I realized I can imagine anything I want! I can dream greater than I once allowed myself to. I can feel whatever I want to feel. So when I lie down to imagine, I think of it as though my body is asleep, and there is nothing to do in the world. Nothing to achieve externally. The only task is to dream a greater dream, and the greatest dream is one where all your desires are fulfilled.

When you make your imaginings specific to your liking, feelings of euphoria naturally spring forth. This is not manufactured emotion or forced positivity, it is the *natural* result of occupying a state where everything is as you wish it to be. Be bold and imagine exactly what you want. Leave the world alone, abandon the idea of "trying to manifest," and change Self by imagining specifics, creating a greater dream within. If we can truly imagine anything we want, as specifically as we want, and if our life truly shapes to our imaginings, then our highest interest should be to imagine better than the best we know!

> *"Mentally feel yourself right into the proposed action, until the single sensation of fulfillment dominates the mind; imagining all the while that you are actually performing the action* ***here and now*** *so that you experience in imagination what you would experience in the flesh were you now to realize your goal."* - ***Neville***

To feel the wish fulfilled, as Neville teaches, you must imagine as though it is *here and now.* The way to do this is to set aside the surface world and the idea of "trying to manifest." Simply adopt the attitude of changing your inner world to your liking, just as if you awakened inside a dream where you can dream anything! There is nothing to do, nothing to force externally. You change it, mold it, feel it, all within yourself. You create a new dream, a perfect dream within.

It is all about *feeling*. To "*try* to manifest" is itself a feeling, a feeling of lack, of separation from what you desire. "Trying to get, trying to resolve, trying to make something happen," these are feelings you carry with you before you imagine. These feelings disrupt you from actually feeling the reality of what you are imagining. Instead, feel that you are simply re-imagining or re-dreaming a new dream within you and changing how you feel inside. These inner changes express themselves in the outer-world naturally and effortlessly.

So go within and change *that world*, the world within. Change *who* you are *there*, what you have *there*, how you are treated *there*. This is not escapism or fantasy, this is an actual change in Self and Self must always express just as it is expressing now. Would not the man who walks with their head down in guilt and that same man walked with their head up free, have a different experience and feeling? Would they not do, act, speak differently? Same man but different! What is different then? The state that man occupies inside himself.

Fantasy, in my view, tends to involve escapism, retreating into worlds that are often more comforting than changing. Imagination, however, involves actively shaping reality, *you*, itself. While both involve conjuring mental images, active imagination seeks to change those images into tangible outcomes. In essence, imagination is not merely mechanically, or purposelessly visualizing but desires to embody itself in you. Not just leave it as a wishful hope. *Fantasy never knows, imagination always does.* So know you are, rather than be uncertain that you are.

> *Once you know you are, you elevate from the depths of self-doubt to the pinnacle of divine authority. The God that emerges is not born of external validation but of internal conviction.*

In your meditation allow others to see you as they would see you were this new concept of self a concrete fact. You always seem to others an embodiment of the ideal you inspire. Therefore, in meditation, when you contemplate others, you must be seen by them mentally as you would be seen by them physically were your concept of self an objective fact; that is, in meditation you imagine that they see you expressing that which you desire to be.

> *"And you can change the dream. Change it by simply daring to assume that you are now, what reason is going to tell you that you're not it now and it's difficult to imagine that they ever will be it. Forget that. All things are possible to God and you have found who he is. He is your own wonderful human imagination. That's God. So assume it and then let it happen in world. I'll give you a little secret: People say, "I work so hard at it."* ***Imagination will do little that we seek from compulsion. It will do little if anything until, we have imagined the wish-fulfilled.*** *It does not move under compulsion. We have to imagine the wish-fulfilled for imagination to take action.*

*So people will tell me, "I work so hard at it." Well that's why you're failing. If you really believe all things are possible to God and God is your own wonderful human imagination and his ways are higher than your mortal level, well then what are you interfering with that state for? Assume the end and don't work it at all. You'll be moving under compulsion to manifest it, if you simply assume it and let it be. What do you do after someone is pregnant? Just let it be. If you don't, if you interfere with it it, you're going to perform a certain miscarriage. Well the same thing is true of a mental miscarriage.* ***You simply assume that you are and go about your business. When you least expect it, you'll feel the evidence of it coming into your world.*** *And then you can speak with the authority of experience. Now let us, that is going into the silence."* - ***Neville***

*"You are dreaming. If you try to make your dream come true while doubting its possibility, you are heading toward a nervous breakdown."* - ***Neville***

Notice how Neville emphasizes that imagination does not work under compulsion. Imagination only takes action after we have fully imagined the wish-fulfilled. This reveals an effortless approach to assuming. It is not about anxiously forcing imaginal acts or nervously anticipating results. Rather, it is about changing our inner reality, changing who we are inside and how we perceive ourselves.

If the evidence we seek comes when we least expect it, then why live in anxious expectation? If when it happens, it will feel like it would have happened anyway then why is the focus not on being feeling natural and relaxed? Why try to control everything? This is why the instruction is always to imagine the end, to dwell in the feeling of the wish-fulfilled, and then to let it go. Not to abandon it as if you do not care about it but to release your grip on how and when it must appear.

Instead, you approach your imaginings with the freedom and playfulness of a dreamer. You ask yourself: "What do I want to dream?

How do I want to see myself? How do I want to be seen by others?" And then you simply dream it, feel it, occupy it within yourself. There is no effort in this because you are not trying to make something happen in the outer, surface world. You are simply changing your depths, and that inner change must express itself outwardly because what we do in our depths must rise to the surface. No compulsion, no nervous break down, just you and your imagination.

> *"The work is to **uncritically observe your reactions to life, as they bind you to a certain level.** Disassociate yourself from your unpleasant thoughts and associate yourself with your aim, thereby rising to its level, for your ideal is on that vertical line you stand upon."* - ***Neville***

> *Expectationless imaginal creating is the foundation of creating anything in imagination.*

This way of being free inside is the way to remove anxiety and compulsion. This is how you cleanse the path to bring forth your true desires, not born out of compulsions. Why? Because expectationless imagining removes judgment. The removal of judgment dissolves anxiety, for you are no longer judging your imaginal act in some future tense. You are not asking "When is this going to happen? Will it happen?" Such questions breed nervousness and doubt. Expectationless imagining removes compulsion because you are not trying to force anything in your imagination. You are allowing yourself to release expectations upon yourself. You are simply letting yourself enjoy what you are and do inside yourself.

When you imagine without expectation, you are not waiting for something to arrive from outside yourself. You are not looking at the outer-world for confirmation. Instead, you are simply being what you desire to be, right now, within yourself. This is the freedom that dissolves compulsion.

Consider the difference between these two states: in one, you imagine your desire while constantly checking the outer-world, asking "Is it here yet? When will it materialize?" This state is filled with tension, anxiety, and effort. In the other, you imagine your desire and simply enjoy the feeling of being it within yourself, without concern for when or how it will appear outwardly. This state is peaceful, effortless, and free. Which state do you think allows imagination to flow more naturally? Which state embodies the wish fulfilled?

The reason expectationless imagining removes compulsion is subtle but profound. When you imagine without expectation, you are not waiting for anything to arrive because *you are already experiencing it within yourself.* You are simply being it, enjoying it, living *from* it internally. There is no gap to bridge, no distance to cross, and therefore no compulsion to force anything.

This is why Neville emphasized imagining *as though it is here and now*. Not as a future event you are waiting for, but as a present reality you are experiencing within yourself. When you do this without the pressure of expectation, without judging whether it is "working" or when it will "express," you allow imagination to move freely. You allow yourself to actually feel the reality of it, rather than feeling the anxiety of wanting it.

The pregnancy analogy Neville uses is perfect. Once conception has occurred, you do not anxiously interfere with the process. You do not "work hard" at being pregnant. You simply let it be, and nature takes its course. The same is true with an assumption. Once you have truly assumed the state, once you have felt the wish-fulfilled within yourself, you let it be. You go about your business in your day.

This is the paradox that many struggle with: the act of trying inside to express reveals that you, the Inner Man, have not truly assumed the state in imagination. Because if you had assumed it, had faith in it, if you truly felt it ***real*** within yourself, there would be nothing to try for. You would simply be it, and being it, you would naturally express it.

*"**If you assume that you are what you want to be your desire is fulfilled, and, in fulfillment, all longing is neutralized.** You cannot continue desiring what you have already realized. Your desire is not something you labor to fulfill, it is recognizing something you already possess. It is assuming the feeling of being that which you desire to be. - **Neville***

*"I know this much: **if you believe (feel) to the point of acceptance, life will be marvelous for you, perfectly wonderful** for this is the one secret in the world that everyone should aspire to solve, for God is that pure imaging in ourselves. He underlies all of our faculties including our perception, but he streams into our surface mind least disguised in the form of productive fantasy.*

*I sit here and have a daydream. Well, that's God in action, but then someone breaks it and I forget it. I didn't occupy it; I simply had a daydream but without occupancy. That's one of the greatest fallacies of the world, 'perpetual construction'. It's a daydream, deferred occupancy. I don't occupy it, I don't go in and possess it and make it mine. If I, in my Imagination, could go right in and possess it and make it mine...*

*If I, in my Imagination, could go right in and possess it and clothe myself with the feeling of the wish fulfilled, actually clothe myself with it by assuming that it's done now, until I feel natural in that assumption and that assumption though at the moment denied by my senses, if persisted in will harden into fact." - **Neville***

**Artwork Commentary:**

This artwork represents a man trying to change what is inside his imagination. In the top image, we see a man contemplating the objects before him, a tree, a door, various elements of his inner landscape. In the bottom image, that same man has made his inner movement, rearranging the objects slightly differently.

We are all this man, engaged in the quiet work of reshaping

what lives inside us. The world might observe his efforts and laugh for after all, he has not accomplished much by conventional measures. He brought a stool, shifted the tree slightly, altered the door's appearance. On the surface, not much seems to have changed. But look closer, he is exercising his imagination, stretching the muscles of possibility within himself, even if only incrementally. The objects are symbols of Self. So he is slightly modifying himself in the bottom image.

What more can we ask of anyone than to try to change what dwells within them, even if those changes appear small? The magnitude of change matters less than the willingness to engage with it at all.

This artwork reminds us that imagination is not just about grand visions or revolutionary ideas. It is also about the daily practice of moving things around inside ourselves, rearranging our words, adjusting our perspectives, experimenting with different configurations of who we might become. Each small shift represents an act of creative agency over our inner world.

The man in the artwork understands that sometimes it is enough to move one piece at a time. To see what changes when we place this here instead of there, when we look at the familiar through a slightly different frame.

Never be discouraged if you feel that all you can make at first are slight modifications to what is within you. The point is not the size of the change, but the fact that you are trying, that you are refusing to accept your inner landscape as fixed and immutable. When you bring that stool, when you move that tree even slightly, you are declaring that you have agency over your imagination. You are saying that what exists within you is not predetermined, but malleable, responsive to you. Every small modification is evidence of your power, proof that change is possible even when it comes in whispers rather than shouts.

# Feel The Imagination As Real

*"Well now, I close my eyes to the obvious and then I see the world as I would see it if I were elsewhere. That's motion. Yet I open my eyes and I am still here. But I went and prepared the place...that is motion. That's psychological motion. So I stand here and I desire something which if it came to pass would find me elsewhere spatially.* ***Well now, I close my eyes to the obvious, I assume that I am there, and make there here...therefore, here vanishes. This room vanishes as I make that place here. Then I look at the world and see it as it is related to the new position that I am now occupying. I feel the reality of this state...so I've moved.*** *I move from where I am now to where I want to be. This is creativity." -* ***Neville***

*WHERE DO you feel it in your body?*

This answer has multiple layers, so bear with me. When I write *feeling*, I am referring to something beyond a simple emotion. It is not just happiness or relief, although those are part of it. I would be dishonest if I claimed that was the *entire* experience. There is a far deeper sensation that I am describing.

I am referring to a *feeling* distinct from ordinary emotions. When you genuinely feel that what you are experiencing in your imagination is *real*, it creates a sensation unlike any conventional emotion or reaction. You do not just imagine it, you *actually feel/accept* its *reality*. This means all concepts of "getting," "achieving," "wondering if it will work," "trying to manifest," or "feeling trapped" simply vanish when you enter into and feel your wish being granted. The goal is not to try to get things but to *feel the reality* of them inside of us. If we wish to have freedom inside, we do not just wish it or try to get it. We *feel the reality* of freedom! It becomes so *real* to us!

For example, if you want to hear specific news, imagine hearing it in your imagination. Can you feel it happening as authentically as if it were occurring in physical reality? Can your imagination feel as real as this outer-world? When you hear good news in everyday life, you naturally respond with genuine feeling. Now imagine hearing exactly what you desire. This creates more than a basic emotion. You experience an internal shift and become completely absorbed in your imaginal act. There is nothing stressful about it, nothing you must force. Simply experience the scenario that implies your success and feel its reality.

I am talking about feeling something as though it is genuinely *real*. Recognizing that what you see in your imagination is not fake. And beyond that, you can shape this reality precisely as you wish. This creates an internal feeling unlike any emotion I know. It is accepting your imaginal experience as real. This feeling creates an opening, a mental shift that transforms you until you lose yourself completely in the imaginal act. It does not happen instantly for me, but I can enter this state faster by simply accepting it as real. It is an unseen reality, yes, unseen by mortal eye, but it is still a reality.

To access this feeling, you must be willing to assume what you are imagining is real. If you are not feeling it, it means you are still bound by your physical senses and the outer-world. To truly lose yourself in imagination, you must accept its reality and release your attachment to the outer-world. You must suspend logical thinking and embrace the reality of your imagination. This liberates your imagination. You expand beyond the self-imposed limitations you have placed within yourself. Allow yourself the freedom to expand beyond the rational mind that prevents you from experiencing your wish being granted. *You cannot be afraid to feel and imagine what you want.*

This experience transcends basic emotion, it is a profound shift in imagination. When the wonderful news you are hearing or the amazing things you are seeing no longer feel "fake" but genuinely real, this sparks within you a feeling that words can barely describe. It is similar to the experience of déjà vu. Would you call déjà vu a basic emotion? It is certainly a feeling, a very peculiar one, but not an emotion in the conventional sense. Similarly, this feeling I am describing, this "entering into the imaginal act and feeling its reality," is not just an emotion but a distinct shift in your state of being. You feel yourself moving into the fulfilled desire. You are *experi-*

*encing* your desire being fulfilled, not hoping for it or working toward it, but living within its reality *now*.

The challenge is that most people experience imagination as something separate from reality, a mental exercise disconnected from the physical world. But when you truly enter this state, that distinction collapses. Your imagination starts to take on the tones of reality because you have accepted it as such. This is not about forcing yourself or using affirmations to override doubt. It is about a fundamental shift in what you accept as real. In that moment, there is no difference between what you imagine and what you experience, they become one and the same. Make it lovely and it becomes heavenly. No fear but just what you love.

This is why this feeling cannot be reduced to happiness, excitement, or relief. Those emotions may arise as byproducts, but the core experience is acceptance, the complete acceptance that what you are imagining is real. When you achieve this, your entire being responds. Your body relaxes, your breath deepens, and you feel an opening in your chest and solar plexus. This is not forced or manufactured. It is the natural response to dwelling in a reality you love, a reality you have chosen to accept as true.

*"It is done,* ***in your imagination.****" -* ***Neville***

In your imagination, see yourself expressing your desire. Can you feel this actually happening? Can you feel that this is you? Can you let go of the outer-world and experience this as if it were real?

Then enhance the feeling by asking, "What if everyone around me was also experienced their desires?" See others having their desire and hear them expressing how wonderful they feel. Can you actually feel them telling you this? When there is no difference between hearing it internally or externally, when both are accepted as equally real, that is the feeling being described here.

When this happens, I experience a distinct effect in my body. Personally, I feel an opening in my solar plexus, in my chest, and in my imagination. I feel alive, ready, and open as my breath naturally deepens into my stomach. My body becomes relaxed and receptive. Anxieties and worries disappear. I do not force this. It is simply the natural *effect* of feeling my imagination to be real.

This bodily response is not manufactured through breathing techniques or physical manipulation. It emerges spontaneously when you genuinely inhabit the reality of your fulfilled desire. Your body responds to what you accept as real, not to what you hope might become real. This is why forced affirmations often feel hollow, they are attempts to convince yourself of something you have not truly accepted. But when acceptance is genuine, your entire being responds accordingly.

I never force anything in my imagination. Instead, I create an internal reality I love to inhabit. I imagine and feel myself there, accepting it as mine. When you create a reality you truly love, thinking from this perspective becomes natural. This only works if you genuinely love it, because love creates passion, which then creates persistence, and life is created by persistent imagining.

Sometimes I experience genuine gratitude, not contrived gratitude aimed at expressing something, but honest gratitude that naturally emerges because I have accepted it as mine in imagination. A gentle self-gratitude, for who else would you thank inside of you, but you? This gratitude is not a technique or a prerequisite. It is simply what happens when you dwell in a reality you love. You do not generate gratitude to try to make something express. Rather, gratitude arises naturally as a byproduct of already feeling it real.

The reason gratitude is not necessary is because the fundamental shift has already occurred through acceptance. Gratitude may accompany this shift, but it is not what creates it. What creates the shift is your willingness to feel the reality of your imagination without reservation. When you do this, you are not trying to get something or make something happen. You are simply experiencing what already is within you. And when you experience something as real, your entire being responds accordingly, whether gratitude arises or not. So the goal is always to feel the reality of what you are imagining.

***Question:*** *I find it difficult to change my concept of self. Why?*

***Answer****: Because your desire to change has not been aroused.* ***If you would fall in love with what you really want to be, you would become it****. It takes an intense hunger to bring about a transformation of self. -* ***Neville***

*"As the hart panteth after the waterbrooks, so panteth my soul after thee, O Lord. "If you would become as thirsty for perfection as the little hart is for water that it braves the anger of the tiger in the forest, you would become perfect." -* ***Neville***

To change, you must fall in love with what you want to imagine. This means giving yourself the freedom to imagine what you truly love. That is the path to transformation. Continue shaping your idea of yourself until you love it completely. Like a potter, you mold and refine until it matches your vision. When you fall in love with this vision, change becomes inevitable because you cannot resist what you love within yourself.

Fear creates stagnation, but love transforms. When you fear what you desire, when you are afraid to fully feel and imagine what you want, you remain bound by your current concept of self. The very act of withholding permission from yourself to imagine freely is what keeps transformation at bay.

Ask yourself: what would you love to have and experience? Do not just contemplate the question abstractly, but act on it right now in your imagination. Give yourself complete freedom to imagine what you truly desire without reservation or fear. Shape this vision of Self until it becomes something you cannot help but return to, something so lovely that thinking from this perspective becomes natural and effortless.

This is why the answer to difficulty in changing your self-concept is always the same: you have not yet fallen deeply enough in love with who you want to become. When that love ignites, when you become as thirsty for your ideal self as the hart is for water, change is no longer difficult. It becomes as natural as breathing.

> *"**It is my hope that you do not wish to die a hero's death or some martyrs death, but that you really want to live fully and graciously in this world of ours, live lovingly**. If you want money, but no one tell you shouldn't have money. If you want to extend yourself and be a great artist in the world, let no one tell you that you shouldn't be a great artist."* - **Neville**

> *There is no other Creator within you. You create everything that you experience within yourself.*

> *"If it be not now," said Shakespeare, "yet it will come. If it be not now, it will come. Readiness is all." **All I need to do is to be ready for it. Well, I'm ready for it the minute I enter into the state and accept it as fact**. That is the readiness, that is all that it takes. So I enter into a state and feel the reality of that state, well then, that is the readiness, then it will come. If it be not now at this very moment yet it will come, and the whole thing will appear in my world. That I know from my own personal experience."* - **Neville**

**Artwork Commentary:**

In this artwork, we see a man contemplating different visions of himself. In some, he appears lost at sea, lonely and afraid. In another, he gazes upon the ocean's vastness.

What he is doing is looking within himself to discover what he holds to be real. While these images are not necessarily pleasant, they represent his truth, his inner reality.

We are not called to avoid our inner realities or distract ourselves with external pleasures. We are called to face them directly and consciously reshape them.

In this moment, he is simply observing what feels real inside of him, without rushing to change it. He is examining what actually exists within him and where he dwells in his inner world. He is not condemning or judging himself. He is simply seeking to understand himself.

When he sees himself lonely, lost, or drowning at sea, he can offer himself compassion by imagining something new, something more inviting, warm, and freeing. But he must first see where he truly is before any change can occur. This inner observation is the foundation of all change. Without honest self-awareness, we cannot know what needs to shift. We remain trapped in patterns we have not fully acknowledged.

This is what Neville means when he speaks of taking an objective view of oneself. He is not suggesting cold detachment or dead intellectual analysis. Rather, he is pointing to a quality of awareness that sees without judgment, that observes our inner states as they are, not as we wish them to be or fear them to be. When Abdullah told Neville, "*You must first start with self. Find self. Don't be ashamed ever of the being you are. Discover it and start the changing of that self.*" He is recognizing that shame and judgment actually prevent us from seeing clearly. They distort our vision and keep us trapped in reactive patterns. Only by setting aside these emotional reactions can we truly see what exists within us and what we have unconsciously accepted as real. From this place of clear seeing, we can then ask: "Can I change this? Can I imagine something different for myself? Can make a new thing real to me?" The question itself becomes an act of creative power, because it acknowledges both our current inner reality and our capacity to reshape it.

# Feel Beyond The Walls Of Reason

*"I will persist in feeling that which if true implies the fulfillment of my dream. And if you do it, no power in the world can stop you from realizing your dream, but no power.* ***Because causation is mental, it isn't physical... You say that is selfish? Forget it! It's all part of your own wonderful imagination.***

*So tonight, you try it. Try it and see how it works, not if it works. Because not "I'll think about it"; try it and see how it works. Take every person's request, and then do it in feeling, not in words. There are million of people across the country who will declare, "I am rich, I am rich, I am rich"; in the depths all they are feeling, where is the next dollar coming from. They are feeling poverty, but declaring in words, "I am rich"- doesn't work that way. As we said earlier, I'll teach one little child to say when someone gives you something, "Thank you." If someone is kind to them, say "Thank you." Teach them how to say "thank you," but I need not ever teach anyone how to feel it.* ***So how do I feel it? Not the words, get below the words into the feeling. Well, what am I feeling? ... You try it." - Neville***

*"Good news is that everything in this world that you want you can have if you clothe yourself with it. Clothe yourself with it. You want to be rich? How would you feel where you rich? You want to be healthy? How would you feel were you healthy? You want to be free of all embarrassment? How would you feel this night if you were not embarrassed, that not a thing in this world could embarrass you? How would you feel where it so? And* ***clothe yourself with these states, one after the other, and be faithful to the clothing that you wear, and let it unfold in your world. It will! It will completely unfold in your world and you will see it." - Neville***

IMAGINING "THE END" is not the problem. Imagining what you want is not the problem. Anyone can imagine anything, but not everyone can *feel the reality* of what they desire. The challenge lies not in thinking but in feeling.

You can imagine all wonderful things, but can you release the feeling of fear? You might be bold enough to declare yourself the greatest being in the world in your imagination, but can you summon that same boldness in your feeling? Can you spend an entire day feeling what you wish to feel, that nothing can harm you, nothing can embarrass you, that you are abundant in all things? You can certainly think these thoughts, but can you feel them to be true? How much longer until you become bold enough to embrace these marvelous feelings? How many more days will you carry this angst with you? Within your imagination, it is all your creation. There is no other creator within you. Just as you are bold in your thinking, become bold in your feeling. When you shy away from those glorious, freeing, blissful feelings, the very feelings you desire, you are rejecting that inner experience itself.

Become selfish in your feeling and feel whatever you desire. Perhaps you want to feel you have a clean slate in life. Maybe you desire to feel that your world continually shows you love. Do these thoughts seem impossible to feel? If so, this is precisely when you must become bold and feel them anyway. Overcome the angst and fear, and simply feel. It is your imagination, and if you do not feel these wonderful states, you will end up feeling something less, you will feel your limitations instead. So how bold can you be in your feeling?

The beauty of this practice is that your imagination is a completely safe space. No one is watching. No one is judging. There are no consequences to feeling whatever you wish to feel in your inner world. Yet so many deny themselves this freedom, as if some invisible force will punish them for daring to feel beyond their current circumstances. This fear is baseless. It is simply another creation of your own imagination that you are choosing to give attention to.

When you catch yourself afraid to feel what you desire, pause and recognize: you are the one creating this fear. You are the one maintaining it. And just as easily as you created it, you can create its opposite. You can create the feeling of safety, of freedom, of abundance. The question is not whether you can, you already are creating feelings moment by moment. So what will you choose to feel real inside of you?

> *"But everyone is falling into states, infinite states; to understand this world you must think in terms of states. He (God) has made everything for its purpose, even the wicked for the day of trouble.*
>
> *And so, use everything, but you don't have to think of which one will do it, forget it, who will play the part... There are those who have chosen to be pickpockets for the rest of their lives, so if they are caught in the act, all right, that's part of the game. They've chosen that part to play...*
>
> *Either wisely or unwisely, we fall into these things; but* ***when the Inner Man begins to awake, he selects his part wisely****. It's entirely up to us, so I tell you, everything in this world that you want to be, you can be if you will know that there are only states. You move into the state because the occupant of the state does not differ from the occupant of any other state."* - **Neville**

When choice is given and then your life changes. Until then life will feel all but predetermined. Why? Because the outer-man acts from compulsion. The outer-man has no free will outside of the Inner Man. So if you associate with the outer-man, life feels choiceless, but that is not true. Once you come back to the Inner Man, you have creative freedom and most importantly choice is restored. The Inner Man is restoration of things lost, like worth, freedom, unconditional love, no judgement, and choice.

You, the Inner Man, have freedom of choice. Do you know that means? You are free entirely free to choose what you do not want to be and free to choose it forever. You are free to choose a different side of you, a different state, you are free to do that as well. You are always free to choose and it will never go away. Even when we forget, it is already there.

And the moment I realize I'm doing it, now I'm given a choice.

But there's always this choice inside your dream, where you can choose to become conscious.

This is why boldness is essential. You must be willing to feel states that your outer senses deny, that your reason contradicts, that your past experience seems to invalidate. This is the definition of faith, to assume a feeling as true before you have any evidence of it. And when you persist in that feeling, when you remain faithful to it despite all appearances, you are performing the highest act of creation.

Remember, Neville is telling you to assume you are God! What senses, what reason, would ever report such a thing? No physical evidence supports this claim. And yet, this is the assumption you are asked to make. So an assumption needs no basis in fact. None whatsoever. It is not built upon evidence, it *creates* the evidence.

If an imaginal act with *no basis in fact*, an act that contradicts everything your senses report, when felt as reality, begins to harden into fact and express in your world, then are you not completely free? If you start to become what you imagine yourself to be, and nothing can stop you from imagining, then your freedom is absolute. You are not bound by circumstances, conditions, or the past. You are not at the mercy of the world. You are the creator of your experience. This is why the boldness to feel beyond reason is so transformative. It breaks the chain of cause and effect as you have known it.

> *Just as you boldly imagine the thoughts you desire, become equally bold in the feeling you crave. Do not merely think beyond your limitations but feel beyond them. Feel beyond reason.*

Feel what might seem "impossible" to your rational mind. Your imagination is your own subjective reality, and you have the power to shape it precisely and feel whatever you desire within it.

You must be willing to feel states that contradict all evidence. An assumption needs no basis in fact whatsoever. This is perhaps the most liberating realization that you do not need permission from your circumstances to feel differently. You do not need proof. You do not need validation. You simply choose the feeling and persist in it, regardless of what your senses tell you.

I once had spoken with someone and they asked me, "What do I do when the circumstance does not allow me to be free? That the circumstance feels like there is no way out?"

My answer was, when people come to me with a problem, I do not see the outer-man struggling with the circumstance. I see the Inner Man who has forgotten their creative power, the Inner Man who believes they have a problem they cannot solve. I see the Inner Man of Imagination telling themselves they cannot find freedom in the World of Imagination. But the truth is, if the Inner Man begins to search for freedom within imagination, they will find it. They must find it, because imagination contains all states, including the state of freedom from a particular situation.

So say they come to me with a problem, I tell them to see their circumstances as chains around their wrists, signaling that they are imprisoned, not free. But understand that these chains exist only because you have accepted them as real. Each time you feel free in imagination, each time you assume you have no such chains, each time you see *through* the chains rather than *at* them, a link in that chain breaks. If you persist in *being* free in spite of all evidence to the contrary, the links will continue breaking until the chains fall away entirely, revealing the freedom you have appropriated within. A chain does not mean a literal metal chain but anything in life that makes you feel in bondage.

What does it mean to persist "in spite of the evidence of the senses"? It means you must learn to look *through* appearances rather than *at* them. The evidence of the senses report only effects, never causes. When you react to the senses, you are reacting to yesterday's creations, to old assumptions hardened into facts. But when you look *through* them, you recognize they have no power to determine what you feel now, in this moment, in your imagination.

Take this example: say your boss or anyone, says something that would typically trigger a feeling of limitation, frustration, or bondage. In the past, you might have fought back with words, with arguments, with emotional reaction. But now you understand a different way, you wield the sword of assumption. Instead of fighting the outer circumstance, you look *through* your boss, *through* their words, *through* the reason, *through* the entire situation, and you feel as though you have never been more free. You do not wait for permission from the external world to feel free. You do not wait for the boss to free you. You claim that freedom now, internally, regardless of what is being said or done.

> *"This is the battle within me, the battle between the outer-man of the senses and the Inner Man of Imagination."* - ***Neville***

This is the real battle. Not against people, not against circumstances, but against the tyranny of the senses, against the belief that what you see and hear has more authority than what you imagine and feel. The opposing senses will always report limitation when you want to imagine beyond them. They will always tell you that you are bound by conditions, by other people, by the past, by lack. But you have the power to reject that report entirely, not by denying what appears, but by feeling beyond it.

When you feel free while your boss speaks words of limitation, you are not pretending the words were not said outwardly. You heard them, there is no denying that. But you are recognizing that those words have no power over your inner state unless you give them that power. You are exercising your freedom to choose what you feel, and in doing so, you break another link in the chain. Do this consistently, feel free when circumstances suggest bondage, feel abundant when appearances suggest lack, feel loved when the world reflects indifference, feel power when the world is scared and you will watch the chains dissolve. Not because you fought against them, but because you stopped giving them reality through your feeling.

This is what it means to fight with the sword of assumption rather than with your words or actions. Words spoken from a state of bondage only reinforce that bondage. Actions taken from limitation only perpetuate limitation. But an assumption, a feeling held as true in imagination despite all contradiction, this cuts through every chain, every obstacle, every seeming impossibility. Because causation is mental, not physical. When you change the feeling, when you change you to being free when world wants you to be prisoner, you change your destiny.

**Feel Beyond Reason Meditation**:

1. Go within *(remove the outer-world, and only change Self)* and ask yourself this simple question: "What do I, the Inner Man, deeply want to feel?"

2. Your answer will likely reveal something that would bring you profound bliss and freedom if you felt it. Perhaps it is feeling free from worry, no longer embarrassed about your life, or knowing a certain problem is resolved. It might be feeling that nothing can harm you, that you no longer need to walk on eggshells. Perhaps you want to feel you always act with love toward others, or that your past no longer haunts you, that you are free to begin with a clean slate. What matters is identifying something that initially brings fear when you try to feel it.

This fear is the threshold. It marks the boundary between your current state and the state you wish to inhabit. The resistance you feel is not a sign that you should turn back, but rather evidence that you are approaching something real, something transformative. The very fact that fear arises tells you that what lies beyond it matters deeply to you.

3. When you encounter that initial fear, recognize that you are denying yourself this wonderful experience. This fear is entirely your creation. There is no deeper meaning behind it. It is simply your creation that you are giving attention to. **I will give you a little secret: "I have never regretted feeling the reality of what I wanted."**

Think about this carefully. Every time you have dared to feel what you truly wanted, despite the fear, has it not brought you relief? Has it not dissolved the anxiety that kept you bound? The fear exists only as long as you refuse to cross into the feeling. The moment you dare to feel it, the fear loses its grip entirely. This is why persistence is so essential, not because the feeling is difficult to sustain, but because you must overcome the initial resistance to enter it in the first place.

4. Once you recognize this fear and understand that you are its Creator, realize that your imagination is a safe space to feel exactly what you want. This is your subjective reality where you can experience whatever you desire.When you overcome this fear, you will experience freedom, bliss, ecstasy, and relief. You will begin to feel like a new person.

Your imagination is not subject to the laws of the physical world. It is not bound by circumstances, by other people's opinions, or by past events. Within imagination, you have absolute authority. No one can stop you from feeling free. No condition can prevent you from feeling loved. No circumstance can keep you from feeling abundant. This is your domain, your subjective reality, and you alone determine what is real within it.

5. You must be *bold* and *feel* beyond your limitations. Summon the same courage with your feeling that you already apply to your thoughts! The reason most people hesitate is that they believe feelings must be justified by facts. This is what it means to feel beyond reason. Your senses will tell you that you have no right to feel this way. Your circumstances will contradict the feeling. Your past will seem to invalidate it. But none of this matters. An assumption needs no basis in fact whatsoever. You do not need evidence to feel differently. You simply choose the feeling and persist in it, knowing that if you remain faithful to it, it must harden into fact.

> *"How do we act? If I tell you that an assumption, a mere assumption, which is God's way of creating, though at the moment that you've assumed it, reason denies it, your senses deny it, if you persist in it, it*

*will harden into fact. If you demand from me proof before you dare to assume, you will never come to action.* ***To act I really must assume, and the assumption is the act of faith****; and without faith it is impossible to please him, as told us in the unknown author's letter to the Hebrews. Without faith it is impossible to please him, and faith is simply this bold assumption. I dare to assume that I am the one that I would like to be. If I would dare to assume, then I have proven to my own satisfaction that I have made the great act of faith."* - ***Neville***

**Artwork Commentary:**

In this artwork, imagine yourself at the center, enclosed by towering concrete walls. These walls symbolize the limitations of your senses, barriers you cannot seem to breach or see beyond. It appears there is no escape. The arches suggest different pathways of reasoning, yet each leads only to dead ends. Above, you glimpse clouds representing freedom, but the walls remain impenetrable, trapping you within.

Then we notice a hand reaching upward toward those clouds. The hand represents feeling, not intellectual analysis or organ perception, but feeling the reality freedom. Escape does not come through battering against the walls of logic or struggling within the confines of our senses. The way out is to feel those clouds, to reach beyond what can be seen or reasoned, to connect with what lies beyond the physical barriers.

Our senses provide us with evidence about the immediate world, creating a structured reality we navigate daily. Reason attempts to organize and make sense of this sensory data, constructing frameworks to obey. But both senses and reason operate within the same bounded space, the courtyard defined by those concrete walls.

Feeling, however, operates on a different plane entirely. It does not require validation from sight, sound, or logical proof. It bypasses the need for evidence or rational justification. When we feel the reality of something deeply, whether it is love, inspiration, or passion, we access a dimension that exists independent of our physical senses and our reason. The hand reaching toward the clouds does not need to understand everything about the clouds or see a clear path to them. It simply extends to them with pure feeling and trust.

This is why the reasoning represented by the arches fails. Each arch promises a solution, a way out to think yourself free, but logic alone cannot transcend its own framework. You cannot reason your way past the fundamental limitations of reason itself. The walls remain because they are built from the material of sensory and rational thought. To escape requires abandoning the insistence on understanding and instead embracing the direct experience of feeling, touching the intangible, connecting with what cannot be proven but can only be known through the heart.

# Hear As Though You Heard

> *"Denying evidence of the senses and* ***appropriate*** *in the feeling of the wish fulfilled is the way to the realization of your desire." -* ***Neville***

> **Appropriate**: *Take something for one's own use, typically without the owner's permission.*

BASED ON THIS DEFINITION, you must see yourself as the rightful owner of everything inside the World of Imagination. We must learn how to appropriate states in imagination, this includes things, words, and feelings. Your imagination is your own subjective reality where you are either its God or its servant. In truth, you are God, but you may believe yourself to be a servant within imagination. You are either the Creator of your assumptions or their follower. There is no other Creator in your imagination. There is only "yes" in the imagination for all things.

Most enter imagination tentatively, as visitors rather than owners. They imagine their desire but hold it at arm's length, afraid to fully claim it. They imagine success but whisper "maybe" instead of declaring "yes." They see their wish-fulfilled but refuse to feel it as their reality. This hesitation is what keeps their desires in the realm of fantasy inside rather than feeling it real.

Now, I want to speak on receptivity. I found this to be crucial when it comes to imagining. I have noticed within myself a resistance that I created. I wanted to understand why I was creating this resistance. What I saw was I am creating resistance because I fear letting go of the outer, surface world and I fear accepting the wonderful things within me.

> ***"You must know what you want before you can ask for it.*** *You must know what you want before you can feel that you have it, and prayer is the feeling of the fulfilled desire. It does not matter what it is you seek in prayer, or where it is, or whom it concerns. You have nothing to do but convince yourself of the truth of that which you desire to see manifested." -* ***Neville***

*"Sit quietly where you are and assume the mental attitude of listening; recall your friend's voice; with this familiar voice established in your consciousness,* ***imagine that you are actually hearing his voice*** *and that he is telling you that he is or has that which you wanted him to be or to have.*

***You assume a receptive attitude of mind****... You remain in this receptive state until you feel the thrill of having heard the good and wonderful news." -* ***Neville***

**Receptivity**: *Willingness to consider or accept new suggestions and ideas.*

Imagine three people walking into a mall where they can take anything they want for free. The first person enters with an attitude of saying "no" to everything they see. Despite the abundance around them, they reject it all, refusing gift after gift. The second person enters uncertain about what they want and can never make a decision. They wander the aisles, picking things up and putting them down, paralyzed by indecision and doubt. The third person enters with the attitude that since they can have anything, they choose precisely what they want. They move with clarity and conviction, selecting exactly what brings them joy.

Notice how both the person who said "no" and the person who was "doubtful" left with nothing. They gained nothing and remained in their present state of mind. But more importantly, notice *why* they left empty-handed: it was not because the gifts were not available, but because they refused to accept them or know what they want.

The person who said "no" represents those who enter imagination already convinced of their unworthiness or impossibility. They see their desire but immediately reject it with thoughts such as, "this isn't for me" or "this is too good to be true." Their rejection is not based on the reality of imagination, where all things exist, but on their past conditioning and current circumstances.

The person who was "doubtful" represents those who fear

commitment to their imaginal act. They touch their desire lightly, imagine it tentatively, but never fully claim it. This hesitation stems from the two fears mentioned earlier: the fear of letting go of the familiar outer-world and the fear of accepting something wonderful that might not express. They protect themselves from potential disappointment by never fully believing, never fully accepting.

The third person, the one who chooses precisely what they want, demonstrates true receptivity. They understand that in imagination, there is only "yes". They do not question whether they deserve it or whether it is possible. They simply accept it as their reality. This is what Neville meant when he said to appropriate in the feeling of the wish-fulfilled, to take possession of it in imagination without asking permission, without waiting for evidence, without hedging your commitment with doubt.

The point of this analogy is to reveal that when you enter the World of Imagination, you must do so with an *attitude of receptivity,* a willingness, even an eagerness, to accept what you truly want. Not to test whether you can have it. Not to peek at it from a safe distance. But to fully claim it, to appropriate it, to make it yours in feeling. The gifts are already there. The only question is whether you will accept them for yourself.

> *"How to believe when reason denies it, my senses deny it, everything denies it? Yet I am haunted with the statement of scripture, "All things are possible to him who believes." So how do I do it? Fawcett said, using the word Imagination, but really you can take the word belief in the same way, he said "The secret of imagining is the greatest of all problems to the solution of which the mystic aspires, for supreme power, supreme wisdom and supreme delight lie in the far off solution of this mystery." Well, if that is true,* ***I should devote all of my energies to the mastery of this art of believing and the art of imagining. For Imagination and believing are the stuff out of which we fashion our worlds... every one of us****. There isn't a thing in this world that comes suddenly upon us that really did not have its cause in some invis-*

*ible imaginal state where we believed it. We forgot it, yes, went about our business, things are active, and suddenly it confronts us, and we don't really recognize our own harvest. But everything comes by reason of the law, and we plant it by believing. We were told the story and we believed it. Others rejected it; we believed it."* - ***Neville***

**Deny**: *A state that one refuses to admit the truth or existence of.*

True denial is not looking at your outer-world and merely repeating, "It does not exist." That is mental struggle, not denial. True denial is the natural result of *accepting* the new reality within you so completely that the outer-world loses its authority over your inner conviction.

You do not deny being unwanted by fighting against the feeling of unwantedness or by affirming "I am not unwanted." That is still acknowledging unwantedness as your reality, even as you resist it. Instead, you deny unwantedness through the complete *acceptance* of being wanted. When you genuinely accept being wanted in your imagination, when you feel it, live from it, and make it your dwelling place, unwantedness is denied automatically. Not through force, but through displacement.

Our *acceptance* of imagination is our *denial* of the senses. The two are not separate actions but two sides of the same coin. Denying is not something you actively do, not a battle you wage against what you see and hear. Rather, it is the natural *implication* of your *acceptance* of imaginal acts. When you truly accept your imaginal act as reality, the evidence of your senses is automatically denied, not through struggle but through the sheer conviction of your inner acceptance.

If someone were to tell you that the sun does not exist, you would not need to fight their claim or repeat to yourself "The sun exists, the sun exists." You would simply be indifferent to their statement because your acceptance of the sun's existence is so complete that contradictory claims hold no power over you. This is the indifference Neville speaks of, not a forced detachment, but a natural byproduct of complete acceptance.

Many worry whether they are "denying" their senses enough, creating unnecessary stress and internal conflict. They monitor themselves constantly thinking, "Am I denying correctly? Am I still too focused on the outer world? Am I doing this right?" This concern reveals that they are still giving authority to the outer-world, still measuring their inner reality against external circumstances.

But you do not need to fight against your senses. You do not need to close your eyes to what you see or cover your ears to what you hear. You simply need to imagine beyond them, to accept a reality in imagination that is more real to you than what your senses dictate. When you do this, denial happens automatically.

> ***"I desire to hear, and then I listen as though I were hearing,*** *and the imagined voice speaks that which I dictate as though it had initiated the message."* - **Neville**

We often find it difficult to let go of our outer-world, even when it causes us pain. We cling to what we know, to what our senses confirm, because it feels safe in its familiarity. Yet the only sacrifice required of us is the willingness to release our grip on the current outer-world and to enter into and *feel* our desired place in imagination.

Be not only willing but eager to accept all the wonderful gifts you are discovering within yourself. If imagination could speak, it would say, "Stop telling me what you don't want and tell me what you *are*." Imagination does not respond to negation or resistance. It responds only to acceptance, to the feeling of already being and having.

There are no restrictions on what you can imagine and feel in your imagination. None. The boundaries you perceive are not laws of imagination but habits of thought carried over from the outer-world. In imagination, you are not bound by logic, by past failure, by current circumstances, or by the judgments of others. You are completely free to be and have whatever you desire.

See your imagination as a place where you are completely safe and free to feel and have what you desire. This perspective cultivates an attitude of receptivity because it removes the fear that blocks acceptance. When you recognize that imagination is your private domain, that no one can enter it to judge you or take from you, that nothing can hurt you there, you naturally become more willing to accept the wonderful.

In imagination, there are no consequences for claiming what you want. There is no risk of disappointment because imagination is not an unpredictable place but a present reality in itself. Whatever your human reasoning says, learn to accept the great gifts that you discover within yourself.

> *"So before you meditate on the things you Love, assume an attitude of receptivity.* ***You are willing and eager to accept the Lovely Reality your are discovering within yourself****. "Do not limit yourself to the past."* - ***Neville***

~

**Artwork Commentary:**

> *"To listen attentively* ***as though*** *you heard is to evoke, to activate."* - ***Neville***

This artwork explores the act of hearing as though you truly heard, listening with intention rather than through the distorted lens of our inner filters. We unconsciously filter what we hear, both from others and from ourselves. Beautiful words of encouragement can be blocked out when all we can hear is judgment. We revise what people say, hearing what we expect or fear rather than what was actually spoken. In certain states, we become so closed off that we cannot truly hear another person at all. This faculty to hear with inner ears is a special ability.

We see the masses gathered in a room, a representation of the countless voices that grumble and speak nonstop within us and outside of us. These voices create such noise that we filter some out entirely, failing to pay attention to what is genuinely being said, whether from ourselves or from another person.

The practice, then, is to consciously hear what you wish to hear. To listen as clearly and deliberately as you would listen to a friend sharing good news in the physical world. We must bring that same quality of attention inward, giving our ear to ourselves with the same care we would give to a trusted person. This is about choosing which voice to amplify, which narrative to feed and trust in.

We can give our ear to ourselves, to a friend, or to the world at large. What we choose to truly listen to becomes the narrative we live within. It shapes our reality, our emotions, and our actions. The external world may be filled with chaos, if you peek in and listen, you can hear the masses only responding to fear and hysteria. But *you, the Inner Man,* have the power to decide what you hear inside yourself.

*Remember it is not about what you, (the Inner Man) have heard in the past or what you are going to hear in the future. It is about what you are hearing **now**.*

# The Persistent Fool Becomes Wise

> *"Now, here is the secret in this little story of believing:* ***You always start at the end. The end is where I begin. In my end is my beginning****. You go to the very end, the thing accomplished, you start there. And then you bounce back here...and then you move across this series of events that lead you to that end that you had already predetermined. Here is something that...of course I don't like to use science to support anything in scripture, because scripture is so far beyond anything in science. It doesn't appeal to the rational mind as science does. It belongs to a depth so deep that reason can't reach it, that's why it still remains undisturbed by all the arguments, all the intellectual criticisms that you can throw at it. It still remains undisturbed..." -* ***Neville***

WE ALL STRIVE to be rational. I have tried to present these ideas logically to help you understand. Yet ultimately, what is being asked is to believe in your imagination as real.

This is the crux of the matter, the point where reason must yield to something deeper. We spend our lives training ourselves to distinguish between "real" and "imaginary," to trust only what our senses, our organs confirm, to dismiss inner experiences as mere fantasy. But what if this distinction is the prison that keeps us from our true power? What if the rational mind, for all its utility in navigating the physical world, is utterly blind to the realm where creation actually occurs?

When you decide to live from imagination, you are making a choice that the rational mind cannot comprehend. You are choosing to privilege your inner experience over outer circumstances. You are declaring that what you feel within yourself has primacy over what your senses and organs say. This is not delusion, it is a recognition that imagination is not separate from reality but is the foundation of it.

The rational mind will protest. It will present evidence, circumstances, facts. It will remind you of your limitations, your past failures, the impossibility of your desires. But reason cannot reach the depth where imagination operates. This is why the teachings remain undisturbed by intellectual criticism, they exist in a dimension that rationality cannot touch.

Do you want to be called brilliant? To acquire that special item? To create magnificent art? To write an extraordinary book? To receive wonderful news? To feel like the most amazing being imaginable? To hear admiration from someone you respect? To experience prestige and diplomacy? To feel universally loved within your imagination? To not fear anything within you? To hear exactly what you wish to hear? To feel what you want to feel, not what circumstances dictate? To stop making excuses for not feeling what you desire? To experience infinity within yourself? To feel oneness? To express yourself freely without fear of judgment? What do you truly want? To know deep down that your imaginal self is real?

What do you truly want? The question itself is radical because it asks you to look past what seems possible, past what circumstances suggest, past what reason deems achievable. It asks you to identify your desire in its purest form, untainted by considerations of "how" or "when" or "if." Then it invites you to do something that seems absurdly simple yet impossibly difficult: to begin it all in your imagination. No one will know, it will be your secret.

This secrecy is important. Your imaginal acts need not be justified to anyone. You need not explain why you feel loved when you are alone. The rational mind cannot make sense of this because it insists on waiting for external validation before permitting the internal experience. But this reverses the actual order of creation, which begins within and moves outward.

> *"I (Neville) said, "You're asking the wrong person for advice because* ***I'm not a rational person when it comes to the world****. To me, I do not go along with the reasoning mind. I am talking of an entirely different principle. I am speaking of imagination...*
>
> *I am not speaking of anything rational in this world. I am speaking of a power that isn't rational. The 'rational mind' is simply the interference between the being that you are, and this so-called world that you think so real. No; the rational mind - let it be what it*

*wants to be. But I'm not talking about that. I'm speaking of something entirely different..." -* ***Neville***

The world may feel imprisoned but you have never felt more free. When the world calls itself wise, it is time to be foolish.

The rational mind operates within the boundaries of sensory evidence. It demands proof, consistency, logical progression before any change has occurred. It is the voice that says, "This is how things are, therefore this is how they must remain." But this voice, reasonable as it sounds, is what that stands between you and the life you desire. It interprets the world through limitation, through past experience, through the accumulated evidence of what has been rather than what could be.

When Neville speaks of a power that is not rational, he is pointing to imagination itself. So expand beyond what is familiar with your feeling in imagination. You are likely denying yourself what you want because it seems impossible. The rational mind whispers its objections: "Be realistic. Don't get your hopes up. That is not for people like you." But these objections are merely the rational mind protecting itself from disappointment by pre-rejecting possibility. Let go of that limitation. Everything is possible in imagination. Imagine it anyway. Just do it. Do what? Whatever you deeply desire. Do this for yourself alone.

Reach for something that seems just out of reach, something that makes the rational mind uncomfortable, something that would require a complete change of your current circumstances. Do it anyway. True fulfillment is not external but within. We are meant to fulfill our desires in the World of Imagination because that is where our *Real Self* exists.

The physical world is not where you truly live. You live in your imagination. Every moment of your conscious experience occurs within imagination. Even what you call "reality" is simply your interpretation, your imaginal construction of sensory data. If you already live in imagination, why would you choose to imagine limitation when you could imagine fulfillment? Why would you choose to feel lack when you could feel abundance? Why would you imagine yourself as powerless when you could imagine yourself as the creative force that shapes that world?

You might say I am being irrational by thinking thoughts and feeling feelings that may never materialize in my life. That sounds reasonable, but I am not interested in being reasonable. I am interested in expanding inside. And this expansion costs me my rationally and so I must pay the price. This is what me, the Inner Man, the *Real Me* desires. I must grant myself these feelings or I suffer. Where do I suffer? In my imagination.

Paradoxically, the greatest challenge in life is allowing ourselves to feel what we want in our imaginations. Is that not strange? The one place where we can have anything, yet we struggle to give ourselves what we desire. We police our own feelings, we censor our own joy, we refuse ourselves the experiences we long for, all because the rational mind insists we must "earn" the right to feel good through external achievement first.

Why would we deny ourselves? Even if the external manifestation seems impossible, why not indulge in the feeling anyway? What is lost by feeling loved, successful, admired, fulfilled in your imagination? The rational mind fears that these feelings without external justification will somehow make you delusional or complacent. But the opposite is true. When you finally allow yourself to feel what you desire inside without reason, you obtain a freedom you have never known before.

Fulfill your desires with feeling and move forward. Just do it. You will not regret satisfying every desire within you. Life is too brief not to experience beauty, honor, wealth, and love in your imagination. These are not "just" imaginary experiences, they are real experiences happening in the only place you, the Inner Man, actually live: Imagination itself.

*"Man is only reacting in his natural or Satan state; he never acts or creates, he only reacts or re-creates.* ***One real creative moment,***

***one real feeling of the wish fulfilled, is worth more than the whole natural life of re-action." - Neville***

Too often we allow excuses to block what we truly want in our imagination. We believe that if some external event happens, we *must* feel a certain feeling within the framework and restrictions of the senses. When something unpleasant occurs, we think we *must* feel bad or angry. Some even believe that not feeling these negative emotions means rejecting their true feelings. This is incorrect for those are typically reactions, not choices. You are actually rejecting your true feelings the moment you deny yourself what you want to feel.

This belief that we must feel according to circumstances is one of the most pervasive forms of self-imprisonment. It suggests that our inner state is at the mercy of external events, that we are merely reactive beings with no sovereignty over our own imaginal experience. But this is a fundamental misunderstanding of where you, the Inner Man, truly live. If you already live in imagination, why would you surrender the choice of what to feel to circumstances that exist outside of you? I am not claiming this is easy, it not about how hard or easy this is. It is more about recognition. Recognize and contemplate on this ideas and see if you are more free than you previously saw yourself moments ago.

If someone says something to me hurtful and I initially feel pain, but I desire to feel peace instead, yet I convince myself I must feel hurt by their words, what am I truly rejecting? Peace. The thing I want! Though I might initially feel hurt, is that what I truly want to experience inside? Does my peace deny the hurt of their words? Not exactly. Knowing something and choosing to experience are two different things. I can understand the hurt while feeling peace and act from the freedom and peace I chose. When I embrace my desire for peace, I transcend the limitations of my senses and enter the world of wants.

*"No, you cannot know this intellectually, you cannot debate it, you cannot substantiate it.* ***You can only feel it. You can only be aware of it.*** *"* **- Neville**

Perhaps others will not understand why I feel peace in such situations, but fulfilling my inner desires does not require anyone's approval or their faith. My rational mind may register hurt as an automatic reaction, but my Inner Self, my True Self, desires to rise above this realm and feel what I want to feel, regardless of what seems rational.

From this perspective, you choose what you feel. You leave a life of mere reactions for a life of choices inside. Then you become proactive in your own life rather than merely reactive. It is not the denial of pain or grief. If an experience of loss, or a natural dark event happens to you that requires you to feel through it then feel it. But if something happens that feels like opposition to you, towards your goal, then ***see*** through it!

*"Now may I tell you, when I invite you to go all out and to imagine that you are now the man, the woman, that you want to be, some will tell you that will lead to madness. May I tell you, it will not! The only thing that would lead to madness would be to doubt it. The minute doubt sets in, and you would like to believe it but reason tells you it isn't true, and you begin to doubt, then descends what the world would call a mental division, a certain madness. For doubt is the only devil in the world...that's doubt.* ***If you could go all out and believe it then regardless of what the whole vast rational world will tell you, you won't go mad. The whole thing will become a part of your dream world. You'll bring it into and fit it in without any difficulty into the world****. Someone born poor, very poor, he began to dream that he had wealth and that he had fame. Well, at the moment it would seem insane, his dream, but he persisted in his dream. But when the dream became true and his fame was established and his wealth established, it seemed perfectly natural to those not knowing his dream. So everyone is dreaming.*

*But if you begin to doubt your dream and still try to make it true, but doubting all the time, you're heading towards a little breakup. But you will not breakup if you go all out in your wonderful claim that you are what you desire to be. Because all things are possible to God and the God spoken of is right where you are seated. That's the God of whom the Bible speaks."* - ***Neville***

Was it rational that Neville believed he could be in two places at once? Was it rational for him to believe everything would align with his desires? Was it rational to consider imagination his real self? None of this seems rational. Was it rational for Neville to discard conventional ideas about how life "should" be lived? Was it rational to simply feel whatever he wanted? Was it rational for him to believe that what he experienced in his imagination was real?

The answer to all these questions is no, it was not rational. And yet, Neville still imagined it anyway as if it was real. The rational mind cannot make this journey because it demands evidence before belief, proof before acceptance. But imagination operates by a different law entirely, one where you must first become what you desire internally before it can express externally.

Are you willing to release your reactions to circumstances and instead embrace your desires within? To walk with the feeling that you are secure? Are you willing to finally live in the mental space where you truly want to be?

I have taken the leap in my imagination to accept that physical reality is not the *only* reality. Reality does not end at the boundary of the senses but extends infinitely into imagination. What does this mean specifically? It means I no longer grant the physical world final authority over what is real or possible. The rational mind insists that only what can be seen, touched, and measured is real. But I have chosen to recognize that my imaginal experiences, my feelings, my inner states are equally real, perhaps more real, because they are where I actually live.

*"The fool who persists in his folly will become wise."* - ***William Blake***

*"Well, I only wrote one little thought from William Blake: "If the fool would persist in his folly, he will become wise." When he got it, it did something to him..."persisting in my folly, for certainly it is folly to assume that I am what the evidence of my senses deny, reason denies it.* ***So I must persist in my folly?" Yes, and if you do, you'll prove it and you'll become wise." - Neville***

**Artwork Commentary:**

Here we see a man playing the piano with no crowd around him. He appears foolish, playing sounds that nobody else can hear, and yet he continues. In life, you always look foolish to those who cannot see what you can, who cannot hear what you can. All sorts of labels are tossed upon the individual who dreams.

The piano is his imagination because imagination, like any instrument, requires practice, dedication, and the courage to produce discordant notes before finding harmony. He tunes it, plays with it, experiments until he strikes the right chords. The chords that resonate in harmony with his soul. These are sounds that others may not hear, and yet he chooses to be foolish anyway, to continue playing beautiful melodies only he can hear.

Most people abandon their instruments the moment they sound foolish. But the dreamer knows that foolishness is not the opposite of wisdom, it is often the path to it. Every teacher was once a fool stumbling through their craft, playing notes that made no sense to anyone, perhaps not even to themselves at first.

The crowd's absence is not a punishment but a filter. It separates those who create for external validation from those who create because they must. The man at the piano has discovered that the greatest audience is not out there, it is within. When you can satisfy that inner listener, when you can move your own soul, you have achieved something far more valuable than outward applause.

This solitary act of creation is not madness, it is faith. Faith in the unseen, in the unheard, in the possibility that what resonates within you has value, even if the world cannot yet recognize it. The dreamer understands something fundamental, that all visible noises brought to the surface began as invisible melodies. So we must leave the surface of noises and come down to the depths of ourselves to tune, and play a new melody.

# The Dreamer And The Dream

*"This is a dream, my dears, this is as much a dream as the dream of last night, only it's more difficult for man to control, because he sees it's so real and so objective and so independent of has own perception of it. But to prove to you that you can control it* ***assume that it is a dream. Then assume that things are as you would like them to be and persuade yourself of the reality of your assumption. Don't make any effort to make it so, just trust the power within you to make it so."*** ***- Neville***

MAN IS TRULY afraid of their dreams. They cling to limitations, mistaking them for safety and salvation. Self-limiting beliefs become the false gods we worship. We convince ourselves that these restrictions keep us alert, cautious, and protected. Fear becomes our home, our family. Worry becomes our father, shame our mother, and indecision our character. We gaze longingly outside this house of fear, yet the thought of leaving terrifies us. Abandoning this familiar home sparks deep terror. In this state, we can neither see nor hear our dreams, for they wrongfully fade into fantasy and falsehood.

Fear infiltrates all our decisions, making escape seem impossible. How do we release this fear? To be free from fear, we must recognize ourselves as the Dreamer, the Inner Man. We created the fear, the house, the family inside.

This outer-man thinks they must work their way out of this fear. They believe if they fight back against their parents of worry and shame then they will overcome their fear. Or they assume accomplishing something in surface world will make their deeper fears subside. Never recognizing themselves as the Dreamer, they inevitably fail. The notion that they do not need to do anything, that they do not need to work their way out, that it is actually impossible for this outer-man to do anything in the outer-world to change their inner state, seems absurd to the outer-man.

They insist, "No, there must be a solution I have not discovered yet." So they continue searching outside themselves, yet they remain a desiring self, and seeing only their reflection, they only see desire. Never obtaining, always pursuing, frustrations, rage, jealousy, and the deadliest sins stir within them. Hating their world, hating what they see, hating their own reflection, they seek to destroy it all. They cannot win because they exist in a state of fear and failure, and what is within will give birth to without because Man can only give what exists within themselves.

The outer-man lives in constant reaction to their reflection. When the mirror shows them lack, they scramble to fix the reflection directly. When the mirror shows them rejection, they fight to change how others see them. But the mirror has no power of its own. It simply reflects what stands before it.

The mirror of your world is faithful. It never lies, never distorts, never adds anything that is not already within you. If you bring fear to the mirror, it shows you fearful circumstances. If you bring shame, it reflects shameful experiences. But the moment you change what you bring to the mirror, the moment you assume the state of having, of being loved, of being worthy, the mirror must reflect this new inner reality. It has no choice. The mirror does not judge whether you deserve what you assume. It does not question whether your assumption is realistic. It simply reflects.

This is why hating your reflection is futile. The reflection is innocent. It is merely doing its job, showing you yourself inside. When you hate what you see in the mirror of your world, you are hating yourself. When you fight against your circumstances, you are fighting against your own mental activity.

If only Man would stop hating their reflection and recognize that the inner, living mirror merely reflects their mental actions, they would be free. If only they would understand that the mirror stands still and does not judge but simply reflects. The mirror cannot initiate. It cannot create. It cannot deny you anything. It can only show you what you are. If only Man would see themselves in the mirror and recognize that they are the Dreamer, the one standing before the mirror with the power to change what they bring to it, they would let go of all these false gods, the gods of circumstance, of other people's opinions and past failures. None of these have any power except the power Man gives them by believing they are the cause of their inner state.

Freedom comes when Man realizes they are not the reflection. They are the reality that the reflection mirrors. They are not the image in the mirror of their world. They are the Dreamer dreaming the dream, the Creator creating the creation, the Cause that gives birth to all effects. When this is truly understood, Man can turn away from their reflection without fear, change their inner state, and trust that the mirror will faithfully reflect their new assumption. This is the death of outer-man and the resurrection of the Dreamer.

> *"You are an eternal dreamer dreaming non-eternal dreams. Your dreams take form as you assume the feeling of their reality."* - ***Neville***

The Dreamer must transform completely! Minor alterations of the Dreamer produce mixed results. You cannot change while one foot in expansion and keeping the other planted in limitation. You cannot let go halfway. Half-measures produce half-results, or worse, they produce continued oscillation between states, leaving you feeling powerless and confused. The old state fights for survival, pulling you back, whispering its familiar fears. This is why complete transformation is required, anything less leaves the door open for the old dream to reclaim you.

The Dreamer does not view their dreaming as fantasy but as actual reality, a reality they fully control. This is the critical distinction that separates the Dreamer from man. Man treats their desires as distant possibilities, things that might happen if circumstances align, if they work hard enough, if they get lucky. But to the Dreamer, their dreams are not distant possibilities they hope to one day realize. No, to the Dreamer, their Dreams are happening now. Not tomorrow, not when conditions change, not when the outer world catches up, *now*.

The mental activity happens *now*, requiring death of the "limiting now". You trade one "now" *(outer-world)* for another "now" *(inner world).* You are not trying to change the future, you are changing what is real to you *now.* The outer-world shows you one testimony, limitation, lack, delay. The inner world offers you another testimony, fulfillment, abundance, completion. Which now will you accept as real? Which testimony will you validate with your attention and feeling?

Typically, Man resists this trade. They cling to limitations "just in case," while hoping for their desire to appear. This is the fundamental error. They want to keep one foot in each world. They want to maintain their awareness of the problem while simultaneously creating the solution. They want to acknowledge the limitation while imagining the freedom. But this divided state produces no transformation. You cannot serve two masters. You cannot occupy two states simultaneously. You must choose.

The choice is always now. Not later, when circumstances improve. Not tomorrow, when you feel more ready. Not next week, when you have more evidence. For our past was once our future and our past was created now. So it is what we do now that matters.

Do not think the passage of time will yield the harvest you want if you do not identify with the state you want to be. Why? Because we are harvesting *ourselves.* We are the yield we are looking for in our future. So if you must change something, change yourself. If you must change in it a time-frame, change yourself *now.*

When you recognize that you are the only operant power, that everything in your world is your imagination is yours, then you understand that changing yourself is not one method among many, it is the *only* method.

> *"Then the entire drama unfolds within you and you will know exactly who you are: that you are the ones spoken of in scripture as the gods who gathered. We agreed then to dream in concert, so that when you and I see a building we may see it differently—you may see it through the eyes of one who would like to own it, I may see it through the eyes of one who admires it with no feeling of possession—but we*

*do see the same building, only we see it differently. So when we descended, we agreed to dream in concert. So while we walk this earth, we see the same streets, therefore, we know the same number; and we can go where we want to go because we are dreaming in concert. But we are dreaming, my dears. This whole vast world is the dream of the gods who descended. But because we agreed to dream in concert there's no confusion. Had we agreed to dream individually and all play solo, this would be the wildest, maddest thing in the world. But we agreed to dream in concert.* ***Now may I tell you, when I invite you to go all out and to imagine that you are now the man, the woman, that you want to be, some will tell you that will lead to madness. May I tell you, it will not! The only thing that would lead to madness would be to doubt it. The minute doubt sets in, and you would like to believe it but reason tells you it isn't true, and you begin to doubt, then descends what the world would call a mental division, a certain madness. For doubt is the only devil in the world...that's doubt. If you could go all out and believe it then regardless of what the whole vast rational world will tell you, you won't go mad. The whole thing will become a part of your dream world****. You'll bring it into and fit it in without any difficulty into the world. Someone born poor, very poor, he began to dream that he had wealth and that he had fame. Well, at the moment it would seem insane, his dream, but he persisted in his dream. But when the dream became true and his fame was established and his wealth established, it seemed perfectly natural to those not knowing his dream. So everyone is dreaming. But if you begin to doubt your dream and still try to make it true, but doubting all the time, you're heading towards a little breakup. But you will not breakup if you go all out in your wonderful claim that you are what you desire to be. Because all things are possible to God and the God spoken of is right where you are seated. That's the God of whom the Bible speaks."* - **Neville**

The awakened Dreamer stops seeing opposition and recognizes

that this reflection only shames them because they have first shamed themselves. The Dreamer does not experience love because they have not yet dreamt themselves into the state of being absolutely loved. The Dreamer does not experience what they want because they have not dreamed themselves *having* what they want.

The Dreamer operates from the highest states because the highest states are theirs to claim. There is no hierarchy of deserving, no ladder to climb, no prerequisites to fulfill. The Dreamer does not ask anyone's permission to dream what they want or to feel what they want. They understand that seeking permission is itself a denial of their power. The Dreamer knows all is theirs, and as it says, *"If I were hungry I would not tell anyone" (Psalm 50:12)*. If they desire an outcome, they give themselves the outcome in imagination. To the Dreamer, this is not wishful thinking or fantasy, this is fact, this is the only fact that matters.

The Dreamer can make demons bow and kings kneel, not through force or manipulation, but through the recognition that all characters in the dream respond to the Dreamer's assumption. The Dreamer can conjure whatever feelings they desire and feel them as deeply as they wish.

*Anxiety is the restriction of feeling new things.*

The Dreamer is unafraid of any thought within themselves. They do not run from "negative" thoughts or police their imagination with fear. They recognize that thoughts have no power except the power they give them through sustained attention and feeling. The Dreamer is unafraid of their own greatness. This is perhaps the most profound fear to overcome, not the fear of failure, but the fear of your own magnitude, the fear of what it would mean if you truly accepted that you are the operant power in your imagination.

The Dreamer abandons limitations and turns toward their desires, giving themselves what they want fully and shamelessly. The key word is "shamelessly." Man is taught to be humble, to not want too much, to not claim too much, to not feel too much. But the

Dreamer recognizes this as just another limitation, another fence around the infinite. The Dreamer gives themselves permission to want everything they desire, and more importantly, to *have* everything they desire in imagination, without guilt, without shame, without apology.

The Dreamer will always dream beyond what their limitations dictate because limitations are not truth, they are simply current assumptions that can be abandoned. You are not bound by your past, by your circumstances, by what seems possible or probable. You are only bound by what you accept as true for yourself. Change that acceptance, and you change everything.

You are the Dreamer and this is your dream. This is not metaphor. This is not spiritual poetry. This is recognition of what you are. You are not a small self navigating a vast, independent world. You are imagination itself, housed in a body, dreaming a world into being through your assumptions and inner states. When you truly accept this, when you truly *assume* this position, you stop asking the world for permission for your worthiness. You stop waiting for circumstances to change. You stop reacting to what appears. You simply dream what you desire, feel its reality now, and watch as the dream reshapes itself to match your inner conviction. Assume this position, not as a technique, but as recognition of what you have always been: the eternal Dreamer, dreaming non-eternal dreams.

*"Well, who is the dreamer? Aren't you a dreamer?"* - ***Neville***

**Artwork Commentary:**

*"I do not bow to the facts of life but I make my imagination the fact."*

Here we see a man sitting above the tiles of black and white. There is a inner door through which he passes through. He is no longer bound by the outer realm, for he has entered into his own imagination. Before him stands a peculiar tree bearing peculiar fruit.

He sits on a chair contemplating, this chair is the true throne of life. The throne of the dreamer who dreams. The fruit hovering above his head, with a bite taken from it, represents the feast he partakes in which is the conception of himself. The floor beneath him which was once his only reality, has now become his footstool, a foundation he is no longer ruled by. That a man can take an image of himself, and by believing in it with conviction, he begins to feast upon it. Through this feast, he changes. He starts to become that image, and in time, he bears the fruit of that conception.

What we see illustrated here is the mechanics of self-change. The outer-world, represented by those black and white tiles, offers its patterns and restrictions. But the man who enters his imagination discovers he is not subject to those patterns. Instead, he becomes the reaper of his own inner reality.

The tree is significant because it grows from within, not from without. Its fruit is not given by circumstance or inheritance, but cultivated through belief. Each time he takes a bite, he is consuming his own assumption about who he is. And assumptions, when persisted in, harden into fact.

In the world below his feet, he must only reap his harvest, while in this world, he sows by feasting on fulfillments. In this world of imagination, there are only ouroboroses. Each new state is the end of the old and the beginning of a new. For the imaginal man never see's seeds but always a fruit bearing tree. There are no buds for the imaginal man, only blossoming flowers.

# Reasonless Imaginal Acts

> *"Tonight, I ask you to take the most fantastic thing in this world and find an inner conviction within yourself that it is yours, for the truth of any concept is known by the feeling of certainty which that conviction inspires.* ***Once you have that inner feeling of certainty, don't ask me to confirm it. What would it matter what I think?*** *Do not be disillusioned if your experience has not been mine.* ***Believe in yourself and trust your inner feeling.*** *Test yourself and if it works on this level it will work in the depths of your being."* - ***Neville***

To truly grasp the freedom attainable within you, you must understand the concept of states. A state is *not* an emotion. A state is a belief, a feeling about how you perceive yourself. Something you feel is true about you. How does one know what state they are in? Well, pay attention to what you feel about yourself inside. *Not* what you want to feel, but what you feel is real inside about yourself.

Many confuse themselves with thinking they are what they want to be, but that is not true. You are what you feel is real to you about you. All day long man can long to think greater about themselves, but until they feel those new words as real to them about them, they remain as they are. And we do not get what we want to be, we get what we *are*.

This state is not merely a passing feeling but a lived reality. It feels fundamentally real to you. While a state can trigger emotional responses, that emotional response is not the essence of the state itself. The goal is to see yourself differently at the level of identity. When you feel the reality of being different, that is when you are.

Emotions are reactions, they are effects, not causes. A state, however, is causal. It is the ground from which your emotions spring. When you occupy the state of being loved, you do not manufacture loving feelings; rather, loving feelings arise *naturally* because you *are* love in that state. The state you animate determines the emotional landscape you experience, not the other way around.

You cannot force emotions that belong to a state you are not currently occupying. Instead, you must accept the *reality* of being the new state *now*, and the corresponding emotions will follow. It is not about believing you *will* be something; it is about accepting that you *are* something in the World of Imagination, which then elicits an emotional response.

You have an emotional reality, a physical reality, a financial reality, all these realities exist as dimensions of your experience. But you also have an imaginal reality, and this imaginal reality is the foundation of all the others.

Your imaginal reality is not a fantasy separate from "real life," it is the creative source from which your outer realities emerge. Why? Because the imaginal reality is one with yourself and you take yourself into all of these realities, and we receive ourselves in all facets of our life.

So imagination is *not* a state. Imagination is the *Real Self*, which I call the Inner Man. This Inner Man can be and have whatever it wishes in the World of Imagination. It cannot be stressed enough that you, the Inner Man, are *not* a state.

The Inner Man is the permanent I AM, the changeless awareness of being and animator of all states. States are temporary garments worn by this eternal Self. You do not become the Inner Man by achieving a certain state, you already *are* the Inner Man, regardless of which state you currently occupy. This is why no state can truly define or limit you. The moment you recognize yourself as the animator rather than the animation, you reclaim your power to choose which state to bring to life inside of you.

If entering into a new state within you is challenging, it is because you have not accepted who you truly are within. You are not a state, but the one occupying it.

Now listen to the words of Neville in the lecture "*Repentance Is A Gift From God*":

> *"But grant me the freedom to change it (my state)– don't leave me in the state if I desire to get out of it. Yet many a person wallows in it, and wallows in it morning, noon, and night, and they are totally unaware they are doing it. They will say, "Oh, yes," and then five*

*seconds later they are back in that state (old man).* ***I have had interviews with people who will say to me, "This is what I would like, but I must first tell you..." Don't tell me anything! Tell me what you want – they are only states!*** *They insist on wallowing in all the things of the past."* - ***Neville***

"Don't tell me anything!" This is the secret. Complete abandonment of your current state is the way to bring life to the new state. This is not a partial letting go or a temporary forgetting, it is a total letting go to everything that constitutes the old state.

Before you assume a new state, understand who is doing the assuming. The Inner Man that *precedes* all states. This understanding is the difference between shame and renewal, between punishment and forgiveness, between being trapped and finding freedom in your imagination. When you realize you are not the state, you realize you can never be damaged by a state. No matter what state you have given life to in the past, you remain untouched, unchanged, free to choose again.

You must completely let go to what you no longer wish to express, which is a true act of surrender. You can do this. It is not beyond your power because *you* are the power that gives life to states. The only thing keeping you bound to an old state is your continued animation of it through attention and identification. Merge with the new idea, while letting go to the old one.

Practice this art daily with others in your world. Imagine the best for your neighbor. See them glowing and radiant. Place *no* conditions on this vision. See them that way without justification or reason, a truly loving, unconditional act. Doing this for others makes it easier to do for yourself because it trains you to animate states without asking "why" or "how" or "do they deserve it?" You simply *see* them as you wish them to be, and in doing so, you practice the art of pure assumption.

The reason practicing with others makes it easier to do for yourself is because when you imagine for another, you have no personal resistance, no questions about worthiness, no concern about "how" it will happen. You simply see them as you wish them to be, and this pure act of imagination is uncontaminated by doubt. When you bring this same simplicity to imagining for yourself, when you see yourself as you wish to be with the same unconditional acceptance you give to others, you discover the true power of assumption. You realize that the only thing standing between you and any state is your willingness to occupy it fully, without question, without condition, *now.*

> *"It depends on the acceptance, the state with which we are identified, how things present themselves. In the fusion of imagination and states is to be found the shaping of the world as it seems. The world is a revelation of the states with which imagination is fused. It is the state from which we think that determines the objective world in which we live. The rich man, the poor man, the good man, the thief are what they are by virtue of the states from which they view the world. On the distinction between these states depends the distinction between the worlds of these men. Individually so different is this same world. It is not the actions and behaviour of the good man that should be matched but his point of view.* ***Outer reforms are useless if the inner state is not changed****. Success is gained not by imitating the outer actions of the successful but by right inner actions and inner talking. If we detach ourselves from a state, and we may at any moment, the conditions and circumstances to which that union gave being vanish."* - ***Neville***

I call this way of imagining "Reasonless Imaginal Acts." You might say, "But I once did this or that," or "I was treated wrongly in my past," or "I am afraid of my future." This is all understandable, but what do you want? Do you want freedom? Peace in your body? Love? To stop fearing life? The counterpart to your current state exists within you, though dormant.

You may have countless reasons why you feel you must remain in a state of being unloved. But I tell you, if you want to be loved, you no longer need to cling to feelings of being unloved. You do not need to reason your way into being loved. There are no physical acts you must perform first to accept this new state! It can be given unconditionally because imagination does not hold anything against you, for it is merely a state, and you are *not* a state.

The beauty of this approach is that it removes the burden of justification entirely. You are not required to prove yourself worthy of the state you wish to occupy. You are not asked to compile evidence of past good behavior or future promises. The state simply *is*, waiting to be occupied, and you, the Inner Man, have the authority to occupy it at will. This is what makes imagination unconditional, reasonless: it does not discriminate based on your history, your circumstances, or your perceived limitations.

Imagination is forgiving because thoughts and feelings create your world, and imagination places *no* conditions on any thought or feeling. It does not ask you why you think you deserve love. It does not require proof that you are worthy of peace. It does not demand that you first resolve every mistake or fear before you can assume a new state. Imagination is unconditional, reasonless by nature because it is not bound by the logic of the outer-world. It operates by a different law: the law of assumption. Whatever you assume in imagination, you *are*. And because you are *not* a state, you are the Inner Man, the animating power behind all states, you are free to choose which state to occupy at any moment, regardless of your reasons or lack thereof.

> *"He holds success in store for the upright, he is a shield to those whose walk is blameless."* - ***Proverbs 2:7***

The "He" is your imagination. If you assume you are blameless, your imagination, will become a shield for you. Who can punish a man who is blameless? Assume you are upright, and success will be in store for you.

When you assume blamelessness, you are not denying past actions or pretending mistakes never occurred. You are choosing to identify with a state that does not carry the weight of condemnation. The outer-world may remember what you did, but imagination does not bind you to any past version of yourself unless you continue to animate that old state with your sense of I AM. The moment you withdraw your awareness from the state of being guilty or flawed and place it into the state of being blameless, free you have performed the only act that matters. You have changed who you are being in imagination, and imagination is the only reality.

> ***"Do it effortlessly. You don't burst a blood vessel to do it, you do it in faith. Well, you're patient, you can wait. If they're anxious, you won't be anxious with them. You're patient, you heard it, you've seen it clearly, and now you go in confidence that it's done. So you rest in confidence that it's done.*** *So here, your faith, if you believe it, is justified not by any argument in the world but by an experience. Let them come and argue. As someone said, "You ministers are making a frightful mistake. In your pulpits you're arguing for Christianity and no one wants to hear your arguments. Does this thing work? Well then, share it with the rest of us." You can get in that pulpit and argue forever. So you are telling me what you believe and you make a confession of faith, and you confess to me what you believe. I'm not interested. Tell me why you believe it."* - ***Neville***

Listen closely: *if they are anxious, you will not be*. Why? Because you, the Inner Man, have already seen the vision of the accomplished work. It is a vision, unseen by the mortal eye, invisible to the senses, but to you, it is real. You became a witness to yourself in imagination. You stood in the reality of the wish-fulfilled, and from that moment forward, you live from that conviction, regardless of the thoughts and emotions swirling around you.

The wish-fulfilled is not found in listening to the voices of everyone around you. It is found in the voices of adversity. When you stay true to what you have imagined, true to how you see yourself, and you live from internal conviction rather than external validation, you cannot help but become it. And so while the voices on the outside may be arranged in a certain fashion that makes you doubt and stumble, you realize the wish-fulfilled is independent of external arrangements.

So when others panic, when they doubt, when they question, *you remain unmoved*. Not because you are ignoring them, but because you are anchored in a different reality. You have already witnessed the accomplished fact in your imagination. To you, it is done. And because it is done within, it *must* appear without.

You do not follow everyone's thoughts, do you? Of course not. You do not adopt every opinion, every belief, every assumption that crosses your path. You discern. You choose what thoughts to accept as true. So why, then, would you follow everyone's emotions? Why would you allow the anxiety, fear, or doubt of another to dictate your inner state?

Emotions are not commands. They are not facts. They are *reactions,* temporary conditions that arise from assumptions. When someone is anxious, they are simply occupying the state of anxiety. That state has a particular feeling-tone, and they are identified with it in that moment. But you are not required to enter that state with them. You are free to choose differently.

The Inner Man does not react automatically to external conditions. The Inner Man *selects and see's through conditions*. They choose which state to occupy, which feeling to assume, which conviction to live from. This is freedom. This is creative power. This is why, when you have seen the vision of the wish-fulfilled, you can remain calm while others panic, not because you are detached or indifferent, but because you are *anchored in a different assumption*.

They might not understand. They may look at you and wonder why you are not afraid. But you hold firm in yourself, because you know something they do not yet see: *feeling is the reality*. What you feel to be true in imagination is more real than what the senses dictate.

Let give a practical example: say you want to imagine success for a friend.

You see them unsuccessful in your day to day but you imagine inside yourself them *expressing* success. Remember, it is present tense. They are *expressing*, not trying to one day express, no. In imagination, there is no "one day." You see them present tense expressing success! Zero conditions or reasons. A complete reasonless imaginal act for them.

But suppose you see them the following day they call you about their failures, what do you do? On the outside, you may express to them empathy but what do you on the inside? Do you take this image of their failure within and accept it? What you do is you keep holding onto the initial reasonless image you created of them. You continue seeing them *expressing* success. Do you have imagine it all day? No, not exactly for you will have to imagine other things in your day. However, say your friend comes into your imagination during the day, all you have to do is maintain the image. Do nothing but just keep seeing them *expressing (present tense)* success without condition or reason.

Are you maintaining the image of them being successful, even when you doubt? You do not have to do it over and over, it is more that you hold the image. You do it once and trust in that inner work that you did. When they appear in your imagination again, you hold the same image, you see the completed work, not to redo the work. You set it in motion; the work is already done inside. You did it the moment you saw them *expressing* their success. It is not about how many times you do it, but to trust in the work you have done. Do you trust your inner work? You see them as that, then hold that. You can repeat if you wish but it is more about letting it develop and if they come expressing the opposite you simply see the work you have done inside.

I do not have to repeat it over and over. Until I feel the reality of it, I do not have to repeat it. Why? Well, if I am mimicking the flesh inside myself, and say you told me some good news in person, would it not be rude for me to keep having you repeat yourself? Maybe I missed what you said and ask you to clarify, but to have you do it over and over after I heard you? That would come across rude. So no, the moment I feel the reality, I feel that I actually heard it, I do not repeat it. I trust what was said the same way I would trust it if you told me externally.

When you practice unconditional imagining for others, you naturally bypass all the mental obstacles that you place on yourself. You see your friend as successful without requiring them to first overcome their flaws or past mistakes. You do not think, "Well, they need to work harder first," or "They do not deserve it yet." You simply see them *expressing* success, and in that act of seeing, you give it to them freely in imagination. This is the purest form of assumption, uncomplicated by judgment, uncorrupted by doubt.

Now apply this same unconditional acceptance to yourself. When you want to be loved, peaceful, or successful, you do not need to audit your past to see if you have earned it. You do not need to create a plan for how it will come about. You simply occupy the state of being loved, peaceful, or successful *now*, in imagination, with the same ease and freedom you gave to your friend. This is unconditional imagining. It is giving yourself permission to *be* what you desire, not because you have justified it, but because imagination itself places no restrictions on what you can assume.

Complete, reasonless, unconditional acceptance of the wish-fulfilled relieves the mental knots of resistance and ushers in a wave of fulfilled bliss. None of this is happening outside of you. It all happens within you, in your own imagination.

> *"You want it, but you condition it. Everyone wants something, but they condition it.* ***They feel they have to lose something, or do something, to get what they want. They don't. They feel there is a catch. There isn't.*** *They have to think of a logical way of getting something, instead of going straight to the end and occupying the state of the wish fulfilled. Don't worry about the how, only the what. But never condition it. Anything is possible, beyond your reasonable comprehension."* - ***Neville***

**Artwork Commentary:**

Here we see a man surrounded by walls, yet above him, clouds drift freely and a castle rises in the distance. Before him is an orb of light, the symbol of his imagination. Though trapped with no visible escape, he chooses to focus intently on this sphere. He decides to imagine beyond his circumstances.

Despite nothing in his physical reality offering freedom or hope, he decides to believe anyway. Where a ceiling should be, creating another barrier, he imagines beyond it and perceives the clouds. Through the power of his intention, he sees through what confines him.

These walls are merely representations of the limiting beliefs he holds about himself. They are not made of stone or iron, but of thoughts, fears, and self-imposed restrictions. The architecture of his prison exists entirely within his own imagination.

The true insight is that the only room he is genuinely enclosed in consists of the ideas and contents within his own imagination. The boundaries of his inner world are determined by his ideas of himself. When he looks at those walls and sees them for what they truly are, projections of his own limiting ideas, they lose their solidity.

So the walls we must see through are the ones we have constructed inside ourselves. We have built them brick by brick with every doubtful thought, every fearful assumption, every moment we chose limitation over possibility. They feel real because we have made them real through by feeling them to be solid and real.

We are all this man, enclosed within invisible barriers. But like him, we possess the power to see through our entrapment. The orb before us, our imagination, is not just a tool for escape, but the instrument of our liberation. When we focus our attention on what lies beyond our perceived limitations, when we imagine with conviction despite contradictory evidence, we begin to dissolve the walls themselves. The act of seeing through them is what makes them transparent, and ultimately, what makes them disappear.

# Change The Feeling Of "I"

> *"And so we start with the "I". Most of us are totally unaware of the self that we really cherish. We have never taken one good look at the Self, so we don't know this Self, for the "I" has neither face, form nor figure, but it does mold itself into structure by all that it consents to, all that it believes, and few of us know really what we do believe. We have no idea of the unnumbered superstitions and prejudices that go to mold this inner, formless "I" into a form which is then projected as a man's environment, as the conditions of life...*
>
> *And now, how do we go about changing the "I". First of all, we must discover the "I" and we do this by an uncritical observation of Self. This will reveal a Self that will shock you. You will be altogether, I wouldn't say afraid, but ashamed to admit you've ever known such a lowly creature. And had it been God Himself who drew near in this despicable form, you would have denied him a thousand times before a single cock would crow. You couldn't believe that this is the Self that you've carried around and protected and excused and justified. Then you start changing this Self after, by an uncritical observation, you make the discovery of that Self.* ***For the acceptance of Self is the essence of the moral problem of the world****. It is the epitome of a true outlook on life, for it is the sole cause of everything you observe.*
>
> *Your description of the world is a confession of the self that you do not know. You describe another, you describe society, you describe anything, and your description of the thing you observe reveals to one who knows this law the being you really are.* ***So you must first accept that self. When that self is accepted, then you can start to change." - Neville***

WHEN YOU LIMIT THE "I" to only what your senses dictate, you create an invisible barrier that creates resistance to transformation. If you believe the "I" is imprisoned by past events, change becomes a struggle against memory rather than a simple shift in imagination. If you confine the "I" to your current state of consciousness, you cannot conceive of inhabiting a different state, for you have made your present limitations the boundary of your being.

When you believe the "I" is shaped irreversibly by childhood experiences, you resist the present moment's power to redefine you. If you believe the "I" is destined for catastrophe, you cannot genuinely feel the reality of something wonderful, for you have already predetermined your trajectory.

If you believe the "I" is bound by habits, you will resist repenting *(radically changing the imagination).* If you limit the "I" to shame, you cannot enter states of dignity and worth. If you limit the "I" to the beliefs of those around you, you become a prisoner of consensus reality, unable to imagine beyond the collective's limitations.

If you limit the "I" to a particular ideology or 'ism,' you struggle to recognize the God within, for you have replaced the infinite with a system. If you believe the "I" cannot be saved, forgiven, or loved, you reject the very gifts that would transform you.

If you limit the "I" to only what reason and the senses dictate, you cannot transcend the evidence of the outer-world. If you believe in anything other than God as the foundation of the "I," you have imposed a false limitation upon your own being.

Understanding what the "I" truly is becomes essential. The "I" is not your circumstances, not your history, not your body, not your thoughts about yourself. The "I" is the Being inside, the fundamental core, the essence and the experiencer. The "I" is what remains when you strip away every label, every story, every limitation you have accepted.

This "I" *creates* reasons rather than being bound by them. This "I" *enters* into states and exits from them, moving through imagination like a traveler through different cities. But here is where most people become confused: they identify the "I" with the state they currently occupy. They say, "I am poor," "I am lonely," "I am sick," as if these states define the essence of what they are. This confusion makes transformation impossible, for if you are the state, how can you leave it?

You must separate the "I" from the state. The "I" is the occupant, not the dwelling. The "I" is the actor, not the role. When you realize this distinction, you understand that there is only One "I" in this world playing all the parts. This "I" of Man is the Inner Man, who is God. And God calls us to use Him as a creative power. This is why Neville said, "None to change but Self." You are not changing the outer-world directly; you are changing the "I", the imagining being within, and the outer-world rearranges itself to reflect that inner change.

The "I" is made of all imagination. Not partially of imagination and partially of something else, but entirely, completely, wholly of imagination. This is not metaphor or poetry; this is the fundamental structure of imagination. Every feeling you have about yourself, every belief you hold, every state you occupy, all of it exists within imagination. Therefore, any change must occur within imagination. You cannot change the "I" by changing external circumstances, because external circumstances are merely the out-picturing of the "I." You change the "I" first, in imagination, and then the external follows as effect follows cause.

When you truly grasp that the "I" is made of imagination, you realize why physical effort cannot transform you. Physical effort operates in the world of effects. But the "I" dwells in the world of causes, in imagination itself. This is why changing the feeling of "I" is an imaginal act, not a physical one. You do not change who you are by doing different things; you do different things because you have changed who you are in imagination. The doing flows from the being, and the being is established in imagination alone.

> *"For the changing of the feeling of "I" results in the change of reaction, which change of reaction results in a change of world. If you like your world and you are complacent about it, you haven't started on the road of the mysteries, for the very first beatitude appeals to one who is not complacent. "Blessed are the poor in spirit". You must be poor in spirit, not complacent, not satisfied. The man who thinks that by reason of birth, the religion that he inherited at birth, is good enough for me, that he is not dissatisfied, he is not, I would say moved that being is complacent and therefore he is not poor in spirit;*

*he is very rich in spirit. Theirs is not the kingdom of God.* ***For if I could stir you, make you dissatisfied with self, then you will recognize that self and set about to change it.*** *For the only field of activity for man is within himself and on himself. You do not work on the other. The day you change self, that day you change your world."* - ***Neville***

Dissatisfied with what Self? Not merely the outer shell, the surface circumstances, the visible conditions of your life. Neville is speaking of something far deeper which is being dissatisfied with the conceptions you have attached to the Inner Self, the "I" that dwells in imagination. This dissatisfaction is not about your job, your relationships, or your possessions, it is about the feeling of "I" itself, the state of consciousness you currently inhabit.

The dissatisfaction Neville speaks of is an inner recognition that you have accepted limitations upon the "I" that are not true. You have bound yourself to states of lack, unworthiness, fear, or limitation, and these self-imposed boundaries have become so familiar that you mistake them for reality itself. This is what must disturb you, not just the external conditions, but the realization that you have been dwelling in a state unworthiness.

Remember, transformation occurs within. We change who we are in that inner world of imagination and sustain that change inside ourselves. This game is not just physical but psychological. Persistent assumption, consistently being, living, and loving a new habitation for the Inner Man in imagination, creates changes in your outer-world. This change of "I" creates a change in your reactions, and this change in your reactions creates a change in your world.

*"But let me warn you now. A little alteration of mood is not a transformation; it's not a real change of consciousness. Because as I change my mood for the moment it can quickly and rapidly be I would say, replaced by another mood in the reverse direction. When I say that I was changed, as that gentleman changed his mood, his basic mood,*

*his* ***state of consciousness, it means that having assumed that I am what the moment denied, what my reason denied, that I remain in that state long enough to make that state stable****. So that all of my energies are flowing from that state. I am no longer thinking of that state. I am thinking from that state. So that wherever a state grows so stable as to definitely expel all of its rivals, then that central, habitual state of consciousness from which I think defines my character and is really a true transformation or change of consciousness. Whenever I reach that state of stability, watch my world mold itself then in harmony with this inner change. And men will come into my world, people will come to aid and they will think they are initiating the urge to help. They are playing only their part. They must do what they do because I have done what I did. Having moved from one state into the other. I have altered my relationship relative to the world round about, and that changed relationship compels a change in behavior relative to my world. So they have to act differently toward me." -* ***Neville***

There are certain moods that I often return to during my day, weeks or year. Years can go by and yet, I remain in the same state of consciousness or the same feeling of "I."

So how do I truly apply this? Well, I change what I am aware of being, my feeling of "I". I start with myself and leave the world exactly as it is. If I do not do this part, if I do not release my grip on it, I will want try to change the outer-world. My urge will be too strong, and I will eventually attempt to force external changes immediately. This might work for an hour or a few days, but like a stretched rubberband suddenly released, everything will snap back to my previous habitual state. Out of frustration, I might try harder and achieve change for a month or even a year. Even though I am not truly satisfied, I may settle for this forced change. Yet inevitably, everything returns to its original shape.

Simply rearranging my physical furniture is not enough! Why? Because I have not changed myself. I am the one reverting to my previous state. I have not truly packed my luggage and moved in imagination. In a sense, I am physically in a new country while mentally imagining the old country I left. Why do I go back? *Self-persuasion.* Without realizing it, I become persuaded of the old patterns again, the old state of consciousness. I may have unconsciously convinced myself that I am not what I, the Inner Man, just changed into but exactly what I was before. If I am not careful, I may not realize this self-persuasion until weeks later. But not all hope is lost, for nothing in this world or any other can stop you, the Inner Man, from deliberately and consciously moving into a new state of inside of imagination. This capacity to change states is your (*the Inner Man*) inheritance that no circumstance can ever remove from you.

When changes occur in imagination, they have occurred in you. When we change inside, we typically find it effortless, because the Inner Man *never* has to struggle to move within imagination. The real struggle for the Inner Man is not movement but remaining faithful that the inner movement. Thinking it was too simple, Man reverts back to their own pattern not seeing that pattern too was once created the same way. It was done all by sustained faith in it. So the struggle within is *not* movement but remaining faithful to that new, effortless change in imagination.

So never allow others to make you feel small within your imagination, you are not small there. Instead, you are the author of size itself. If you dislike what you see in your imagination, if you feel small inside and see only giants, understand that these giants need not be changed. They will remain giants not because they truly are, but because you have made yourself, your feeling of "I", small. Do you see the difference? Many attempt to reformulate thoughts without recognizing they stem from the thinker. The thought and its thinker are one. However, thoughts reveal rather than oppress. To change what you see inside, leave those frightening thoughts alone and instead change your feeling of "I." For only grasshoppers see giants. Change not the giants but you, the grasshopper, to transform what you see.

When you feel powerless in imagination, the world appears

filled with forces beyond your control and power. But this is a great deception. The Inner Man of Imagination, your *Real Self*, is never actually powerless. This feeling of powerlessness is itself an assumed state, a costume you have temporarily donned.

> *"Now, how will I know that I have changed the feeling of "I"? By beginning first with an uncritical observation of my reactions to life and then noticing my reactions when I think I am identified with my choice. If I assume that I am the man that I want to be, let me observe my reactions. If they are as they were, I have not identified myself with my choice, for my reactions are automatic and so if I am changed I would automatically change my reactions to life.* ***So the changing of the feeling of "I" results in a change of reaction, which change of reaction is a change of environment and behavior." - Neville***

We often carelessly claim to be various things and hold onto self-concepts we do not want, yet we must express them. This is inevitable because Man is expressor of mental states. You must express whatsoever state you feeling to be true about you because you are the agent through which mental states express. So do not take this expressive power, your I AM, in vain.

When I enter imagination, I find myself in a place completely different from my physical location. I did not struggle to get there. Speaking as the Inner Man, my *Real Self,* I simply arrived there effortlessly. Unlike the outer-man who must physically struggle and open doors to move around, my Inner Self faces no such barriers. In imagination, the moment I (*the Inner Man*) decide to be something, I become it instantly.

This is not from my outer-man's perspective. The outer-man protests, "But you are not that! Look with your organs! Look around!" But I must set aside this perspective and see through the eyes of the Inner Man. Through these inner eyes, I witness myself expressing something new and desirable. This Inner Man is also "I AM," and that is God. When someone asks my name, I respond, "I am Edward." When you ask your Inner Man, "Who is hearing the fulfillment?" The answer is the same: "I am." Do you see it? There is only one "I" in you and in me. Therefore, to change anything, I leave the external world alone and focus solely on changing the "I."

You may argue or congratulate someone in your imagination. You put words in their mouth and you reply. All of this happening within you. But who is hearing it? Who is seeing it? Naturally Man says, "Well, nobody is seeing it or hearing it, but I am." Who is I AM? God! So when you catch yourself arguing, congratulating or any interaction, at the moment you have caught God creating! So who is doing the seeing and hearing? "I am." That is God. So it is God who sees it and hears it. But is that not me and is that not you? Of course. So what Neville is telling us is that the core of our being is God.

> *"So you and I can be anything in this world we desire to be if we will clearly define our aim in life and constantly occupy that aim. It must be habitual.* ***The concept we hold of self that is noble must not be put on just for a moment and taken off when we leave this church. We feel free here; we feel that we have something in common, that's why we are here, but are we going to wear the noble concept we now hold of self when we go through the door and enter that bus, or are we going to return to the restrictions that were ours prior to coming here?*** *The choice is ours and the hardest lesson to learn is that there is no one in this world that can be drawn into your world unless you, and you alone, call him.*
>
> *So do not do what they did thousands of years ago, for that is the beginning of the secession of the great truth. So we are told they turned away from it, never again to walk with it, and the few who remained didn't like it either, but where would they go if this is the word of eternal truth? Not that it's true for this day and age, but if this is the law of being, and in all the dimensions of my being it holds good, if this is eternally true, then let me learn the lesson now, though I wrestle with myself as he did for three years.*

*So, the changing of the feeling of "I" is a selective thing because unnumbered states are infinite states, but the "I" is not the state. The "I" believes itself to be the state when it enters and fuses with it, so he was presented with a state and without the faculty of discrimination in his youth, he fused with the state and believed these restrictions were true, and it took him three years to disentangle the "I" from these fixed ideas with which he had lived for so many years. Now you may take only a moment or you, too, may take your three years. I can't tell you how long it's going to take you but I'll tell you this much. It can be measured by the feeling of naturalness. You can wear a feeling until it's natural. The moment the feeling becomes natural, it will begin to bear fruit within your world."* - ***Neville***

**Artwork Commentary:**

The internal houses in the imagination of this man represent the feeling of "I," the sense of self we all inhabit. We do not just live in physical homes; we also dwell in psychological ones. This mental home is not constructed from bricks and mortar. Instead, its foundation is built from conviction, the beliefs we hold about ourselves and our place in the world.

Just as we can physically move from one house to another, relocating to different cities or states, we can do the same mentally. We can shift from one state of consciousness to another, from one version of ourselves to a new one.

However, in the mental realm, things are far more fluid. They lack the concrete solidity of physical structures. The only way to make them solid is through feeling, by fully experiencing and accepting them as real.

When we discover a new feeling of "I," a new mental home, we must genuinely feel that we have moved in. We must allow ourselves to settle in and become comfortable living there, just as we would in any new physical residence.

You may have inhabited one mental home for years, even

decades. The walls became familiar, the rooms comfortable. But now you feel a stirring, an urge to move, to leave behind what no longer serves you. The new home you are moving into will feel unfamiliar at first. It may seem strange or uncomfortable simply because it is new. But this discomfort is not a sign that you have made a mistake or you do not belong. Over time, as you persist in dwelling there, this new mental home will become just as comfortable and familiar as the old one once was. The key is to remain patient with yourself during this change in feeling of "I."

# Signs Follow, They Do Not Precede

*"So you tell a man I'll show you how to try to prove it...and you see what isn't there to be seen, and you look at it, it isn't there, but in your Imagination you can see it.* ***And you persuade yourself of the reality of what you're seeing in your Imagination, and to the degree that you are self-persuaded of the reality of what you are imagining it will take on an objective form.*** *Well, it may take it on in twenty-four hours or two years if you really believe in the reality of what you are imagining. Well, when it takes on that objective form and becomes an objective fact, between your imaginal act and the objective fact so many things happen that seem to you outside of yourself and so natural and so real that it's outside, you can't relate it to your imaginal act. And so, you deny your own harvest. You can't believe that what you're doing there, what you now see on the outside, is in any way related to what you did on the inside. Yet all ends run true to origins, and you and I today are bearing the fruit of some forgotten blossom time. We don't remember it."* - ***Neville***

THE INNER MAN does not work on facts, but with *persuasion*. Why do we seek to feel the reality of what we imagine? What are we doing this for? We are trying to convince ourselves that we already possess or have fulfilled what we believe we lack.

The way I have found the best to become self-persuaded is to identify with the Inner Man of imagination. See life through their eyes as if they are your very own eyes, which they are. Accept what you are hearing with their ears. *Feel them to be real.*

The first step is to release the outer-man completely and embrace being the Inner Man. Make this Inner Man your only reality by assuming you are them. This I have found to be the most effective approach. To assume you are the being inside who both hears and sees in imagination. This method of self-persuasion works best because you are no longer desperately trying to convince yourself/another, or engaging in empty repetitions.

*"Now this is the Inner Man and the Inner Man has powers beyond the wildest dream of anything on earth." - **Neville***

Never let anyone come in the way of changing your feeling of "I" because the obstacle that presents itself, that stops you, is an illusion. It must be, because *nothing* can stop the Inner Man from imagining nothing.

Once you identify with the Inner Man, accepting what you imagine becomes natural. After this acceptance, you may notice a change in mood, maybe you are feeling more elated or free. This change in mood is a sign that you have moved to a new state, and remember: *signs follow, they do not precede*. Any actions you take will then flow automatically from this new state. All you need to do is trust what you have accomplished internally. And what did you, the Inner Man, do? You moved to a new position within your imagination. Now trust in that work, and it will, in its own strange way, come into your world.

So never try to devise the means by which your desire will come into your world. Your goal is to become self-persuaded of the reality of what you imagine. As you begin identifying with the Inner Man, assuming a new state and trusting in it becomes increasingly natural. This is the essential nature of the Inner Man, to move internally and have complete faith in that new position. You accept it all entirely on blind faith that you are what the Inner Man is.

Do you see the importance of the statement Neville made, "*signs follow, they do not precede*"? For Man will try to open their eyes *(organs)* and try to find the movement. They seek and seek and seek, aimlessly looking outside for their signs. Not seeing that the change in imagination is what makes signs follow. So then the focus solely becomes on imagination. The questions arise, "Am I where I want to be in imagination?" So when you start to see changes in your world, that means you have successfully moved inside. Just continue in trust that the Inner Man will keep expressing it. The first change always is a change in the feeling of "I".

> *"Now, others may not believe, but you don't have to appeal to anyone in this world. God sees the heart. Man sees the outward appearance of a man, but God sees the heart.* ***You can't lie; you can't fool the inner man. When you lie you know you've lied. When you make a claim you know it****, and that's God who knows that you lie, so you can't lie."* - ***Neville***

So there is nothing to seek on the outside. For the outside *follows* changes in consciousness, not precedes it. There is not be something that will happen first before you move into a state. So do not wait to changes outside of you, to move on the inside. This shifts our focus entirely to imagination. The question becomes, "What state of imagination am in? What is my feeling of "I"?"

The outside changes will never come before inner persuasion/conviction. The "signs" (*actions, changes in your world, validating conversations, opportunities that appear, proof*) are the *effects* of changing imagination, they are not the cause.

Most people are seeking outwardly for validation first because they move inside of imagination. Ever seeking validation/confirmation but never finding it in their world for they are not imagining it in their inner world. They seek signs rather than their own inner conviction. They are trying, in a sense, to run away from their state in hopes something outside of them tells them the opposite. However, this running away will be done in vain for they will never accept truly what they desire to be if their feeling of "I" contradicts it.

So Neville says to reverse the order. Without any proof, no proof whatsoever, you assume a new feeling of "I"! You must understand the Inner Man needs no external validation or proof to dream anything! You do not need to know the right people. You do not need more knowledge. You do not need to have everything in order. You only need your faith. Your faith in what? In the change of feeling of "I". You change that feeling and have complete faith that you that. What is faith? Faith is the assurance of things imagined. So you imagined a new idea of Self, do you have faith in this unseen you?

If you are waiting for signs to appear before changing the feeling of "I", you will remain stuck in imagination. For the world echoes was we yell inside. It shouts the we whisper within. It tells us, who we are claiming to be. However when you change the feeling "I" to something desirable, when you *feel* yourself to be it, the world, filled with signs, will follow. The signs come *after* the inner claim, not before. So you can start from scratch without anything in the world but a new assumption of Self.

If you assume you are and then find yourself being shown the opposite. Do not become discouraged. Remember, it is a change in imagination that results in a change in your world. The world is not causative. So the way you fight the world is through persistence. Persistence is not giving upon on the assumption, the new feeling of "I". Signs are not something you manufacture or devise the means of. The appear to you and simply come based on that state.

> *"But you can build exactly what you want. You want wealth? You can build it. You want health? You can build it. You want to be known? You want to fulfill a great ambition to be someone important in the eyes of others? You could have it if you are willing to assume that you are already such a person, and in spite of the evidence of your senses and your reason that contradict it, and if you walk and sleep in that assumption, it will harden into fact. But in the end, when it hardens into fact and you experience it and revel in it, it will turn to ash. You will depart and leave it behind you and the whole thing will collapse. For, it was brought into being by an imaginal act and it can only be sustained in being by an imaginal act. When that imaginal act is withdrawn or modified, it just collapses in your world."* - ***Neville***

The first step is to imagine being what you desire, not imagining that one day you might become it. For signs *follow*, so imagination must be the first step in change. Then you begin by imagining that you *already* are that thing in your inner world. This becomes your desire, and then you make it feel real through self-persuasion.

Once you have become convinced, even if only momentarily, you experience that feeling of conviction. You have persuaded yourself through this act of communion with yourself inside *(The true communion of life, not the symbolic wine and bread of Sunday services).*

After that self-persuasion, signs *follow*; they do not precede. You do not spot a sign and think, "This means I will become it someday." You would not see the sign unless you were already in that state. You do not manufacture these signs or deliberate force them. You do not devise the means or the signs themselves. They simply appear as a natural result of the change in your imagination. That is the truth.

***Question:*** *This evening you stressed inner talking, on other occasions you emphasized picturing with the inner eye, are both of these components necessary to...?*

***Answer:*** *"No, you can take one or the other, or take a combination. For instance, if I sit down to listen to a friend's voice, I not only hear his voice but I see him.* ***So that it helps if I can bring many senses to play, but any one will do it. But the more that I can bring, the more real it seems to me****. So I can take any of the five senses and bring them. There are certain fellows who have a certain touch. I can discriminate between the feeling in certain hands, or if I, say, the flesh of certain friends of mine who I would kiss. No two are alike, really, so you can discriminate between that sense of touch. All right, take as many as you can, but any one will do. But inner talking I find very effective. I spoke of it tonight because a friend of mine this past Sunday night at dinner asked me why don't I speak on inner talking, and I promised him I would. And so it's for him that I spoke tonight on inner talking. Only to have confirmation of it from another friend, not the one who heard the experience. It's another friend altogether who asked me to speak on inner talking, and then in that interval comes a friend (who's here tonight) who*

> *tells me his experience of inner talking. He went home and carried on these inner conversations where he is speaking to a large crowd. All things being relative, if the average crowd would be eighteen and sixty-four would come, that's an enormous increase. So he did have sixty-four, and then to get invitations from others.* ***So that was inner talking. I would say to anyone, because you can't stop talking anyway, observe carefully your inner talking. You carry on mental visions, but I mean this inner talking. You don't think of anyone in the course of a day but you're saying something, you're talking to them. Inwardly, you're saying...or if things aren't as they should be, you're justifying it****. That in itself is the acceptance of failure by justification. And so, if one could only observe what they're saying in the course of a day. Don't delay one second; the minute you become aware that it's not what it ought to be, stop it, and just put on a new record, and play the new record..."* - **Neville**

In response to a question about whether one should use inner talking, visualization, or both in imagination, Neville emphasizes, *"But the more that I can bring, the more* ***real*** *it seems to me."* This directly relates to self-persuasion. Neville incorporates multiple senses, hearing someone's voice, seeing them, feeling their touch, simply to enhance the feeling of reality. For Neville, feeling the reality of the imaginal act is paramount, as this approach works effectively for him.

In my experience, I have found that identifying with the one who is hearing, what I call the Inner Man, creates that sense of reality for me. Regardless of method, the objective remains the same: *Making imagination feel real.* You can either combine multiple senses to give dimension to your imaginal act, or identify yourself as the one experiencing it. Both techniques achieve the same purpose. If you are still afraid while imagining it, then you are not making it feel real to you. It is not about being afraid or feeling as if you are doing something wrong. It is about making it feel real to you. The great secret is that anything in imagination can be made to feel real to you. So why not imagine the most lovely things for yourself and others, and make them feel real?

*The idea that signs follow, they do not precede, is the difference between one who changes and one who remains the same.* This is not a small distinction. The one who waits for signs is a prisoner to signs. They are reactive, not creative. They scan the outer-world for permission to feel differently, to assume a new state, to believe in a new reality. And because they are waiting for external validation, they never move. They remain locked in the same state, perpetually seeking proof that has not yet appeared, because they have not yet assumed the state that would produce it.

So they wait and wait and wait for the stars to align, for circumstances to shift, for conditions to become favorable, *before* they allow themselves to move into a new state of Self. But this is the trap. The stars will never align for someone who has not first aligned themselves internally. You are not waiting for some universe to grant you permission. You are the operant power.

Signs are confirmations of states already occupied, not invitations to occupy them. If you wait for signs before you assume the state, you will wait forever, because the sign cannot appear until the state is first assumed.

Until you accept this you will wait for the stars, wait for the circumstances to change and you will bow before man made sculptures and gods for good luck.

> *"For, to the degree I am self-persuaded of what I'm imagining, to that degree the thing works. So the secret is how to imagine to the point of self-persuasion. Can I really believe it? Well, it's like having a being that's one being, not you and something, you aren't working on a piece of putty, you aren't molding it, you're working on yourself. You are actually adjusting yourself to what you want to see, and you'll not stop until you see exactly what you want to see, and then try to fix it. Well, you'll project it on the screen of space in this world that really passes away. But as long as you hold that fixed state within you, it keeps on perpetuating itself in the world. And the whole vast*

*world is yours for the taking if you want it, but there, too, the outer world of effects and the inner world of causation." -* ***Neville***

*You take a dream (state) within your imagination and then you make that state of imagination real to you.*

**Artwork Commentary:**

Without realizing it, Man can look at something and see something entirely different than their neighbor. And yet we are both looking at the exact same object. So what eye are we truly seeing with? Do these physical organs, called eyes, only see that which is in front of them, or do they see more? If they do see more, what eye is it that sees more?

In this artwork, we see a cubic reality. There are two eyes that represent the organs that only see the senses. We see a door that enters inward, which represents the entering of your imagination. And in the shadows, in the invisible side of this cubic reality, we see another eye, looking elsewhere. This inward eye sees all that we do inside ourselves.

We see a cloud that connects from the inside to the outside, and this represents the sign, the feeling that follows, it does not precede. What this inner eye perceives is connected to what you feel. And so what we acknowledge to be real within us, our feelings will flow from that perception, and it will decide what we see.

The physical eyes are merely instruments. They receive light, shapes, and colors. But the inner eye, the eye of imagination, has the power to see beyond and make a dream feel real. Two people can stand before the same painting, the same sunset, the same moment, and one sees beauty while the other sees emptiness. This is because the inner eye is shaped by what we have chosen to feel as real about ourselves.

Do not think there is anything wrong with you or your inner eyes. Your inner eyes see perfectly fine. What needs examination is what you have accepted as real within yourself about yourself. Because your feelings do not arise from nowhere, they flow from your inner perception, from what your imagination has deemed true. If you feel the world is hostile, you will see hostility everywhere. If you feel the world is abundant with meaning, you will discover it in the smallest details. The organs merely report; the inner eye decides what the report means. And that decision, that interpretation, is what shapes the reality you live in. Your feelings are the evidence of what your inner eye has chosen to see as real. So we feel a certain way, because we perceive ourselves a certain way.

# The Potter & The Clay

> *"So the great magician is the Father, the great alchemist, the great artist that is he. He'll take every misshaped concept of man and he'll work it for good. He doesn't discard the vessel, as we brought out last Monday night. "It was spoiled in the potter's hand, but he re-worked it into another vessel, as it seemed good to the potter to do" (Jer. 18:2). The word potter means "Imagination."* ***So he doesn't discard anyone in the world; he simply reshapes it****. But he allows us the freedom to continue in our ambition that will keep playing the part all over and over and over again, until one day from all the hard blows we think the whole thing is stupid, anyway. We really will believe it is a tale told by an idiot and I was the idiot telling it all the time, full of sound and fury, signifying nothing." -* ***Neville***

Just as explorers discover new lands, your imagination is a mental land waiting to be explored. When you go within to explore you may discover dark frightening caves, nightmarish dreams and disharmonious images. This mental land, remember is your throne, your temple. Throughout life we have collected beliefs, ism's, idols, devils etc. We become hoarders and reluctant to let these go. Our inner temple then becomes dirty and we lose sight of who we are. We are the Inner Man, yet we are bowing to false idols in our imagination *(time, reason, doubt).*

These false gods appear convincing because we have worshiped them for so long. Time tells us that change requires duration, that we must wait for circumstances to align. Reason insists that logic must explain the bridge between here and there before we can cross it. Doubt whispers that we are unworthy of the throne we ourselves have created. But these are merely states we have accepted as our masters when they should be our servants. The Inner Man exists beyond these limitations, limitless, unconditional, and fearless.

Similar to clay on a potter's wheel that becomes misshapen, your imagination might seem flawed. But do not discard it as something unworthy of redemption! Instead of abandoning it to seek answers in the illusions of leaders, priests, holy men, or false gods, rework your imagination into a new vessel. Mold and reshape it daily to conform to the images you love. Remember, never giving up on your imagination means never giving up on yourself, because *you and your imagination are one.*

> *"Now, it brings me to this. You sit down to change your world, you want something better than you have, and so you begin to conjure a certain scene that would imply the fulfillment of your dream. You begin to conjure it. The average person cannot control their mind long enough to go from A to B. If, for instance I assume that I am what reason denies and my senses deny, and at that very moment of assumption* ***I think of all the debts and what people know me to be...I take it off. That doesn't fit, it's like a tight shoe, it just doesn't fit me; so I take off the assumption. If I could only put on the assumption!*** *Now what's the next step? I assume that I am the one that I want to be. If it were true, my friends would know it. I wouldn't hide it from them. In fact, it should be so obvious if it were true that they should see it. Well, the next step, the B step, would be to bring them into my mind's eye and let them see me as they would see me were it true."-* ***Neville***

If only we could stop living in poverty in our imagination thinking we cannot afford states. The name of "I AM," our awareness of what were are being, is the price for all states and you have infinite coin. If people only knew who they were in their imagination. If they truly knew who they were within it, they would stop the feasting on spoiled foods. If a piece of food smells bad, you do not eat it. If a thought makes you feel bad, why do you accept it? When I tell you that everything within you is clay, and can be reworked into anything you please, you will let go of fear.

You want to stop being judged? Then enter into imagination and walk around feeling nobody in here can judge you. You experience it, that is what you do. Everywhere you go within your imagination you take with you the feelings you want. Realize, truly, I urge you to realize this: when you say to yourself, "I no longer want to feel judged." You have to see that the "I" in that statement is the

Inner Man speaking. Why? Because the desire is *within* you and the "I" is within you. Since the desire is within, and there must be an agent in order for there to be a desire, then who is this agent feeling this internal desire? The Inner Man.

We eat when we are hungry. We drink when we are thirsty. And if we are in desire, let us give ourselves fulfillment. If only we can see the our desires are *in us* then we can see that we need to fulfill them *in us*. Another way of phrasing this is realizing our fears are not "out there" but "in here," then we know where the fear must be neutralized. If we can see that one who is desiring is not this outer-man but this Inner Man, and this Inner Man lives in the World of Imagination where all things are possible, then the Inner Man can appropriate whatsoever he desires.

When you, the Inner Man, desire within, you are simply wanting a different experience. Everything is *already* finished in your imagination. Since this is the case, your desire is not there to "improve" you as though you lack something. No, you lack nothing in imagination. There are only experiences inside here and the ones you give the attention to is what starts to grow. If you knew who you were inside of your imagination, if you only knew were the potter, then you would stop feeling desperate inside. Desiring itself is natural and beautiful, but allowing desires to remain unfulfilled internally is what generates feelings of lack and desperation. Then the outward approach to controlling the world becomes attractive. Yet, like Sisyphus, you may appear to make progress only for your boulder to roll back to the beginning. And what is the beginning of change? The imagination. So you the potter, start to change the desires inside of you into fulfillment. Do not discard them as silly, but honor them by fulfilling them. You do this *not* on the outside but within. For remember, the desire is within you, not outside of you. And what is within, will be without for everything must be expressed even the undesirable. What is whispered inside gets shouted on the rooftops.

The potter is not interested in these doubts of "What if...?" The potter only interested in reshaping the clay into something beautiful, lovely. The imagination is this malleable clay and this clay always reveals the ends. It shows you the destination, not the journey. It shows you the blossoming flower, not how it grew. To personify the imagination, another way of saying it is that He provides the ends and you must trust him. The clay does not provide the middle, it shows you the end of you being what you desire, not how you got there. When it starts to express in your world, reason will come and reveal to you *how* it came into being, but reason was not the cause.

This is why imagination works primarily in the language of completion rather than process. It deals in finished states, not lukewarm changes. When your inner vision begins to materialize in your outer world, reason will eventually explain *how* it all unfolded, the "logical" sequence of events that bridged your former state to your present reality. But make no mistake: Reason merely explains the how *after* the fact in imagination; it was never the creative power that initiated the transformation. The true cause was always your assumption of the end, a completed idea of yourself.

> *"Now, what's the next step? Well, C...could they keep that secret? No, they would have to discuss it with friends. I would eavesdrop and listen to their discussion of the good fortune that befell me. And so I would listen... "Have you heard the good news?" one would say to the other. "You know what has happened to him? Who would have thought that he could ever get that?" Well, listen to it...then they tell a story.* ***I'm conjuring the whole thing, I know I am, but can I endow it with reality and not say it's a fantasy?*** *It's not an apparition, because not a person is before me, not a thing is before me, it's not an apparition. So, I would say it is fantasy, sheer fantasy, all conjured in my Imagination."* - ***Neville***

Neville is asking you to let go of feeling that you are only imagining it, that is only a fantasy. To try to accept the reality of what you just imagined. In order to truly experience the awareness of the Inner Man, you have to surrender everything. You surrender your concepts of time. You surrender what you think is possible. You surrender what labels you have put on yourself or what labels others have put on you. You surrender your physical location and your body. You surrender what happened just moments ago. You surrender what you think you are and are not worthy of. You surrender believing in outer-reality. You surrender every fear. You surrender everything for that is the price to changing oneself. All must be fully be dropped in order to fully accept the new reality within, knowing that when you accept this you will change and that change must automatically express.

Do not be ashamed to accept the Inner Man. You may conjure up an image of the Inner Man that is outstandingly beautiful, and you may think, "That is far too great for me to be." Then you have not fully surrendered, not fully died. To fully surrender you would be it. Every image you can conjure up of the Inner Man can be realized in you if you die to your old feeling of "I". Nothing is sabotaging you in this inner world for it cannot. It does not tempt you, but is merely reflecting you the "I AM," your current idea of self.

We cannot help but express or share to the world that is within us. So if we can only express what is within us then you can see how success lies in being exactly who we want to be in this inner reality as a present fact. We can express ideas and theories we have but the most important expression you hold is the concept of yourself. It is in this where your life will be tuned. Your self-concept is the song you sing to your world, and if you feel you are out of tune, then change your concept and your song will become harmonious.

Dying to the self-concept is where every doubt arises. Man can die to their concepts of time and space if they lose themselves in imagination. However, to die to their self-concept that they have held onto for so long, this is where all their doubts arise. It does not matter to people how limiting their self-concept may be, they find comfort in a routinely horrific inner life. If there is repetition, a routine to it, they would rather stick with that than die to their limited self-concept, if and only if, they do not see the benefit of dying to it. So this is why it is imperative that you create a self-image that is far lovelier than what you are now. Once you see the wonder and benefit of being this new self-concept you would feel genuinely grateful to die to your old self.

Ask yourself, whose ears are you willing to trust? The outer or Inner? Whose eyes are you willing to believe? The outer or Inner? Whose awareness are you willing immerse to yourself in? The outer or Inner? Rejuvenate yourself by accepting the Inner, where no lack lies. Reality can be reworked, changed and is fluid inside. Reality does not question the wrongness of the potter changing it. Reality does not question the worthiness of the potter who wants to change it. You are this potter. It is impersonal. Reality *(your inner world)* awaits upon to you make your own mark upon it by using the name of "I AM" beautifully. Never be ashamed of bearing this name nor changing it as clay.

> *"So man, if he can only control his Imagination between A and B, doesn't have to go to C, just from A to B. Take the first step: You assume the end. The end is where we begin: "In my end is my beginning." So I assume the end, I am the man that I want to be. And were it true, I would be known by my friends first, so I bring them into my mind's eye and they see me. I let them see me.* ***If I want to talk with them, accept their congratulations and not duck but really hold my head high and proud of what has happened to me; alright, accept the congratulations. And then I turn from that to the third step, and let them talk between themselves, and I'm listening. All of that is making it real to me****. And then I go on in my wonderful state that it is true. I begin to make plans of the things I would do and am going to do now. And then, in this simple little drama I now credit it, I give it reality... And so, we must test it, and test it by giving it reality. I try to give it all the tones of reality, all the sensory vividness that I can muster. And when I do it, it works."* - ***Neville***

If you created a throne in your imagination, is it not your right to sit upon it? If you do not sit upon it then who else will? If you created a state, an image of yourself that you would love to be, is it not your right to take it? If you do not take everything that you find lovely within yourself, then who else will?

So you must see that what you imagine is your right to take inside of you. Do not duck what you imagine, do not hide from it. Look at it and keep looking until you actually see the change in you.

**Artwork Commentary:**

In this surreal artwork, the water and ladder represent the person entering into their own imagination, a deliberate decision inward to explore new possibilities of Self.

The pot that sits atop the water is the vessel, the conception they have formed of themselves. It represents their current identity, the way they see and understand who they are in this moment. But the person is curious about a new idea, a new conception, a new pot. They sense there is more to discover, more to become.

The person does not discard everything and go to a different body of water. They do not break the pot that is sitting on top of the water either. There is no need for destruction. No, they go to look for a new conception of themselves, one that feels truer, more aligned, more alive.

And so they open one door and peek in and see an idea. They close it and choose a different door and see another idea. They close that door, open another, and see a different idea. This is the process of exploration in imagination: trying on different states, seeing what is fulfillment to you.

The first two conceptions are similar in nature to the one they already embody. It is not until they reach the last conception that they see blossoming flowers, a symbol of change and full expression.

That symbolizes that they hit their mark and found the door that shows them expressing the conception in fulfillment, while the others seem to be only partially expressing. The flowers represent the difference between merely existing as an idea and fully blooming into it.

This process is not always immediate. It might take some work to discover what idea you would love to hold about yourself, which ones stir within you feelings of peace and love. But if you keep opening doors, you keep peeking in, you will eventually find it.

The key is persistence and trust. Each door you open teaches you something. Each conception you try on reveals what you are not, or what you are only partially. And through this process of elimination and exploration, you arrive at the one that makes your heart open.

Imagination is not a passive place, it is the workshop of yourself. What you conceive there, what you commit to feeling and embodying there, begins to shape the clay of yourself. For what you seek in imagination, you will always become. And that is a promise. Imagination is faithful. It does not withhold. It reflects back to you exactly what you are willing to assume and feel as true about yourself. Every single door can be opened imagination.

Always remember, you are the potter, never the clay; the dreamer, never the dream. You are not *solely* molded by circumstances, nor are you *solely* confined to a single conception of yourself. You are the one who molds, the one who imagines, the one who chooses which door to open inside of you.

# The Art Of Dying & Rising

*"But man is afraid; he dare not so abandon himself to a dream, and so never "dies." -* ***Neville***

*"There must be someone in this room who will so completely transform himself in this world that his close immediate circle of friends will not recognize him." -* ***Neville***

I ONCE HAD an experience that changed my view on entering into the state. You see, I can give lip service to the idea that "You must feel yourself into your imaginal act," but unless I actually do it, then I should not speak. At the time, I thought I was doing it, and in some cases I did do it, but this experience showed me that I was not going deep enough. I saw how afraid I truly am in giving up my present limitations.

When you imagine and you do not feel "present" with your fulfilled desire it is because you have not died to your present conception, the limited conception of your Self.

Now this is what happened to me, how I died to a concept of myself: I began breathing deeply and noticed something unexpected. The deeper my breath became, the more my body shook. I felt that my breathing was not smooth. There was this turbulence in my breath. So I tried to make it smoother. What I realized was that if I accepted certain assumptions to myself such as: "There is nothing to do. I am allowed to feel relaxed. I am in control of my body. These wonderful feelings of relaxation are mine. I can take as much as I want." If I accepted these assumptions without reason, I found my breathing becoming deeper and smoother.

I also noticed that through my fast acceptance of these assumptions, *("fast" meaning I do not allow myself to reason with it, I did not force it, I just accepted it as true to me)* I am able to control my feelings. When I simply felt into these assumptions as already true, my feelings quickly aligned with them. I saw that I had complete control of my feelings and body if I simply assumed what I wanted was already true.

After developing this deep breathing, I began observing my thoughts. I noticed I often think things I do not want to think, or I have thoughts I want to explore but feel somehow prohibited from entertaining. I discovered I am afraid of truly experiencing certain feelings of relaxation, peace, pleasure, comfort, the feeling that there is nothing to worry about. Surprisingly, I resisted these feelings not because I dislike them, but precisely because I desire them! Inside myself, I have created a belief system that says I cannot allow myself to feel these wonderful feelings because something bad might happen if do. This system warns me that if I embrace good feelings, they will inevitably be taken away.

What I ultimately realized was that I feared experiencing the deepest and most wonderful feelings. I decided then to allow myself to feel them fully. These wonderful gifts inside belong to me, available whenever I choose. This decision initiated a profound relaxation within me.

Then I decided to truly let go of everything, knowing I will be fine and everything will be fine, my imagination became blank. It became almost like an empty void of blackness. From here, I felt that I truly let go of my current reality, even my current body and I am now existing in this void. I then realize I am still alive and I can do anything.

I decided to imagine a scene that I would love to experience. I imagined myself writing by a body of water. Something that felt wonderful to me. I noticed something different about being in this scene. I noticed that I did not take with me *any* of my present limiting state with me. When I was in my scene, I was not thinking about my past or my worries or fears. I was simply *experiencing* my scene just as though it is *the only truth.* That there was *no other truth.* All my thoughts were naturally *from* that scene. Meaning I saw the water beneath me. I saw my keyboard and I felt the keys. I felt the feelings of writing in this lovely space.

Then I decided to make it lovelier. I got rid of all shame in this reality. In this inner reality that I am in, I assumed there was no shame. I assumed all my love that I would show would be accepted. I got rid of all rejection. I assumed the feeling of complete security. I assumed I was completely and utterly loved and there nothing to hide, nothing to be afraid of. I was loved in full and accepted. I imagined others doing well and this moment was wonderful.

> ***"So I meet you on the street or I hear of you, so I meet you and you don't look well, or someone writes me and they tell me that you are not well, that's an impression. So thereafter if I think of you that impression comes into my mind's eye. I must learn the art of dying to that impression. I must bring you into my mind's eye and put you into an entirely different light and see you as I ought to see you were you the one that I would love you to be. When I am self-persuaded that you are that new impression, I have died to the other impression****. So every kindness on my part, every little kindness, is a little death in the Divine Image. That Divine Image is death...it must die and die all through love. For what is the Divine Image? Listen to it carefully as Blake defines it: "Mercy, pity, peace and love is God, our Father dear; and mercy, pity, peace and love is man his child and care.*
>
> *So was it a merciful thing to do? Yes, it was merciful. Prompted by pity? Yes. Was it done lovingly? Yes. And now am I at peace because of it? Yes. Then I fulfill the Divine Image—mercy, pity, peace and love. So, I took all these aspects of the Divine Image. It was merciful to do it; why leave him distressed when I could exercise this power? And so every time that man exercises this creative power of his lovingly, he is simply performing this little act of death. Every kindness to another is a little death in the Divine Image. This is called in scripture repentance. Repentance means "to become another person." Didn't I become another person? Because if I am made up of all of my impressions, all of my beliefs, and I believe you to be injured; and that injury need not be physical, in the sense that you are physically hurt, it could be that you are financially hurt. It could be that you are now being disgraced. It could be in a thousand ways. So if I believe this because here are the facts, I'm confronted with facts, I'm called upon to exercise my talent and put something in its place. Therefore, if I put something in its place, I've got to give up that*

> *impression that I hold of you.* ***Giving it up, if I am the sum total of all of my beliefs, in giving up any belief I die. I die by giving up any belief that I now entertain."* - Neville**

What I am going to say here, I believe is the most important concept when it comes to changing Self. Now I have spoken much on doing what you please in your mind, feeling what you please in your mind. I have spoken on creation being finished and how that can change your thinking and accepting. I have spoken on your Imagination being the one and only reality. But what I have not spoken about is, the art of dying to oneself.

From this experience, I've discovered that dying to your current self is the greatest thing you can do. You cannot inhabit the state you desire unless you die to your present state. What I said at the beginning remains true, if I merely speak about this without practicing it, I should not speak at all. Previously, I thought I was entering the state of my wish-fulfilled. Sometimes I did and felt different, but now I have found a method that works for me every time. It requires only my willingness to die to my current self.

> ***"Many people only age, but never change inwardly. They only mature physically, but they have not died in the mystical sense.*** *There is no transforming power in the physical death, and they will still be anchored in a larger world with all the trends of this world. To our senses they seem to be dead but they will still, on another plane, have to learn the art of dying. I can anywhere so completely detach myself from what is taking place that I can "die" to that state. So every little death is the lifting of the divine image. This means dying as the mystic means it. It means dying mentally. Man dies to ill health, or poverty, or to disharmony, etc., but he does it by yielding to the other states.*
>
> *Blake looks on all states as permanent, as in his great poem regarding the Halls of Los: "I curse the earth for man and made it permanent." So states remain and man passes through states, as though cities. If I do not pass through some state but remain in it, I*

*think [it] is the only reality. You cannot conceive of a state that is not, for the whole is finished; but man is awakening only by dying to state after state." -* ***Neville***

Again, you cannot be in one state and not suffer the consequences of being in another. If you wish to be loved, are you willing to die entirely to the state of being unloved? Here is what I do not mean when I say "die." I do not mean you repeat hundreds of affirmations that you are loved, or to repeat an imaginal scene hundreds of times before sleep to overcome the state of being unloved. No. I am speaking of something far simpler, far greater. I am asking you to die to it, to let it go. What does it mean to die to it? If you died to your present limited state, how can you take with you those worries, those fears, that limited thinking with you anywhere in your imagination? Those worries and fear no longer exist, they cease to be.

Here is the indicator on whether or not you have died to your present limiting state. Suppose you imagined a lovely image that you would love to experience. The more *real* your imagination it feels to you, the more you have died to your present limiting state. Conversely, the more *unreal* your imagination feels to you, the more you are holding onto your present limitations.

This is what I am asking: "Are you willing to die entirely to your present limited thinking and feeling and enter a new reality within yourself? Can you make this new reality feel real to you? Are you willing to let go of questioning whether it is possible or if you are worthy? Are you willing to abandon every limiting thought and feeling you have? Can you release these limitations and fully accept your desire?" If you can do this at will, you will control your thinking and feeling, which is your destiny. You are always destined to experience whatever you feel is real about yourself. These questions must be answered continuously throughout your life, not just once. They require your daily attention and response.

*"What does it mean? If I am poverty-ridden and frightened and then you meet me and see me as free as a bird and happy, then I am*

*not the man you knew who was frightened. Then where is that other man buried? For Moses is the power in man (generic man, male-female) to draw out of himself anything in this world he desires, and to so enact the drama that he dies to what he was, that he may live to what he is enacting...* ***I do not wait for signs to appear; it is when I am most aware of my restrictions and feel the pressures, then is when I must learn to die. I must learn to let go of what my senses dictate and "go mad" and yield to what is only a dream. But sustaining it and living in it, I die to what was physically real as I gradually lift up what was only the dream. You knew only the frightened man and not the other one. No one can tell where the other has gone.***

*So this is how the art of dying is dramatized in the Bible as the death of a man. But it has nothing to do with any certain man, for the story of the Bible takes place in the mind of every man." -* ***Neville***

Let me walk through an example. Imagine you want to hear someone tell you how brilliant you are. You want this because may have been feeling like a failure in life, and this feeling has caused suffering in your imagination. Remember, your first goal is not to force this praise into existence, but to relieve desire by *feeling the reality that your wish has already been granted.*

So you imagine this person telling you how brilliant you are. If you do not feel what you would feel if that person truly called you brilliant, if you have not *lost* yourself in that scene and fallen in love with it, it is because you are still holding onto your current limited state of "I am *(feel like)* a failure."

To truly feel the imaginary act of someone calling you brilliant, you must die to the feeling of being a failure. This means completely dropping the thoughts and feelings attached to that state and its expression in your current reality. This is not always easy, not because it is inherently difficult, but because we are often less willing to give up our limitations than we think. We find comfort in limitations because they provide a sense of predictability. Being brilliant involves stepping into the unknown, which may frightens us.

But when you are willing to face everything within yourself without fear, and you truly taste the reality of your wish being granted, you will find that this death to your old self is the best gift you can give yourself.

In this example, once the individual dies to being a failure, they approach the imaginal act with nothing but receptivity. There are no feelings or thoughts of failure in their imagination. Having died entirely to that state, they can now fully accept being called brilliant. They can feel it as their true reality, as if there is no other reality but the one they are experiencing in imagination.

There is no "overcoming" the feeling of failure. You do not overcome it because you have died to it completely. All that remains is accepting being called brilliant.

This process does not necessarily require hours of your time. You do not need to lie down and meditate to die to a feeling *(though this may help initially)*. Once you have practiced this art of dying, you can release any limiting feeling in an instant.

Imagine you are in a crowded place and suddenly feel insecure. Knowing the art of dying, you can completely release that feeling. You can let go *(detach)* of this limiting state *(any state, even the ones you find difficult letting go of)*, and immediately bring forth a new feeling. All you need to do is surrender that insecurity and fully embrace security. No justification needed. You do not need to go outward for permission.

> *"No man can be born in one environment and ever realize another if he does not yield to the state desired. So Blake was right: "The best thing in life is death but it takes man so long to die that his friends never see him rise from the grave."* ***Can you not see then how it is with your friend who always tells you the same things, even though you have not seen him for ten years? Everything is still recurring, nothing is new, but that makes him feel secure. Man does not want change; it frightens him.***
>
> *I tell you that your Imagination is God. Believe it. Exercise it. It is keyed low, but as you lift it up you intensify it and then vision*

> *after vision will be yours as you begin to awake. Do not think you are greedy because you are demanding things or the changing of things. You are here to create as your Father creates.* ***Want what you want and yield to it and create it. Then you will want higher and higher things****. But nothing blesses a man unless it comes down from its heavenly state and takes on flesh.* ***You are the only one who can clothe it in reality. But it remains a state unless you yield to it." - Neville***

Remember that every wonderful feeling, in this case, 'security' belongs to *you*. You deserve to fully experience these feelings. But to *truly* accept this new state, you must die to your current condition. Turn away mentally from what you do not want, abandon it, and fully embrace your fulfilled desire because you love this new state. *Lose* yourself in that new state *(new feeling of "I")* until you forget you are even imagining and experience the new change *now*. Do not wait for signs to appear or believe the passage of time will allow you to become what you wish. It is not by the passage of time do we become anything, but only by the appropriation of states in imagination.

I must stress this: *Do not be afraid of rising to higher levels Self.* Do not fear dying to your present conception. When you encounter a grand, great thought and trying to fully accept it in your imagination sparks fear, remember there is nothing to fear within your imagination. Nothing. You are *allowed* to die to your limitations and resurrect that wonderful new state within you. Not only are you allowed to, it is the most noble act you can do for yourself! You need no one's permission, nor must you consult anyone outside yourself to feel and do what you want in your imagination. The only reason you do not feel you are what you want to be is your refusal to die to your present state.

When I say "die to it," I mean that literally. You no longer associate your identity with the state you just left. This feeling of change will be specific to you, there is no single way to feel something. I give myself that feeling in my imagination without fear or hesitation. I allow myself the freedom to feel it fully and to die to my worries. I see myself doing and having what I would love to experience.

Even if a part of me wants to hold onto insecurity, worry, and stress, I allow myself the freedom to feel deeply what I want. I keep dying to these limitations until I resurrect within me the true feeling of my desire being completely fulfilled. "My desire being fulfilled" means I *actually* experience what I would experience if my desire was already fulfilled. To me, it is *not* a distant future but a current fact in my imagination. I imagine it in the here and now.

The moment I *lose* myself in that imaginal act or words that *imply* my desire is fulfilled, I have successfully died to my current limitation. I die to feeling ashamed and enter a reality where shame does not exist. I give love without shame and without fear of rejection. I feel the comfort of acceptance and the wonderful feeling of giving love freely, expecting nothing in return.

Can I truly enter a reality and feel there is no shame? Can I sustain that glorious feeling until I *lose* myself in it completely, until I forget I was ever ashamed? You cannot take your limiting past or your limiting present with you into your imaginal act that fulfills your desire. You must drop it completely, and there you will find bliss.

What would it be like to wake up in a reality where your past no longer has power over you, where it is completely forgotten? Can you die to your past and your present expression, and simply experience this wonderful reality as though it is the only one that exists? Can you give yourself entirely to it with feeling?

Do you fear a future event? Can you die to that fear and give yourself to your desired outcome instead? It is my imagination, and I am allowed to feel and do as I wish. I must die to what I do not want and assume I am what I want. I die to the feeling that I cannot control my body, and I assume that I can. I die to the feeling that I cannot control my feelings, and I assume that I can. My assumption is not something I take lightly, I feel it fully. I do this because I can in my imagination.

The idea of releasing your limitations sounds appealing when you first hear it, but when you try to apply it, you may find yourself gripping tighter to limiting beliefs *(feelings of "I").* The moment you start to let them go, you might cling even harder. This is precisely when you learn why this release is so powerful. *The moment you find yourself gripping harder to your limitations is the moment you must release everything you think you are.* Be willing to cross to the other side, the liberating side, in your imagination without fear. There, you will discover a space with no shameful past, no embarrassing present, just your fulfilled desire waiting for you to immerse yourself in until you forget you are imagining it because to you, it becomes the only reality that exists.

Practice this art of dying daily, and you will resurrect within yourself the images, words, and feelings that bring you joy. These pleasing words and images will no longer be mere fantasies if you have truly released your limitations. They will become your only reality, your truth. Since you have abandoned your limitations, the imaginal acts of liberation will feel *real* to you, and because they feel real, you will receive thoughts and feelings *from* that new state. Then you will master your inner reality through this process of dying and resurrecting. The old state completely ceases as the new state emerges.

So the greatest gift you can give yourself is to completely release your limitations, allowing yourself a new change of "I".

> ***"If I could yield myself to my dream and it would not become flesh, it would be complete tyranny over this wonderful concept of life. But you cannot fail if you yield. If you hold back within yourself, wondering "What will I play as my last card if this doesn't work?" then you have not yielded, you have not nailed yourself to it. It is a complete yielding****. It is the great cry "My God! My God! Why hast Thou forsaken me?"* ***If you know that you're God doing it, you can yield. But there must be complete abandonment as though it were true and then you make it a reality****. The cost is that form*

*of mental abandonment that Blake calls "madness." But man is afraid; he dare not so abandon himself to a dream, and so never "dies." So Blake was right when he said: "There is nothing like death: the best thing in life is death."* - ***Neville***

*"Well, do practice the art of dying...and you won't really die. You will die and not really die. You will die to what you now believe and live to what you want to believe, and become the greater for the dying."* - ***Neville***

**Artwork Commentary:**

As with the other artworks, we see a man in communion with himself. This time, the man is looking down at the clouds symbolizing the imagination within us. That vast inner world where all possibilities exist. His face, peaceful and downward-gazing, represents the act of self-surrender, the willingness to release what no longer serves. Letting go completely of all thinking and doubting and releasing himself to feeling.

Taking the inner leap can feel terrifying. You sense you are going to lose something, and you are not wrong. You will lose the state you are in, the idea you have held of yourself for so long. That can feel like a profound loss, like dying to who you thought you were.

But communion with yourself does not end there. It is not about death and destruction; it is about redemption and life. While the figure on the left decides to let go and release, feeling as though he might die, he discovers himself on the other side of the table. Not dead at all, but risen.

He is still the same person, the same essential being, yet what has risen is a different state of imagination. He has moved into a new state of imagination, a new version of himself. This is the harvest we receive: ourselves, changed yet identical in essence.

This is why I say we receive an identical harvest. The harvest is always yourself, not some external reward or changed circumstance, but you, embodying a different state. You plant a seed by assuming a new state of being, and what grows from that seed is you, expressing that assumption. The man on the right is the same man on the left, but he surrendered to communion with his true self, and in doing so, became the version of himself he was always meant to be. You will always harvest yourself. The question is only which state you choose to plant and surrender too.

# Meditations

### Pharaoh Meditation

The goal of this meditation is to get to the ***feeling***. I made this for fun and it should be fun. It should not be stressful or forceful. This is simply to change your feeling and discover new feelings inside of you. This is about becoming greater in your imagination and no longer a fearful dreamer. So think of it as you are changing who you are ***in*** imagination. Make it fun and enjoy it! When I speak of feeling in this mediation, I mean a mix between feeling and acceptance. Acceptance meaning there are no more questions. You simply accept and let the feelings the arise be.

1. Lay down, and relax. Any stresses in the body, release them with ease. Breathe and release. If you have pains in your chest, gut or feeling tightness, just try to relax.

2. Close your eyes and start to feel yourself to be the Dreamer in this world within you. Now let's create a dream to the best of your ability, *it does not have to be perfect*: Dream yourself (first-person) sitting on a throne. Dream yourself into the Pharaoh. Notice the implication of the throne. That you must be the highest here. Notice the power and the stillness it brings. Notice the authority you have. By your own words, what you say goes in here.

3. Now let's focus on feeling from this dream: Imagine someone feeding you grapes. See someone massaging your feet. Hear someone tell you it is an honor for them to serve you. Hear them call you, "Your Grace." Say, "No" to something and let it be a "No." *Feel* the power of your words and the power of your presence. *Feel* the power of being high above. Do not resist this, simply accept what you are dreaming. *Feel* the calmness and intensity of being the highest. *Feel* the power of being the Pharaoh. *Feel* you are divine. *Feel* you have ears that hear beyond the physical. *Feel* you have eyes that see beyond the physical. *Feel* the calmness of abundance. *Feel* that others are inspired by your presence. *Feel* the deepness, the stillness and strength in yourself. You do not have to fear but *feel* intense confidence in every word you speak.

4. You have no fear and you speak with the highest authority. There is no need for insecurity, for you are abundant in everything

for you are the dreamer. The only lack you have is the lack of fear. You do not waste time dreaming punishing for yourself but you uplift yourself. Punishing, fear, guilt and shame are for the unenlightened dreamer but you are enlightened. You are far beyond that and you see how this is your dream world. You can dream the dream to your heart's desire and it must happen. Everything you desire, become fulfilled. You have all you desire inside yourself. You have no enemies, no oppressors, no opposition, no adversaries. There is one greater than you inside of you. The Dreamer is the Creator of everything in here. You only dream all that is loving, all that is the highest, all that is noble, all that is brilliant, all that is powerful, and you only worship your name which is "I AM" by attaching the highest of words to "I AM."

5. Focus intensely on these *feelings*. Feel them and do not allow the lowly feelings of fear to hold you down. If you are not willing to feel to an ever increasing intensity of beauty, power, love and brilliance, then why do you even have an imagination? You are the Dreamer who can do anything in imagination, then why not do anything?

This Meditation is to actually change how you dream about yourself. It is to rework the clay (your imagination) and shape to what you want. This meditation will teach you how much you (the Dreamer) hinder yourself in imagination. It will reveal to you how much you can actually have within. It will teach you to trust yourself and to say the words, "Why not dream this?" and it will give you the confidence to dream it. The only times I have ever changed reality and myself is when I actually dream what I want in my imagination. When you free yourself, your whole feeling changes and as Neville says:

*"A change in feeling is a change in destiny."* - ***Neville***

**In Here - Meditation**

1. Lay down, and relax. Maybe find a comfortable chair and sit up right. Try to relax yourself in this stance.

2. Close your eyes and start to think of your imagination as a place at houses everything. That this place has no limit of expansion and cannot be exhausted of its imaginal resources.

3. Now begin to focus on what you want. Think about anything you desire. From the smallest object, to the largest one. Do not just limit yourself to things made my Man, but also feelings. Think of things you want to feel about yourself. The goal is to have absolute zero judgment on what you are desiring.

4. Then use this phrase "In here (*meaning your imagination*)," to be able to effortlessly accept the idea of having it. Now the goal is to not force yourself into becoming anything or forcing yourself to feel you have things. No. The goal is to acknowledge that imagination holds these things. So start to think of any desire. From hearing good news about a friend, to hearing your own good news. From some object you desire. To a feeling you want to feel. Do not try to get these things. Simply acknowledge their existence in imagination.

5. So then begin to think of it and say "In here, I have..." This allows to to acknowledge the existence and the having at the same time. So you can start to say "In here, I have my confidence. In here, I have my freedom. In here, I have inherent worth. In here, I have my house. In here, I have my money. In here, I have my joy. In here, I have my throne. In here, I have my achieved goals. In here, I have my peace. In here, I have persistence. In here, I have my acceptance. In here, I have my love.

You are acknowledging not trying to create anything. If you accept completely that the statement is entirely true, you will start to feel a bliss entering your yourself. This is not a random occurrence. It still should be acknowledged and accepted without judgment but it is you coming back to your true nature of abundance. Since you are one with imagination, the greater you make your imagination, the greater you make yourself.

**Artwork Commentary:**

Here we see a statue symbolizing strength and stillness embodied in stone. Yet it stands behind a curtain, suggesting that to access this calmness, one must turn inward. The stillness resembles power, a power that can only be discovered behind the veil, for true strength resides not outside of man but within him.

The statue, frozen in its eternal pose, represents an ideal we chase, but the curtain reminds us that ideals are only realized through introspection and personal conviction.

When we seek power externally, through possessions, status, or the approval of others, we find ourselves perpetually unsatisfied. These external markers shift and fade, leaving us grasping at shadows. But the power within, the kind symbolized by the hidden statue, remains constant and unshakeable. It is the power of choosing one's response to life.

Anyone can part it the curtain and look within. Yet most never do, distracted by the spectacle of the external world. The statue behind the curtain represents the paradox that what we seek is simultaneously hidden and accessible, obscured only by our unwillingness to look past the surface. True power cannot be displayed or demonstrated in the conventional sense; it must be cultivated in silence and solitude, then expressed naturally through one's being. The strength we admire in the stone is merely a reflection of the strength we must discover within ourselves.

# It Is Within

This is excerpt from a lecture that Neville gave called "*It Is Within*." This excerpt is an incredible piece that I feel summarizes this whole book. It mixes the spiritual and the practical understandings and weaves these threads together to create a mental sweater of comfort in imagination. Let the words sink into yourself and allow yourself to not try to understand everything but to more be present with what you are reading. So I want to end this series with his own words alone:

It is Within:

"You take a dream, a daydream, of something you want for yourself, or something you want for another, and you represent to yourself a scene which, if true, implies the fulfillment of that dream.

You like to do this, that, and the other, and so you construct a scene, any kind of a scene implying the fulfillment of your desire, and then *to the degree that you are self-persuaded of the reality of that imaginal act, it will become fact in your world*.

I could tell you a number of stories to support that claim. It's not theory for me anymore. This is fact based upon experience.

So when we are told in the book of Luke, "*The kingdom of God is within you*," you can take it literally. These garments that you and I wear are parts of the eternal structure of the universe. You are wearing the garment as an actor wears a costume. You are not the garment you wear. You are doing this for a purpose, a heavenly purpose, but you are not these garments.

You are that being that my friend discovered who sees it from above, and to see this universe from above is so completely unlike what it appears to be seen from this angle. It's not this way at all, but you come down into this world of death for a purpose.

Now William Blake made this observation, and he claims he did not write it from his conscious reasoning mind, that the words were dictated by the spirit of love. Well, God is love. Therefore if the spirit of love dictated the words of Jerusalem, then it's God dictating it.

And in this he said,

*"Then those in Great Eternity who contemplate on Death*
*Said thus. What seems to Be: Is: To those to whom*
*It seems to Be, & is productive of the most dreadful*
*Consequences to those to whom it seems to Be: even of*
*Torments, Despair, Eternal Death; but the Divine Mercy*
*Steps beyond and Redeems Man in the Body of Jesus"*
***Jerusalem***

Now that's something that Man can't grasp on this level, but I tell you it is true. To stand in the presence of the risen Christ, and commune with him face to face, and voice to voice, then to have love, his infinite love, embrace you, and as he embraces you, you fuse with him, without loss of identity, no change in your identity, and yet you're one with the body of Christ.

And then he sends you, and he can't send you without himself, because you're one with him. There's no divorcement, no separation from that moment on. So when he makes the statement, "*Divine mercy steps beyond, and redeems man in the body of Christ.*"

So in my last little pamphlet, I made this statement, and I made it from experience, that you and I are resurrected one by one, to unite into a single man who is God. So here is a reflection that he saw in his dream, a man proud, containing infinity, and the deadest thing he'd ever seen (*A man who told Neville of his dream*).

God places a limitation, and then takes upon himself that limitation, and reaches in this act the very limit of contraction, that he may then expand beyond what he was. He takes upon himself the limit of opacity, and then begins to expand, and there's no limit to translucence, to transparency.

This is the world called the world of death. But while we're in it, and we ourselves are animating it, we can take any state we desire. There are an infinite number of states.

You can be in a poor state, or a wealthy state. You're no better off, as far as the height goes, because one is poor, and one is wealthy. Not from a spiritual point of view. But while you're in the world of Caesar, why not be comfortable? Why not take a state that cushions, and comforts?

And so you can take a state of affluence, if you know what it would be like, were you affluent. Assume that you are, and see the world as you would see it were it true. And then, I would say, accept it. *Believe in the reality of that unseen, imaginal act.* And if you do, it will come to pass.

Because the whole vast world, really, is within you. I don't care what others will tell you, it's all within you. And everyone moving in your world moves because of you.

William James made the statement, that the greatest revolution in his time, was the discovery that man, by changing the inner attitudes of his mind, could change the outer aspects of his life.

Now, James belongs to our generation, this century. He's gone from the world, but he was the great educator of the 20th century. And he said the greatest revolution *in his* time was this discovery.

Well, the great book of books, the Bible, makes that statement. Not as James made it, but how would you interpret this? "*Whatever you desire, believe that you have received it, and you will.*" Isn't that the one condition imposed upon me, or you, is to persuade self that we have it?

How can I persuade myself, when at the moment, reason denies it, and my senses deny it? But James said, he could change the inner attitudes of his mind. Can anyone stop you from changing your attitude towards the speaker?

You may like him or dislike him, and if your dislike of him causes him to act to confirm your dislike, and you like the dislike, well then keep it up. If you don't like that reaction, you could change your attitude towards him, and he automatically and unknowingly would act in the way that you would like. And you can do this with any person in this world.

So if I am that free, that I don't have to get your permission to hold an opinion of you, but I can hold it regardless of you, and if I hold it and persuade myself of the reality of that opinion of you, and you conform to it, am I not free? *I am free to entertain any thought, and if I am, and it produces results, well then I'm a free person, even in the world of Caesar.*

So here, I do hope that I have persuaded you, that the whole vast world, for you seem so small and insignificant to yourself, the whole vast universe is really within you. And so you can take it this day, and test it.

You're invited to test it, and when you get the results, share it with me. Tell me about it, write me a letter, and explain what you did, and how it worked. And if you're blessed this night with a vision, I would love to hear it. For God makes himself known to man in vision, and he speaks with a man through a dream.

Don't try to interpret the dream, tell me just what happened. My friend did not attempt to interpret it, he told me exactly what happened when my lecture, that he was about to record, triggered the memory of the dream. But all from his experiences, what lesson he was learning was this: "I have forgotten, I must remember."

If everyone could now persuade themselves you're trying to remember something, you lost the memory of it when you came this low in the scale. And you're trying to remember. What he was trying to remember was that exalted position where he saw the whole thing as dead, and he came down into the body of death and completely forgot who he really was.

And people are shocked when you tell them that they are Christ. All aims run true to origins. If my origin is God, my end must be God. As the poet (*Sir Edwin Arnold*) said,

*"That which ye sow ye reap. See yonder fields!*
*The sesamum was sesamum, the corn*
*Was corn. The Silence and the Darkness knew!*
*So is a man's fate born."*
***The Light Of Asia***

If I believe what scientists tell me, that my origin is a worm, my end is a worm. If I believe the Bible, and my origin is God, then my end is God. *And I don't have to choose that anymore. I know that from experience.*

I don't have to speculate about the risen Christ. I don't have to speculate about God being love. I stood in the presence of God, and he's infinite love. I'm not bending my head when I say God is Man. As Blake said,

*"Thou art a man. God is no more.*
*Thy own humanity learn to adore."*
***The Everlasting Gospel***

*"God appears and God is light*
*To those poor souls who dwell in night,*
*But does a human form display*
*To those who dwell in realms of day."*
***Auguries of Innocence***

So here you're wearing the form of God. You are God. He gave you his name, and the name that he reveals to the whole vast world, if you'll take it, is I Am.

So that's my name forever. It'll be known, I'll be known by it throughout all generations. But we don't stop there. We say "I am John," "A poor John," "An unknown John," "An unwanted John," and these are the limitations and the restrictions we put upon the name of God.

But if I will remember the name, I will glorify the name, and only put upon it that which is noble, that which is free, and if I did it, I would walk in that light. So do me a favor and try it. Try it, and I promise you from my own experience that you'll get the results. You won't have to harm anyone in this world, but no one." - ***Neville***

**Artwork Commentary:**

We all enter this world perceiving only the exterior, seeing, touching, hearing the surfaces of things. Yet paradoxically, everything we experience is actually occurring within us.

In this artwork, two eggs present contrasting perspectives on life. One egg remains sealed, its shell intact and impenetrable. The other reveals an opening, an invitation inward. These forms symbolize two fundamental ways we can approach life: as observers of an external world, or as explorers of an internal one.

The ladder and door represent our entry into this world. Initially, we begin on the left side enclosed, confined within the sealed egg. We cannot see beyond the walls that surround us. Our senses bind us to surfaces, to the outer shell of experience. This is the perspective most of us inhabit: looking outward, seeking meaning in the material world, believing that life happens "out there."

There is also a fork in the road, a single path that divides into two distinct directions. This is not merely a physical split, but a metaphor for the fundamental choice we face at every moment: which perspective will we take as ours? We can waver between these paths, oscillating between viewpoints, never fully committing to either.

We can return to the left side, retreating to the familiar territory of sensory experience. Here, life appears as our five senses report it: solid, external and objective. From this vantage point, we remain outside the shell, pressing our hands against its surface, feeling its texture, observing its color, but never penetrating deeper. We mistake the symbol for the thing symbolized. This is not fully wrong, but it is simply incomplete. The senses provide information, but they reveal only one dimension of reality.

Or we can choose the right path, the inward path represented by the opened egg. This direction requires us to question everything we have been taught about where life actually occurs. Going inside means recognizing that the external world, as vivid as it appears, is fundamentally a symbolized projection of internal states. What lies beyond the senses is not emptiness or abstraction, but the living, imaginal substance of experience.

But as we walk the road of life, accumulating experiences, facing struggles, questioning our assumptions. Gradually, we discover the opening, the doorway inward. We begin to recognize that the outer-world is a symbolic representation of feelings, that the true theater of existence unfolds within our own imagination. The world we thought was "outside" has always been within.

Printed in Dunstable, United Kingdom

76026108R00181